Nottingham's Millennium

Nottingham's Millennium

The story of the 1,000 years in which a riverside settlement became a thriving city

EVENING POST

The Breedon Books
Publishing Company
Derby

First published in Great Britain by
The Breedon Books Publishing Company Limited
Breedon House, 44 Friar Gate, Derby, DE1 1DA.
1999

ISBN 1 85983 169 9

Printed and bound by Butler & Tanner Ltd., Selwood Printing
Works, Caxton Road, Frome, Somerset.

Colour separations and jacket printing by GreenShires Group
Ltd, Leicester.

Contents

Foreword

THIS BOOK celebrates the turn of the second millennium AD, and the completion of 1,000 years which have seen a small riverside settlement grow into a thriving modern city.

It tells the stories of Nottingham from the Norman Conquest and the Domesday Book through to the events of 1999.

Nottingham's Millennium is not a definitive history.

Nor is it intended as a reference work.

It is a compendium of stories about the events, the ideas and the people that have shaped the city we know ... presented in a style today's newspaper readers will be familiar with.

So expect to read about the landmark events. Like the Civil War, the Luddite riots and the Nottingham Blitz. But look out, too, for some of the quirky and bizarre incidents that have been forgotten as the decades have rolled by.

Our principal source of reference is the Nottingham *Evening Post*, which was founded in 1878.

Which means *Nottingham's Millennium* has been researched and written not just by the team whose names are listed in these pages, but also by hundreds who went before them ... journalists whose job it was to record the events of the day and present them to the people of Nottingham.

We hope you enjoy their work.

Research and Text

JOHN BRUNTON, JEREMY LEWIS, DAVID McVAY, MARK PATTERSON,
ANDY SMART, SIMON WILSON ... and countless journalists, past and present,
who have worked for the Nottingham *Evening Post* and associated publications

Design and Production

CARL BRUNT, KAREN BULLWIN, CHRIS COOPER, MARTIN DONE,
ELAINE GLEADELL, JEREMY LEWIS, SIMON LOWIS, NIGEL MARSHALL,
ROB NAYLOR, ANDY NEAL, RODGER PAGE, MALCOLM PAIN, TONY ROSE,
OLIVER SANDERSON, ANTHONY SCARBOROUGH, COLIN SMITHSON

Project Editor

JEREMY LEWIS

Nottingham before the Normans

EXACTLY when early man first appeared in what we now think of as Nottingham is impossible to say. But we do know that Neolithic man roamed the area, as did people of the Bronze Age, and the later invaders, the Celts.

In all probability, when the Roman armies of Claudius invaded England in 43AD, Notts was under the control of the Coritani.

The Romans built what we now call Fosse Way, linking fortified posts from Devon to Lincoln.

In 868, the Danish army wintered in Nottingham, an event leading to the first references to the town appearing in *The Anglo Saxon Chronicles* and Asser's *Life of Alfred*.

In its early form it was *Snotengaham*, 'the place of the people of Snot'.

Around 920 the first bridge across the Trent was built. The sandstone cliffs above the marshes that bordered the river provided Nottingham with its *raison d'etre*, with early settlement around St Mary's Hill.

However, on the eve of the Norman Conquest in 1066 it wasn't even a town. There were just 192 inhabitants ...

Canute lays down the law

THE Danish king, Canute, acquired the kingdom of Mercia in 1017. The land included Nottinghamshire and the two provinces of East Anglia and Northumberland.

One of his earliest acts was to establish the first Charter of the Forests — the formal codifying of a loose collection of regulations concerning royal lands.

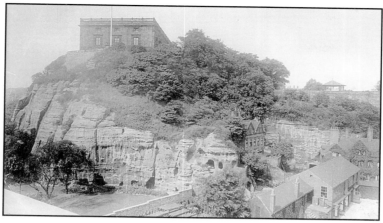

IDEAL SITE: Castle Rock, with caves below

Castle for the Conqueror

WILLIAM the Conqueror ordered the construction of Nottingham Castle in 1067.

Built by William de Peverel, the fortress guaranteed the town's importance throughout the Middle Ages.

King William I, who had defeated King Harold's army at Hastings the previous year, was anxious to quell the rebellion of northern earls under William of Morcar, and visited Nottingham as he made his way to York.

The campaign was typical of the Conqueror's determination to make his mark on his new kingdom.

The site for the castle was ideal: A 130ft rocky sandstone promontory with steep cliffs falling away to the east, south and west sides.

It provided a strong defensive position, commanding views in all directions, but notably across the course of the newly-diverted River Leen, and further south towards the River Trent.

At the northern end of the site, William's men constructed a rampart and ditch and the whole area was enclosed first by an inner, then an outer bailey.

During its early days, it is

BUILDER: William takes the crown of England in a fanciful retrospective view

unlikely that stone was used in the walls. They were probably a mix of earthworks and timber construction.

Stone was introduced on the site in the following century, with the appearance of a tower.

Over the years, Nottingham flourished as the 'Gateway to the North'. It was the chief royal fortress in the Midlands, a position it occupied for the next 500 years. By the time of the English Civil War, the building was partly ruined.

Domesday Book lists 30 owners

THE Conqueror's great survey, the Domesday Book of 1085, listed 30 landholders in Notts — including the King himself, the Archbishop of York and the Bishops of Lincoln and Bayeux, Normandy.

Nottingham is referred to as 'Snotinghsure' in the document, which William's researchers compiled to discover the true and probable future value of his new lands.

Royal officials travelled throughout the country making a detailed inventory of who owned what, and completed the the task with remarkable speed, accuracy and detail.

The place names are familiar now — Bramcote, Beeston, Chilwell, Trowell, Lenton, Stapleford and Basford all emerge from the pages of the Domesday Book.

Populations and livestock were also recorded, and the value of local landholdings.

The Domesday record also reveals much of the customs and laws of the time: "In Nottinghamshire and in Derbyshire ... if anyone be exiled according to the law for any crime, no one but the King can restore peace to him."

❑ ❑ ❑

TOWNSFOLK in Nottingham diverted the course of the River Leen in 1066, allowing the stream to flow under Castle Rock.

The aim was to supply fresh water for brewers, and the river was later dammed to provide fish ponds.

❑ ❑ ❑

POSSIBLY the first church bells to ring out over Nottinghamshire were heard in 1023 when Alfred, Bishop of York, presented two bells to Southwell Church. Building of the Minster began later in the century.

Anglo-Norman tension splits town of 217 houses

THE Anglo-Saxon and Danish inhabitants of Nottingham resented the authority of the Norman invaders. It led to a division of the two communities in 1090.

Separate courts were established, and there were separate markets. The Saxons traded on a site adjacent to what is now the Lace Market, while the Normans did business in what is now Old Market Square.

Records show that in 1083, there were 217 houses in Nottingham.

King John's slaughter of the Welsh innocents ➜ Page 3

Belleme hounded into exile

KING Henry I arrived in Nottingham in 1102 to receive the submission of Blyth, the chief northern fiefdom of the brilliant soldier Robert of Belleme, now accused of treason.

Belleme, whose great estates and military power made him one of England's most prominent citizens, had sided with Henry's older brother Robert of Normandy.

The Duke had landed the previous year determined to take Henry's crown — which Henry had himself seized on the sudden, mysterious death of William II (William Rufus) in a hunting accident in the New Forest.

Henry soon bought off his brother, leaving him free to pursue Belleme.

After Blyth had capitulated, the Bishop of Lincoln, on Henry's behalf, besieged Belleme's strongholds first at Tickhill, then Bridgnorth.

Belleme finally gave up and was allowed into exile in Normandy, having been stripped of his lands.

In 1104 another Notts landowner, William, Count of Mortain, fled to Normandy to join Duke Robert and Belleme to plot against the King.

Mortain was captured in France, and was condemned to be blinded and imprisoned. He was liberated, and later became a monk.

KING Henry II, *pictured above*, gave Nottingham a charter in 1155. The market place, now Old Market Square, was described as "the biggest buying and selling place in England."

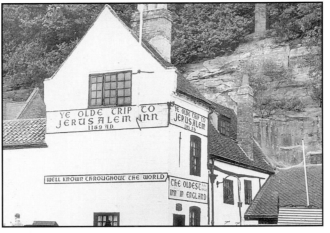

YE OLDE TRIP TO JERUSALEM INN 1189 AD

WELL KNOWN THROUGHOUT THE WORLD

THE OLDEST INN IN ENGLAND

Ye Olde Trip... ye very long trip

LEFT: Crusaders met in Nottingham en route to the Holy Land — hence the 1189 inscription at Ye Olde Trip to Jerusalem pub. The building is of later vintage.

❑ ❑ ❑

KING Richard I met King William of Scotland near Clipstone in 1194.

❑ ❑ ❑

A CHARITY hospital for lepers was founded, possibly in 1179, just east of Gonalston on the Nottingham-to-Southwell road.

Town in flames as cousins go to war

COUSINS Stephen and Matilda fought for the crown of England, and Nottingham suffered.

Stephen, grandson of William the Conqueror, was brought up by King Henry I, his mother's brother, and was given vast holdings in England and France.

Henry wanted his daughter Matilda to succeed him, and Stephen had pledged his support.

But when the old king died in 1135, Stephen sailed to England and took the crown, backed by barons who didn't want a woman in power, and by the Pope, who was promised more influence.

Stephen was able to count on the support of the Custodian of Nottingham Castle.

In 1140, Matilda's half-brother — Robert, Earl of Gloucester — tried to attack the stronghold. It held, but Gloucester's army set fire to the town. According to a chronicler: "The whole city was destroyed by the flames."

Nottingham was torched again in 1153. This time the castle was under siege from Matilda's son, later Henry II.

William Peverel, who had lost control of the castle in 1141, tried to regain it, and set fire to the town to drive out the pro-Matilda invaders.

After the war, Peverel was forced out of England following an attempt to poison the Earl of Chester.

The story went that Chester and his men had been guests of Peverel, who had administered poisoned wine. Three men died, but Chester survived.

RICHLY CARVED: The 12th Century font from Lenton Priory

Priory built at 'Leen tun'

BUILDING work started on Lenton Abbey in 1103. It was founded by William Peverel as a daughter-house of the Benedictine monastery at Cluny — reputed to be the largest building in the world.

The new priory, built by the River Leen (Lenton means settlement, tun, on the Leen), became an ordered home for around 30 monks at a time for the next 400 years or more.

Financed by the livings of St Mary's, and the newer St Peter's and St Nicholas's Churches in Nottingham, and with substantial land-holdings, it became the most important monastery in the county.

Revenues were drawn from sources in seven counties.

Life was an unending round of prayer, contemplation and minor day-to-day issues.

While not entirely inward looking, because monks could find themselves sent to distant parishes, it was governed from within the monastery walls and was to remain so until the Reformation.

King orders £2,454 refit for castle

KING Henry III, during a visit to the castle, ordered that the reduced outer bailey should be encircled by stone and that a gatehouse with twin towers be built.

This was almost the last military improvement to the building.

As Prof John Beckett points out in his *Centenary History of Nottingham*, with the end of the barons' war in the mid-13th Century, castles not situated on borders or in areas of unrest gradually lost their military significance ...

"At Nottingham, the martial front was maintained, but inwardly the accent was on comfort: the Castle was converted into a palace."

From then, King Henry threw himself into supervising a general overhaul of the building, taking great pains to ensure work met his specifications.

These included "a new and becoming door" for his own chamber.

He ordered a new tower to be built on the motte, with windows "looking towards the cliff" and another window overlooking the town.

The refit cost £2,454 — at 1999 rates, a refurbishment of more than £1million.

Jews hit by expulsion order

IN 1264, gallows were erected in what is now Shakespeare Street solely for hanging Jews.

By the mid-13th Century there was an established Jewish community in Nottingham.

They suffered periodically from anti-Semitism. Massacres happened during the barons' revolt of 1264, and again in 1279.

In 1290, Jews were no longer considered necessary to the Crown for money-lending — since money was on offer from other European sources. King Edward I issued his Decree of Expulsion, confiscating Jewish property and assets.

RIGHT: The date 1240 is displayed on Ye Olde Salutation in Houndsgate.

It is thought to be one of the oldest known trading establishments in the town. But a TV survey in 1998 concluded that it was not the oldest inn in Nottingham.

Slaughter of the innocents

KING John wrote a cruel chapter in the history of Nottingham in June 1212 when 28 Welsh 'princes' were hanged at the castle.

They were sons of nobility and had been held hostage to prevent further rebellion in Wales.

The oldest of the prisoners was said to be 14, and the youngest just eight years old.

They were executed on the castle wall, under the supervision of Philip Marc, King John's trusted castellan.

It was seen as a gesture of defiance at a time when the king was under pressure both at home and abroad.

Serious foreign policy reverses included the loss of Normandy to France; at home, high taxation and trouble with the barons meant that King John's prestige was waning.

As a reward for his part in this grim work, as well as other tasks he performed for his royal master, Castellan Philip Marc

END OF THE ROAD: Newark Castle, where King John died in 1216

was granted the manor of Bulwell.

King John, humiliated by his barons with the presentation of the Magna Carta at Runnymede in 1215, died at Newark Castle, aged 48, in 1216.

TWO prominent religious orders were established in Nottingham in the 13th Century.

The Franciscans, or Greyfriars, arrived in about 1230 and settled in one of the town's poorest areas.

At the south-western end of Broad Marsh, not far from the foot of Castle Rock, they lodged in a house possibly belonging to the king. Later, they built their own chapel and later a quay by the banks of the River Leen.

The Carmelites, or Whitefriars, are thought to have arrived in 1270-75.

They established themselves on a site between the roads now known as Friar Lane and St James's Street.

🔲🔲🔲

THE town celebrated in 1230 when Henry III added four days to the Lenton Priory Fair, held at the feast of St Martin, around November 21.

In 1284, Edward I granted a charter to the burgesses of Nottingham which mentioned the St Matthew's Day Fair — and granted them a new one of 15 days, beginning on November 20, the Eve of St Edmund.

The first known written reference to 'Goose Fair' dates from 1542.

🔲🔲🔲

IN 1247 the Constable of Nottingham Castle was ordered to supply wheat to the army in Wales.

🔲🔲🔲

PERMISSION was granted in 1267 to collect a levy to start building a defensive wall round Nottingham.

🔲🔲🔲

THE Bugge family, merchants of Nottingham, bought the lordship of Willoughby-on-the-Wolds in the 13th Century and changed their surname to Willoughby.

John fines sheriff ... but saves him from prison

GREED nearly proved the downfall of the Sheriff of Nottingham, Robert de Vieuxpont, in 1207.

King John imposed harsh terms on those who sought public office.

At the same time as the sheriffship of Nottingham, de Vieuxpont held the same posts in Derbyshire and Westmoreland, custodies of the vacant sees of York and Durham, and the honours of Brough, Sarum, Tickhill and Peverel.

His financial problems began to multiply, and despite the fact he was a personal friend of the king, he was fined 4,000 marks for the royal 'benevolence'.

King John then demanded that de Vieuxpont hand over part of his Westmoreland inheritance and that his nephew should be held hostage by the king for de Vieuxpont's future good conduct.

The sheriff could have been imprisoned, but his friendship with John saved him.

Backgammon gamblers squabble over money Page 5

MORTIMER'S HOLE: The drama recaptured by a much later artist. Inset left: King Edward II, whose widow Isabella was detained

Castle coup: Queen and lover arrested

IN 1367, King Edward III recognised the quality of Nottingham alabaster work by ordering an altarpiece for St George's Chapel, Windsor, from Peter the Mason.

Peter's altarpiece was big enough to require ten carts, each drawn by eight horses, for its 17-day journey. The cost was £200 — more than £65,000 at 1999 prices.

☐ ☐ ☐

MORE than a dozen Notts noblemen, knights, squires and archers are known to have fought at Crecy in 1346.

☐ ☐ ☐

THE Black Death left its mark in 1349. Of 161 livings for priests in the archdeaconry of Nottingham, 59 were left vacant by the plague.

☐ ☐ ☐

EARLY in the 14th Century the Willoughby family acquired the manor of Wollaton, to the west of Nottingham.

YOUNG King Edward III secured his throne in 1330 after the dramatic arrest at Nottingham Castle of his mother, Queen Isabella, and her lover Roger Mortimer.

A small band, including the 17-year-old Edward, entered via a passage through the rock.

The arrest of the powerful magnate Mortimer gave the young king the freedom to rule. It also enabled him to avenge the horrific murder of his father, Edward II, three years earlier.

Isabella had become increasingly alienated from her husband, who favoured the Dispenser family. The ambitious Mortimer disapproved, clashed with Edward II, and was imprisoned. He fled to France in 1324. Isabella fled a year later, and their romance was soon the scandal of Europe.

At home, the king's flagrant homosexuality and the Dispensers' increasing power made him so unpopular that when Isabella and Mortimer returned, they forced him to abdicate and put young Edward on the throne.

Isabella and Mortimer came to Nottingham for a special council, and seemed to know there was a plot.

That night the young king and his lieutenants approached the deputy constable of the castle, William Eland. He told them of a way into the castle by one of two passages through the rock.

Their daring move worked. Mortimer was sent under close arrest to London and was executed at Tyburn. Isabella was ordered into dignified seclusion. She died 28 years later. Eland was made constable for life.

Weavers quit town after trading slump

THE weaving trade suffered a serious decline during the early 14th Century. By 1348 several had left Nottingham.

Other trades were flourishing — and street names give clues as to the town's commerce in the 14th Century. For instance, Barker Gate would have been the street of tanners; Bridlesmith Gate was where makers or bridles worked; Fletcher Gate denoted either butchers ('flesh') or makers of arrows; Lister Gate refers to dyers.

Sheriff Brett collars 200 law-breakers

THE Sheriff of Nottingham, John Brett, rounded up 200 robbers and murderers in 1333 and personally escorted them to London to stand trial.

But all, with a few minor exceptions, were let off free — including the bandits' leader, Eustace Folville.

King Edward III had tried getting to grips with a major crime problem — in existence since the days of his grandfather, King Edward I — by giving more power to the judiciary.

The problem was that felons were freed if they could afford big fines — and the most successful law-breakers had plenty of riches to spare.

The previously respectable Folville family, from Leicestershire, embarked on a life of murder, kidnapping, rape and robbery with

CRIME CRACKDOWN: King Edward III at court

violence. They evaded justice from 1326 to 1342.

The sheriffs of Nottingham, Derby and Leicestershire had a special writ to catch them, but each time they tried, the gang would flee to their hideouts in Rockingham Forest or the Peak District.

A commission was appointed, but then came the war with Scotland. By the time the 200 had been rounded up, most had pardons because of their involvement in the Scottish campaign.

At the trial, the judges examined every indictment but the pardons meant the men, including their ringleaders, were acquitted. Just two minor figures stood trial.

Richard III marches out from Nottingham Page 6

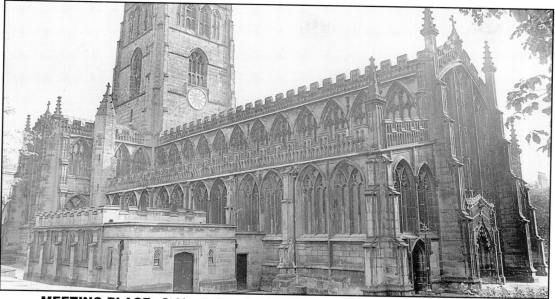

MEETING PLACE: St Mary's Church, where the mayoral election of 1412 led to riots

Guns arrive for war on Welsh

NOTTINGHAM was on a war footing in 1407 when King Henry IV, determined to quell Owen Glendower's Welsh rebellion, started preparations for another military expedition.

Siege guns and other campaign material were brought to the town from the Yorkshire stronghold of Pontefract.

The king had recovered from illness and was ready to take charge of operations — but then news arrived of an outbreak of bubonic plague in the West Country.

He retired to Pontefract, but when he heard rumours that trouble was brewing in Scotland he sent orders to the Sheriff of Nottingham, as well as the sheriffs of Lincolnshire, Lancashire and Yorkshire, that they should muster every man between 16 and 60 and have them ready to march.

The Scottish threat evaporated, but in October the Sheriff of Nottingham received another royal demand to supply men as King Henry once again turned his attention to Glendower.

The Notts men made their way to Evesham for the rendezvous of forces from all over the country, but once again Henry had a change of heart and the muster was dismissed.

Charter lifts town's status

IN 1449, King Henry VI granted Nottingham a new charter, confirming county borough status on the area — a reflection of the town's growing economic importance.

In addition to a mayor, Nottingham was now to have an escheator, whose office concerned certain land and property issues, two sheriffs and seven aldermen.

Senior civic figures were allowed to wear ermine-trimmed robes, in the manner of the lord mayor and aldermen of London.

The aldermen were elected by the burgesses, and from their ranks came the mayor, chosen each year on Michaelmas Day.

After the charter was granted, a new Guildhall was built at Weekday Cross.

The election of mayor had already been the subject of controversy.

CORONATION: The young King Henry VI

In 1412, 49 burgesses met at St Mary's Church to elect the new mayor and bailiffs. Opponents objected to so small a number of men having such a relatively great amount of power, and a riot ensued.

Backgammon conmen fall out

TWO gamblers set out to cheat others — but when they fell out over a debt, one took the other to court.

Henry Bonnington told the jury in 1432 that John Balthwaite had asked him deliberately to lose at backgammon so he could use his winnings against other players.

In return, Bonnington alleged, Balthwaite promised to return the lost money and half his winnings.

Bonnington demanded payment from Balthwaite, who counter-claimed that the plaintiff had also cheated.

The mayor dismissed the case, saying there were no proper legal grounds for it.

SERVANT Margaret Pope was acquitted by a jury in 1408 of allegations that she had stolen 30 gallons of wine from her master, Nottingham tavern owner John de Bothall.

Bothall told the court that she had used false keys to break into the tavern, had taken the wine without his knowledge, and had given it away to her neighbours.

▢ ▢ ▢

IN 1409 a chapel was built near St Ann's Well, which had been a place of pilgrimage for the sick — especially for those with eye disorders — for several centuries.

Another holy well, considered to have healing properties, was reputedly situated in Basford churchyard.

▢ ▢ ▢

THE town was empowered by the charter of 1399 to seize the belongings of people who had been executed.

An inventory of goods confiscated in 1411 included a brandiron worth fivepence, a muck fork worth twopence and a frying pan valued at fourpence.

▢ ▢ ▢

A MAN was fined in October 1418 after a row over the cost of paving Pepper Street. Thomas del Street said John Crophill owed him three shillings [15p] for the paving, and a further nine shillings [45p] for some woollen cloth.

Crophill was told to hand over the full 12 shillings. He was ordered to pay another shilling in fines and costs.

▢ ▢ ▢

BUTCHER John Smith took John Daniel to court in 1423 in a dispute over his Saturday market stall.

Smith leased the stall from Daniel, but he complained that he was having to pay the ground rent as well as his rent to Daniel ... who was told to pay five shillings [25p], with twopence damages.

▢ ▢ ▢

GLAZIER Hugh Hopwell of Lenton went to court in Nottingham in 1408 for the recovery of five shillings [25p] he said was owed him by Gedling Church. The parish acknowledged its debt and paid up.

Rise and fall of 'king's man' Thomas Cranmer Page 7

ACCORDING to the *Nottingham Date Book,* the town's first tiled roof was constructed in 1494 at the Unicorn Inn on Long Row.

The record says: "This inn was for many years distinguished as one of the most famous alehouses in the town.

"A club of 'hearty good fellows' called the Peep 'O Day Club used to meet at this house.

"One of its rules was that every member should have his first quart mug of ale drunk clean off before six o'clock in the morning, or forfeit a shilling for the club box."

The *Date Book* continues: "Nor was this society composed of scavengers or men of low occupation in life, whose callings required them to be on the alert at an early hour of the morning.

"It consisted principally of men of business residing in the market place or parts immediately adjacent."

❑ ❑ ❑

IN 1458 the wealthy wool merchant Alderman Thomas Thurland began building his new home, Thurland Hall.

It was to become the largest private house in Nottingham and was situated on what is now Pelham Street.

It became the town house of Sir Francis Willoughby who, in 1588, entertained his well-to-do friends before taking them to his new country home, Wollaton Hall.

The house was later acquired by the Stanhope family, and visited by Kings James I and Charles I. It was demolished in 1831.

❑ ❑ ❑

THE town approved new measures against prostitutes, brothels and disorderly ale houses in 1463. At that time an alehouse would be considered 'disorderly' if it stayed open after 9pm.

❑ ❑ ❑

SIR Thomas Rempstone, constable of the Tower of London and admiral of the fleet, was buried in an alabaster tomb in Bingham Church in 1458.

KING EDWARD IV:
Rejected plea in Star Chamber

Edward snubs mayor

IN a series of riots in Nottingham in 1471, two people were killed and several seriously injured. City officials, including mayor Robert English, were shot at with arrows.

Blame was placed on demobilised Yorkist soldiers, wearing the livery of Henry, Lord Grey of Codnor — a former Lancastrian who had become a supporter of King Edward IV.

Nottingham itself was broadly pro-Yorkist, but it seems English had sympathy with the Lancastrian restoration.

Lengthy legal action followed, instituted by the mayor, fearful that his authority would be undermined.

English appealed directly to the king, but when Edward heard the case in Star Chamber, he dismissed the mayor's request that the rioters should be imprisoned, and instead ordered the case to be dealt with by Nottingham justices.

The story took various twists and turns after that — but in the end the rioters escaped unpunished, and there was nothing the civic authorities of Nottingham could do about it.

Wars of the Roses: The final conflicts

KING Richard III moved his command centre to Nottingham in 1485, in response to the expected invasion of England by Henry Tudor.

Although Tudor's claim to the throne was tenuous, he was the only realistic Lancastrian candidate.

Furthermore the possibility of a marriage with the king's niece, Elizabeth of York, drew together an unlikely alliance of supporters — Elizabeth's maternal family, the Woodvilles, and older nobility alienated by Richard's *coup d'etat* in 1483.

The king took up residence at Nottingham Castle in June. Early in August he learned — via his network of couriers posted every 20 miles on the major highways — that Tudor had landed at Milford Haven with 2,000 French mercenaries.

Tudor gathered the support of kinsmen and marched via Shrewsbury to Lichfield.

On August 19, King Richard decided he could no longer wait for reinforcements. Astride a white horse, he led his army of 8,000 out of Nottingham to Leicester.

The two armies met at Bosworth Field in Leicestershire on August 22.

The king was killed in the battle, and his body was stripped and taken on horseback to Leicester, where his remains were buried.

Tudor's throne was not

COMMAND CENTRE: Nottingham Castle as it may have looked at the height of its military importance. Below: King Richard III, as interpreted in James Butler's statue for the city of Leicester

secured until 1487, when the final battle of the Wars of the Roses was fought at Stoke Field, south of Newark.

Renewed conflict was caused by the 'coronation' in Ireland of a youth presented as Edward, Earl of Warwick —

nephew of the Yorkist kings Edward IV and Richard III.

In fact he was the impostor Lambert Simnel, but his cause was championed by two diehard Yorkists, the Earl of Lincoln and Lord Lovel.

They landed in Lancashire in June with 1,500 German mercenaries. King Henry VII, who was in Warwickshire, summoned troops and arrived in Nottingham on June 14.

The two manoeuvring armies met just south of East Stoke.

Lincoln was killed in the battle, and Lovel was never seen again. Simnel was sent to work in the royal kitchens.

Rebel soldiers were slaughtered in a marshy gully close to the banks of the Trent.

● Sir Henry Willoughby of Wollaton was created a knight banneret by the new king for his support in crushing the rebellion of 1487.

New mansion for the Willoughbys of Wollaton Page 8

Rise and fall of Thomas Cranmer

THOMAS Cranmer, born in the Notts village of Aslockton in 1489, became the first Protestant Archbishop of Canterbury in 1532.

Cranmer was educated at Jesus College, Cambridge, where he obtained a fellowship and later took holy orders.

In 1529, when the plague hit Cambridge, Cranmer left for nearby Waltham and there found favour with Henry VIII, who made him royal chaplain and Archdeacon of Taunton.

He was then sent on two embassies, to Italy and Germany, and on his return, in May 1532, was appointed Archbishop.

Cranmer served Henry well, pronouncing his marriage to Catherine of Aragon null and void and declaring his marriage to Anne Boleyn valid. He annulled the latter marriage in 1536 and divorced him from her successor, Anne of Cleves, in 1540.

It was Cranmer who told the king that Catherine Howard had pre-marital affairs, and which in turn prompted

KING'S MAN:
Archbishop Cranmer

Henry to marry Catherine Parr.

Meanwhile, Cranmer also promoted the translation of the Bible, and when Henry died he compiled King Edward VI's prayer book.

However, with the king's ill-health ever-threatening, Cranmer supported the claim of Lady Jane Grey as his successor. So when Mary Tudor took the throne, his fate was sealed.

In September 1553, he was found guilty of conscious perjury and arraigned for treason. In 1556 he was taken to the stake.

ROYAL PALACE: Nottingham Castle in the 16th Century

First signs of castle decay

IN 1511, King Henry VIII stayed at Nottingham Castle.

His visit occasioned £100 worth of repairs, which included the relining of some tapestries, and was supervised by the king's clerk of works, Henry Smyth.

But by now the castle was in decline. In 1525 a survey told of 'decay and ruin' ...

● Part of the Great Hall's roof had fallen in.

● The leading and glass of the state apartments were in need of repair.

● The King's Chapel and staff lodgings were decrepit.

● Bridges at the upper bailey, middle and outer gates were in a ruinous state and there were problems with masonry, timber and tiles.

In 1536, the castle was re-armed because of a rebellion in Lincolnshire.

Under the orders of Thomas, Earl of Rutland, fortifications were put up at Trent Bridge in case the rebels considered crossing into Nottingham.

The castle was garrisoned with between 400 and 500 men under the command of Captain Leonard Skevington.

Pay was constantly in arrears, even when the size of the garrison was reduced. By 1542 the force was down to a captain and three men.

Rutland continually stressed the advisability of carrying out repairs he saw as so vital. In a letter of 1538 he wrote: "Forty shillings [£2] spent now will

KING HENRY VIII:
Castle improved for royal visit

save £40 in the future."

The following year, £100 was spent, although by 1546 a new report outlined the extent of decay to 40 tapestries, many depicting classical and biblical scenes, some of them badly affected by mildew.

Later in the 16th Century, money was spent on castle repairs, including £544 in advance of a meeting that had been planned — but never took place — between Elizabeth I and Mary, Queen of Scots.

A letter from the Lord Chancellor in 1560 indicated that some buildings were damaged beyond repair. Mills at the castle were demolished around 1564-5.

There was more investment ahead of a Royal Progress planned for the mid-1570s — but the queen chose to stay elsewhere.

THE Prior of Lenton, Nicholas Heath, was hanged, drawn and quartered in 1538.

A monk, Pentriche, had sworn that Heath and eight others had slandered Henry VIII and his advisor, Thomas Cromwell, who was then masterminding the dissolution of the monasteries.

Heath, who had been appointed by Cromwell, had promised £100 to the latter's nephew for the favour, but had failed to pay in full.

The priory had an income of more than £350 a year. That was tempting enough for Cromwell, acting on behalf of a bankrupt monarchy.

Throughout his ordeal, Heath had a strong ally in Sir John Willoughby of Wollaton, a believer in 'the old religion'.

Willoughby pressed the case that Pentriche had made up the allegations, but Cromwell would have none of it. In 1538, Heath was imprisoned and executed. His remains were displayed outside the priory.

The monks were thrown out and the estate was seized for the king.

● Newstead Priory was dissolved in 1539, and the 750-acre estate was bought for £810 the following year by Sir John Byron of Colwick.

❑ ❑ ❑

DAME Agnes Mellers, widow of mayor Richard Mellers, founded what is now called Nottingham High School in 1513.

The original site was on Stoney Street, near St Mary's Church. It soon established links with Oxford and Cambridge universities.

❑ ❑ ❑

HENRY Norris, lord of the manors of Stoke Bardolph, Gedling, Cropwell Bishop, Newton and Carlton, was convicted of high treason in 1536 — accused of an 'undue intimacy' with Anne Boleyn, wife of King Henry VIII.

He was offered life if he confessed, or implicated others. He refused, and was immediately executed. His lands passed into the hands of the Stanhope family.

Henry Ireton, soldier, scholar and statesman Page 9

IN 1578, Thomas Nix came before Guildhall court charged with practising the trade of ironmonger without being properly qualified.

Under the guild system, men learning trades had to serve obligatory apprenticeships of up to seven years.

Nix was fined £2 for each of the 11 months he had traded as an ironmonger.

□ □ □

THE Bell Inn, just off what is now Old Market Square, is believed to have been an alehouse by 1536, although its origins go back further.

It was then known as The Angel, a refectory for the Carmelite monastery on Beastmarket Hill. After the dissolution it became a secular tavern.

The name derived from the Latin *angelus*, the noon-day bell. The name 'The Bell' was probably in use by the Civil War.

□ □ □

IN 1576, officials showed increasing concern about the disrepair of wells at Weekday Cross and St Mary's Church.

Mention was also made of "offensive and unsightly objects" — dunghills and cesspools — in public thoroughfares.

At the time, the population of Nottingham was about 3,000.

□ □ □

AN outbreak of bubonic plague claimed 138 lives in Beeston in 1593-4, probably caused by insanitary conditions in homes on marshy land near the River Trent. A mass grave was dug at the eastern end of the churchyard.

□ □ □

IN one of the earliest topographical records of Nottingham, about 1540, John Leland reported "a large town, welle buildid for tymber and plaster, and standeth stately on a clyminge hille."

□ □ □

A STORM claimed the lives of several people in 1558. It was reported that hailstones of up to 15in circumference fell. Properties between Wilford and Lenton were damaged.

Courting curate invents the stocking frame

NOTTS clergyman William Lee invented the stocking frame in 1589.

According to legend, the Calverton curate was courting a woman who was so busy hand-knitting stockings that she had no time to respond to his advances.

He set his mind to creating a machine that would replicate the movement of needles. He came up with a device that could knit wool stockings 15 times faster than a skilled pair of hands.

The machine was demonstrated to Queen Elizabeth I, but she declined to grant a patent — reputedly because she feared for the livelihoods of her own hand knitters.

However the Queen did ask if Lee could produce a similar machine that could create silk stockings. He obliged, and several years later was able to

INNOVATOR: William Lee ponders his problem

present her with a pair of machine-made silk stockings.

However he never secured the patent he needed to develop the machine, and emigrated to France to found a workshop in Rouen. The year of death his disputed, but reckoned to be between 1610 and 1614.

Lee's brother James later introduced the machines to London.

Wollaton setting for magnate's mansion

WORK began on the construction of Wollaton Hall in 1580 — and the English Renaissance-style home of the Willoughby family was completed eight years later.

Sir Francis Willoughby was a provincial magnate. He kept about 50 servants and spent about £1,200 a year on domestic expenses — an enormous sum in the late 16th Century.

The principal figure concerned with the building of Wollaton was Robert Smythson, who had been one of the masonry contractors at Longleat in Wiltshire.

He was associated with Wollaton from at least 1582 and, having overseen the building project, he remained in the area until his death in 1614, acting both as an estate manager as well as a freelance architect.

Up to 76 men, women and child labourers worked on the building site at any one time, earning up to 6d [about 2p] a day.

Specialist contractors earned more — plumbers received 1s 2d a day [about 6p] and one mason received £16 for a year's work.

Situated on the crest of a hill, Wollaton Hall, finished in honey-coloured Ancaster limestone,

WOLLATON: 'Splendid and curious',according to one critic

was the most magnificent building for miles around — but not everyone appreciated its splendour.

"Sir Francis, out of ostentation to show his great riches," wrote one observer acidly, "built at vast charge a very stately home, both for the splendid appearance and curious workmanship of it."

He might have been referring to the excessive amount of external decorative motifs, which may

have been included on the insistence of Sir Francis himself.

In November, 1596, Sir Francis died in London — possibly as a result of food poisoning. His illness began the morning after he had dined at The Fleet — the debtor's prison where one of his in-laws was employed.

Although rich in estates, he died cash-poor, owing about £20,000.

Embattled King Charles raises his standard Page 10

£70 feast fit for James's queen

WOLLATON Hall welcomed royalty for the first time immediately after the death of Queen Elizabeth I in 1603.

King James I had travelled to London, and was followed south by Queen Anne and her eldest son, Prince Henry. They stayed the night of June 21 at Wollaton, home of Sir Percival Willoughby.

The banquet that night included eight fish, six capons, a dozen chickens and four pigs. The total catering bill came to £70.

The following year, Wollaton welcomed the king's second son, the Duke of York. He was to succeed his father as King Charles I.

Britain's first wooden 'rail way' was built at Wollaton pit, and the nearby Strelley mine was leased — but still the Willoughby debts mounted.

Sir Percival also lost out in investments in New World real estate and in glassmaking.

● Sir Francis Willoughby, descendant of the builder of Wollaton Hall, became a founder member of the Royal Society in 1662.

One of the most distinguished naturalists of his age, he travelled abroad and was vulnerable to a recurring fever. He died, aged 37, in 1672.

Repair problem at new gaol

A NEW gaol was built behind the old Shire Hall in about 1618, but there was concern about its condition by mid-century.

The keeper presented a petition in 1660 complaining that it was so ruinous that it was hard to guarantee the custody of prisoners.

The repair bill was estimated at £300. In 1686, another £9 was spent, but the next year the custodian reported that bricks were decaying and that "some prisoners will leave no means unattempted to make their escape."

POWER BASE: Henry Ireton's house at Attenborough, above. Right: The general himself, Oliver Cromwell's son-in-law

Henry Ireton, statesman

HENRY Ireton, later to become a soldier, statesman and leader of the Parliamentary cause, was born in Attenborough in 1611.

Educated at Oxford and trained in law, Ireton joined the Parliamentary army at the outbreak of the Civil War in 1642 and went on to command a cavalry force at the battle of Edgehill, Worcestershire.

He befriended Oliver Cromwell, then a colonel in the army of Eastern England, who in 1644 appointed him deputy governor of the Isle of Ely.

Cromwell became a regular visitor to the Ireton family home in Attenborough.

Ireton's military reputation grew as the Parliamentary forces scored decisive victories at the battles of Marston Moor and Naseby.

In 1646 he married Cromwell's eldest daughter, Bridget — the year after he had been elected to Parliament where he was to gain the reputation of being the most profound thinker the Puritans had.

Indeed, he produced a compromise that, had it been accepted by King Charles I, might have resolved the key issues of the Civil War.

Instead, he ended up helping bring the king to trial and being one of the signatories to his death warrant.

Later, after the king's execution, Ireton pursued the Government's cause against Roman Catholic rebels in Ireland, and became Lord Deputy and acting commander-in-chief. He died in Limerick in 1651.

Sherwood: A forest of 50,000 oaks

RIGHT: A gnarled oak in Sherwood Forest. Records of 1609 show there were 50,000 oaks in the forest, as well as thousands of other trees. There was no reference to the ancient Major Oak, near Edwinstowe, which is closely associated with the Robin Hood legend.

A SNEINTON butcher was brought before the courts in 1615 for selling meat during Lent. Seven years later a Nottingham alehouse keeper was charged with eating meat during Lent. He was fined sixpence [about 2p].

☐ ☐ ☐

NOTTINGHAM brick, made from the clay of Mapperley Plains, began to be a common building material in the early 1600s, gradually replacing timber and clay.

☐ ☐ ☐

THE Whyte Lion pub in Clumber Street was first referred to in 1675. Later called simply the Lion, it became a highly significant coaching inn by the early 19th Century.

☐ ☐ ☐

THE Manor House at Beeston was rebuilt in brick by Nicholas Strey, lord of the manor, in about 1665.

☐ ☐ ☐

ONE of the earliest known maps of Nottingham was drawn in 1610 by John Speed. The town covered an area from the Castle in the west to Bellar Gate in the east, with most of the buildings between Parliament Street and what is now Canal Street.

King gives in and orders Newark to submit Page 11

ROYAL STANDARD: Contrasting views of events of August 22, 1642. Above, a romantic interpretation, showing the stormy sky above Nottingham. Right, a retouched scene, looking from Standard Hill towards the town

THE Royalist garrison at Newark sent raiding parties into the pro-Parliament stronghold of Nottingham on at least three occasions — with only limited success.

● Sir Richard Byron led a force of 600 which captured Trent Bridge and shot at the castle from the tower of St Nicholas's Church.

● Sir Charles Lucas led a large force into Nottingham. It was seen off by charges led by Colonel Francis Thornhagh.

● In February 1644, the Nottingham garrison confounded a plot to infiltrate troops disguised as farm women and traders heading for the market. One of the captured Royalists, a defector from Parliament's cause, was court-martialled and executed.

A ROYALIST garrison at Thurgarton Priory, commanded by Sir Roger Cooper, was overcome by Nottingham-based Roundheads in 1644.

In 1645 a siege at a moated house in Norwell, garrisoned by Newark-supplied Royalists, ended when Roundhead troops were redeployed.

□ □ □

ON September 17, 1644, Parliamentarian and Royalist soldiers fought a running battle between Rempstone and East Leake. Two men from each side were buried at East Leake Church.

Monarch declares war on Parliament

NOTTINGHAM was witness in 1642 to one of the most fateful moments in the history of England — the call to arms by King Charles I against the forces of Parliament.

The dramatic moment happened at about 6pm on August 22 at a windblown Nottingham Castle.

The King, who arrived in the town on August 19, stayed at Thurland Hall.

On August 22, he and his retinue travelled across the town centre to the walls of the ancient castle.

Awaiting him were 1,000 lords, gentlemen and soldiers who had responded to his summons, of August 12, to "all subjects who can bear arms northwards of the Trent, and southwards for 20 miles."

A proclamation was read, and the king's personal standard was hoisted. A contemporary print suggests it

EMBATTLED KING: Charles, by Van Dyck

was a huge pennant with two tapering tails. Probably red in colour, it showed the royal arms. According to one source, it included the legend: "Give Caesar his due".

As the pennant flew in the stiffening wind, courtiers

shouted: "God save King Charles, and hang up the Roundheads."

That night, though, the standard was blown down in the gale. It was, according to the king's adviser Clarendon, "an ill omen".

And so it proved. Although the king attended further proclamations on August 23 and 24, and a recruiting centre was opened nearby at the site of the Salutation Inn, only a few hundred men enrolled.

King Charles left Nottingham on September 13. Ever since, the high ground at the castle walls has been known as Standard Hill.

King and Parliament had been in conflict over his freedom to raise taxes. Charles dismissed Parliament in 1629, and there was a further stand-off in January 1642 when he tried to arrest five members of the Commons. This challenge to his "divine right" led to the proclamation in Nottingham.

● There were some early successes for the King in Notts. Late in 1642, Sir John Digby occupied Newark, and governor Sir John Henderson turned the town into a Royalist stronghold.

But in Nottingham, Colonel Hutchinson rallied Parliamentarian sympathisers and formed a defence committee, whose members included Henry Ireton.

Hutchinson became Governor of Nottingham and organised a force of 700 men.

Stay sober, defenders are warned

RELATIONS between the Nottingham garrison and townsfolk were strained, mainly because defences were concentrated on the castle, and outlying streets were vulnerable to Royalist skirmishers.

There were also complaints about the behaviour of soldiers, which prompted orders from the military governor,

Colonel Hutchinson, and the Mayor, William Nix.

Soldiers were threatened with fines of ...

● A half-crown [about 12p] for idling in the street while sermons were being preached.

● Ten shillings [50p] for being caught in taverns on Sundays.

● Five shillings [25p] for drunkenness.

Newark holds firm for crown

THE people of Newark suffered in the last of three sieges of the Royalist garrison town.

Although the King's contingent regularly menaced the Parliamentarian stronghold of Nottingham in the early years of the war, Newark came under increasing pressure.

Early in 1643, Major-General Ballard's army was humiliated by the town's defenders — a force of just 2,000 men led by the governor, Sir John Henderson.

Sir John Meldrum, with 5,000 footsoldiers and 2,000 cavalry, laid siege to Newark once again.

This time the Royalist hero was the king's nephew Prince Rupert, whose troops arrived from Chester and took up positions on Beacon Hill.

On the night of March 22, 1644, they charged down the hill at Meldrum's men, who were routed. The booty included a huge gun, a 12ft cannon known to soldiers as "Sweetlips".

The third siege began in November 1645 and lasted for six months.

Newark's garrison, now commanded by Lord John Belasyse (or Bellasis), numbered just 4,000. It was surrounded by an army four

STRONGHOLD:
Newark Castle

times stronger — General Poyntz's Parliamentarian regiments being supplemented by the Earl of Leven's Scottish troops, based at nearby Kelham.

The will of defenders and townsfolk was tested by skirmishers, hunger and plague. When Newark did surrender, in May 1646, it was on the express order of the king.

UNDER ATTACK: A clash during the 1643 siege of Newark, enacted by the Sealed Knot Society

Broken King surrenders

THE king's war against Parliament began and ended in Nottinghamshire.

In 1642, Charles I had stayed at the King's Arms Inn at Southwell on his way to Nottingham, where he rallied supporters to his cause.

On May 5, 1646, an odd figure arrived at the same hostelry in Southwell, his beard shaven and his hair cropped in the style of a priest.

It was the embattled king, whose armies had been beaten at Naseby (1645) and in Scotland (March 1646). Acknowledging that, militarily, his position was hopeless, he decided while in Oxford to surrender ... but not to Parliament.

After travelling through the night from Stamford, the king arrived in Southwell at 7am and presented himself at the inn now known as the Saracen's Head.

There he dined with two Scottish commissioners, having earlier received private assurances that he would be well received. Later, the king was escorted to Kelham, where he became a prisoner of the

JOURNEY'S END: The Saracen's Head, then the King's Arms

Scottish general, David Leslie.

King Charles was compelled to order the surrender of his Newark garrison ("I can give you no hope of relief," he wrote to the governor, Lord John Belasyse). On May 7, he was taken north with the Scots army.

Hopes of a French-brokered accord between the king and the Scots came to nothing. Charles was handed over to the English Parliament in 1647.

Celebrations in Nottingham were cut short by an outbreak of plague.

THE second Civil War erupted in 1648, with King Charles hoping to regain the throne with Scottish help.

At Willoughby on July 5, Colonel Rossiter's Roundheads overwhelmed Royalist forces led by General Sir Philip Monckton.

Royalist prisoners included Monckton, two other generals, three colonels and some 600 other officers and men. Ten king's colours were captured.

❏❏❏

THE remains of Nottingham Castle were demolished in 1651 after an application to Parliament.

❏❏❏

JOHN, 1st Lord Byron, died in Paris in 1652. He had been raised to the peerage for his services to the Royalist cause.

❏❏❏

COLONEL John Hutchinson, 49, governor of Nottingham during the war, died in 1664 at Sandown Castle in Kent — where he was imprisoned on suspicion of plotting against King Charles II.

❏❏❏

FRANCIS Hacker of East Bridgford escorted King Charles I to his execution in Whitehall on January 30, 1649. After the Restoration he was declared a traitor and executed at Tyburn.

John Deane, the 'secret agent' from Wilford ➡ Page 13

Legend of 'the royal children'

IN 1688 King James II was ousted in the revolution which saw the accession of William and Mary.

That same year, Mary's sister Princess Anne — later Queen Anne — stayed in Nottingham.

One story survives her stay. Her young offspring reputedly played with the children of a local innkeeper — hence the name of the pub, The Royal Children.

A story, though, is all it is likely to be. Anne had five children from a total of 17 confinements. Four of them died before the age of two.

THE rebuilding of St Nicholas's Church began in 1671. During the Civil War it had been damaged by the Parliamentarian garrison at Nottingham Castle because it was a vantage point for Royalist skirmishers.

Rebuilding was completed in 1678. St Nicholas's gained the nickname of 'the Drawing Room Church' because of its well-to-do parishioners.

A RIOT broke out in 1678 after the appointment of a new burgess.

Mayor Ralph Edge claimed the nominee, William Drury, was ineligible. The burgesses refused to nominate another candidate, so Edge swore in Robert Whortley. The mayor and aldermen were pelted with bread and cheese.

Whortley himself became mayor in 1685.

THE *Antiquities of Nottinghamshire,* by Dr Robert Thoroton, was published in 1677. It is one of the classic local history works.

Thoroton was a country doctor who lived at Car Colston, near Bingham. His name is perpetuated by the influential history group, the Thoroton Society.

TRENT BRIDGE: A rustic scene on the banks of the Trent, showing the stone bridge. Its predecessor, built of wood on stone piers, was seriously damaged by the floods of 1683

Baronet who loved rough and tumble

SIR Thomas Parkyns, who became "the Wrestling Baronet of Bunny", was born in 1662.

The story goes that he would not employ any man on his estates who was not a proficient wrestler.

Sir Thomas was a classicist, mathematician — he studied under Sir Isaac Newton — physician, man of letters, architect and builder. But his greatest love was wrestling — he even wrote a book about the sport.

A product of his time, and a true eccentric, he combined the characteristics of country gentleman and man of affairs with a taste for rough and tumble.

And he was kind-hearted, too. In 1700 he initiated a series of charitable bequests which now combine as the Bunny with Bradmore Charities. Another bequest provided a books grant to apprentices who went to university.

MONUMENTAL FIGURE: The Thomas Parkyns memorial at Bunny

Thomas was educated at Westminster School and Trinity College, Cambridge, and went on to study law at Gray's Inn.

He succeeded to the baronetcy in 1684, and took possession of property in Costock, Bradmore, Ruddington, East Leake and Bunny.

Later he rebuilt Bunny Hall, where his family had been living since before the English Civil War.

Building, and designing buildings, he would often add extravagant touches and Latin mottos as a hallmark of his self-taught architectural style.

He organised annual wrestling tournaments in the yard of the Rancliffe Arms, with a fancy lace hat as first prize. He would even grapple with his own staff. In 1713 wrote a short book, *The Inn-Play or The Cornish Hugg-Wrestler*.

Sir Thomas was also one of the first people in Britain to introduce a minimum wage.

Married twice, and the father of two children, he died in 1741 but not before he had seen a monument to his achievements put up in Bunny church.

Joan Phillips hanged for crimes on the highway

THE highwaywoman Joan Phillips, 29, was hanged in 1685 at a scaffold on the junction of Loughborough Road and Wilford Lane.

The daughter of a wealthy farmer, she had become involved with a rogue called Edward Bracey. They ran a tavern in Bristol, then came to Nottingham and robbed coach travellers.

But during the course of one robbery, they made a mistake. The coach occupants were armed and overpowered Joan, though not before, according to the story, she had killed two of them.

She did her best to conceal her identity, claiming she was Bracey. But the truth soon emerged.

According to legend, Bracey made a desperate bid to rescue her as she was led to the scaffold. He was shot dead.

Notts landowners' dispute ends in bloodshed Page 14

Brother's conscience traps killer

MASS murderer William Andrew Horne was executed in Nottingham in 1759, on his 74th birthday.

His first victim was a young woman he had seduced and the second was a beggar who knocked at his door. But it was his third murder which led to his downfall.

Horne had made his sister pregnant, and three days after the birth of their son he took the infant to Annesley and left him in a haystack, tied in a sack.

His brother Charles shared the guilty secret for years. But finally he could stand it no more and informed the authorities.

Horne was arrested, tried, convicted and hanged in front of a huge crowd at Gallows Hill, at the top of Mansfield Road. His body was taken away for dissection.

❏❏❏

COUNT Tallard, a French marshal captured at the Battle of Bleinheim in 1704, was kept under arrest in Nottingham for six years, although he was allowed the liberty of the town.

He lived at Newdigate House, Castle Gate, where he reputedly laid out the gardens and cultivated flowers and vegetables.

❏❏❏

FIVE prisoners escaped from the County Gaol at Shire Hall on June 13, 1786. One used a false key, while the other four clambered on to a roof and descended into the Narrow Marsh.

❏❏❏

THE floor of Nottingham Assizes collapsed in 1724, and several people fell into the cellar. The judge fined the county £2,000 for the hall's shortcomings — but the penalty was overturned by the Privy Council.

SEAMAN-SPY: John Deane's grave. Below: Wilford Church

Daring sailor, special agent

ADVENTURER John Deane, 82, died in 1761 after a colourful life which embraced naval glory, cannibalism and espionage. He is buried at Wilford Churchyard.

Deane had been born into a wealthy Nottingham family in 1679. He ran away to sea, took part in the Siege of Gibraltar (1704) and was promoted captain at the comparatively young age of 25.

Resigning his commission, he entered the merchant trade and in 1709 bought his own cargo ship, which he called *The Nottingham Galley*.

The following year she was wrecked off New England and a valuable cargo was lost. Fourteen men were marooned on Boon Island for 24 days, and news reached home that the survivors had fed on the body of a dead shipmate.

Deane was criticised at the official inquiry — but he was soon off on a new adventure. In 1714 he joined Tsar Peter the Great's navy during Russia's war against Sweden.

He captured more than 20 vessels, but his luck ran out when he was caught between English and Dutch ships. Two of

his own ships were lost.

There was a court martial, but the Tsar stepped in and reduced his punishment to a year's detention and demotion to the rank of lieutenant.

Deane returned to England in 1723 and was recruited by the Government to spy on Jacobite sympathisers (under the cover of the British consulship at St Petersburg). He remained in the diplomatic service until 1738.

Deane and his wife Sarah built two houses facing Wilford village green. His retirement was almost cut short in 1748 when he was attacked in his grounds and left for dead. His assailant, a thief named Miller, was later hanged.

Needles swallower survives

THE case of Kitty Hudson caused great excitement in medical circles in 1783.

From the age of six she lived with the sexton of St Mary's Church. It became her job to collect pins and needles, which she kept in her mouth.

As the years passed, she became addicted to the practice, and could not go to sleep without a mouthful of pins and needles.

In a series of operations over more than a year, dozens of pins and needles were removed from various parts of her body.

Kitty survived the ordeal to marry and bear 19 children.

❏❏❏

ACTOR-manager James Whitley founded the Theatre Royal in St Mary's Gate in about 1760.

The company staged seasons in Nottingham to coincide with the August racing festival, and Goose Fair in the autumn.

❏❏❏

TEXTILE trader Abel Collin died in 1705, aged 52, leaving a bequest to the needy. The capital was so well managed that it later funded almshouses and a ten-bed maternity home in Waverley Street.

❏❏❏

THE Nottingham Lighting Act of 1762 placed responsibility for the town's street lighting in the hands of a local committee, whose first members included the Vicar of St Mary's and the rectors of St Peter's and St Nicholas's. Lamps were lit by whale oil, stored in a cellar at Weekday Cross.

❏❏❏

KITTY Riley, inmate of Nottingham Work House, died aged 100 in 1739. Three years earlier she had walked to London to visit her children. Her plans to settle in the capital did not work out ... so she walked back.

Cotton stockings 'first' for town's knitting trade

A PAIR of machine-made cotton stockings, reputedly the first, were produced in 1730 by a knitter named Draper.

Over the next 20 years there was a huge expansion of the framework knitting trade, with several operators moving from London. By 1750 there were 50 local manufacturers, owning 1,200 frames.

"I can tell stockingers by their appearance," a doctor wrote. "There is a paleness and emaciation about them."

'Old General' Ben Mayo, master of mischief ➡ Page 15

Radical's effigy is hanged

AN effigy of the radical writer Tom Paine, author of *The Rights of Man*, was 'tried' for treason at Lenton.

It was hanged from a tree and later cut down and burned. The 'executioners' retired to a coffee house and repeatedly toasted the health of king, queen and the local gentry.

The context was the growing fear of a French invasion, and there were clashes throughout the Nottingham area between 'Royalist' factions and groups wearing paper imitations of the French cap cockade.

The Royal Navy, army regiments and the fencible units (home defence regiments, forerunners of the 1940s Home Guard) were constantly recruiting.

The bounty for local fencible regiments in 1794 was reputedly eight guineas [£8.40].

□ □ □

THE town council agreed in 1706 to a charity school, and voted £5 a year to the subscription fund.

Initially, it allowed for 26 boys and 14 girls, aged seven to 14. Half came from the parish of St Mary's, and the remaining 20 from the parishes of St Peter and St Nicholas.

Bluecoat School insisted that the children wear the uniform of coat, white bands and breeches. The uniform, in various forms, was retained until 1950.

□ □ □

THOMAS Hammond was credited with producing the first piece of machine-made lace, in 1768. Twenty years later, the term "Nottingham lace" became used.

□ □ □

NOTTINGHAM Cricket Club played the Gentlemen of Mary-le-bone at Upper Meadow in 1791. The visitors won, with local batsmen falling to the superior bowling skills of Lord Winchelsea, Colonel Lenox and Captain Cumberland.

COCKPIT: The 'cockpit' at the Lion Hotel, Clumber Street

Dope row over fighting cocks

OUTRAGED breeders of fighting cocks met in Nottingham to stop corruption.

Owners congregated at the Red Lion Inn in Pelham Street and formed an association to prosecute anyone caught nobbling members' birds.

The action followed several instances of fowl secretly being injured by gamblers who had backed rival cocks.

The most serious incident, at the White Lion Inn, concerned birds brought from the capital for a 'Nottingham v London' match.

Their water was laced with arsenic — not enough to kill, but enough to weaken them. A £50 reward was offered for the arrest of the perpetrator.

Poaching debate ends in fatal duel

WILLIAM Chaworth of Annesley Hall died in 1765 after a duel with fellow Notts landowner Lord Byron, uncle of the poet.

Both were members of 'the Nottinghamshire Club', which met at the Star and Garter Tavern in Pall Mall.

The club convened for dinner and during the evening there was an argument between the two men over the conservation of game and the severity of the poaching laws.

Tempers became frayed, and according to one account, they asked a waiter to show them an empty room.

When the bell in the chamber was rung, the waiter returned to the room to find the men with swords in hands.

Mr Chaworth had a wound in his belly. Swords were

SLAIN: William Chaworth

surrendered and doctors were called. Mr Chaworth was moved to his London home, where he died after giving

instructions for his will. Lord Byron, as was the custom of the time, submitted himself for judgment by his peers. He denied murder, and the two-day trail at Westminster Hall ended with him being found guilty of the lesser offence of manslaughter. He was released.

Aged 85, Lord Byron died in 1798. He was succeeded to the title and the Newstead Abbey estate by his ten-year-old nephew.

George Gordon Byron, the sixth baron, visited Newstead for the first time later that year, but he and his mother settled first in Nottingham and later in Southwell.

He was educated at Harrow and Trinity College, Cambridge, before embarking on a life of writing and foreign travel.

Prison reformer Howard raps 'offensive' dungeons

PENAL reformer John Howard visited the County Gaol, High Pavement, in 1782.

He complained about the unhealthy state of the dungeons, but expressed confidence that the justices would improve them.

Howard returned in 1788 and again expressed reservations about conditions for prisoners. "The prison is too small," he recorded. "Felons lie in two dark,

offensive dungeons, down 36 steps, called pits, which are never whitewashed."

At last there was action in 1798, when the jail was criticised by the grand jury at the March Assizes ...

"The inhabitants of the county ought to make, build, repair and amend the gaol to make the same healthy, safe and convenient for the confinement of prisoners."

Royal Navy hero who became 'the happy man' ➡ Page 16

Etonian highwayman is hanged at Tyburn

BARONET'S son William Parsons was executed for escaping transportation in the colonies.

Parsons, 33, black sheep of a Nottingham family, had received seven years for fraud.

After being shipped to North America, he took advantage of a family contact in Maryland, stole his horse, turned highwayman — and with the proceeds bought his passage home.

Back in England he again became a highway robber, but was detained at Hounslow. He was hanged at Tyburn, London, in February 1751.

Parsons was educated at Eton, but criminal tendencies showed themselves at an early age. After being caught robbing a bookseller, his father sent him to sea — only for him to desert his midshipman's post in the West Indies.

Between periods of poverty, his subsequent career included spells in the colonial service, the infantry and the marines..

Parsons later turned to forgery, for which he sentenced to transportation by Rochester Assizes.

'Old General' makes mischief

BENJAMIN Mayo, the eccentric nicknamed 'the Old General', was born in Nottingham in the 1770s. He was the unofficial leader of the town's urchins, and encouraged children to play truant.

He even organised youngsters to pelt schools with mud, and would

'HARMLESS': Urchins' leader Benjamin Mayo

accept bribes from teachers to end the sieges.

Ben was regarded as a harmless idiot and spent most of his life in St Peter's Poorhouse. He enjoyed his ale, but every Sunday he worshipped at St Peter's Church.

Bands play as canal opens

THE Nottingham Canal, connecting the town with the River Trent, was opened in 1794.

Thousands watched as three vessels passed through, and bands played *Rule, Britannia* and *Hearts of Oak*.

Pay: Knitters attack bosses

VIOLENCE flared in Nottingham when Parliament twice rejected a bid to improve pay and conditions for thousands of struggling frame knitters.

The workers' petition for higher pay and lower frame rents was first ruled out by a Westminster committee in 1778.

Nottingham hosiers and their lawyer had their windows smashed by rioters.

The following year the committee allowed time for the debate on legislation which one MP said had been "saturated with the tears of the poor and their distressed families."

However, the Bill failed, prompting rioting in Nottingham from June 10. Crowds damaged the homes of hosiers and their managers, the master stockingers.

Riots continued sporadically throughout the rest of the century, causing mistrust between stocking framers and the local army garrison.

When a contingent of soldiers was withdrawn from Nottingham in 1791, residents stood on a rock above a narrow street — armed, according to

'WORLD'S FIRST': The cotton mill off Wollaton Street

one historian, with "night-soil in vessels from the privies."

● The Lancashire inventors Arkwright and Hargreaves both set up shop in Nottingham in the second half of the 18th Century. Arkwright created a cotton mill near Hockley in 1768; Hargreaves ran what was later claimed to be the world's first cotton mill in Mill Street, off Wollaton Street.

Troops quell food price riots

RELATIONS between townsfolk and the military were further strained by clashes over food prices.

In 1766, farmers raised the price of cheese, causing disturbances in Nottingham that October.

Protesters knocked over displays in the market place, sending whole cheeses rolling down Wheeler Gate. One knocked over the mayor, Alderman Swann, who had been trying to restore order.

The 15th Dragoons were summoned, and dealt harshly with the mob. A man from Car Colston was shot and others were hurt.

In 1788, townsfolk burned butchers' property because of the price of meat. There were riots over bread prices in 1794.

A DARING burglary was the talk of the town in November 1773. Long Row confectioner Mr Topott found one of his bedroom windows open, and a ladder resting against it. A bureau had been broken into and 265 gold guineas and a gold watch stolen.

Suspicion fell on the young joiner who, earlier in the autumn, had hung paper in the room. Joseph Shaw's lodgings were searched, and town constables pressed their ears to the cellar floor. They heard a ticking noise, and the watch and money were discovered.

Shaw, convicted on the strength of his accomplice's evidence, was sentenced to death. He and another criminal, named as Wheatley, were the last two men who were required to walk through the town to the gallows.

IN 1781, the foundation stone was laid for the General Hospital on land given by the Duke of Newcastle. The Duke also gave £300, and other benefactors included mill owner Richard Arkwright, the Archbishop of York and the Duke of Devonshire.

SIX people drowned when a temporary ferry capsized at Wilford during a gale on July 31, 1784.

THE London mail service was improved in 1785. The new timetable allowed for a coach leaving the capital at 8pm to arrive in Nottingham by noon next day. The return service left Nottingham at 4pm, arriving in London at 8am next day.

THE corporation mace was stolen in 1785 from the mayor's home in Beastmarket Hill. James Shipley was sentenced to seven years' transportation to Nova Scotia — but he escaped and fled to France.

A PUBLIC meeting at the Exchange Room in 1795 pledged £1,200 for the relief of Nottingham's poor.

How Clifton Grove inspired 'Unhappy White'   ➡ Page 17

THE Nottingham racing meeting in August 1799 was attended by King George III's brother, the Duke of Cumberland. He left after his own horse, Pomona, was defeated.

□ □ □

THE legendary Nottingham poacher Thomas Booth died in March 1752, aged 75. His headstone, which he approved before his death, read: "Here lies a marksman who with art and skill, When young and strong, fat bucks and does did kill."

□ □ □

SHEEP were roasted in the market place in 1789 when Nottingham celebrated the recovery from mental illness of King George III.

□ □ □

WORKMEN dug up human bones while pulling down a house in Beastmarket Hill in 1762. They were thought to be the remains of monks from the medieval Carmelite friary.

□ □ □

WHEN hosier's daughter Fanny Melville married merchant Charles Copeland at Bulwell in 1769, she was attended by *sixteen* of her surviving brothers and sisters, all dressed in white. According to the *Journal*, later that year Fanny's 45-year-old mother later gave birth to her *thirtieth* child!

□ □ □

A WOMAN convicted in 1770 of stealing handkerchiefs from a draper's shop was ordered to be strapped to a wagon and whipped from Weekday Cross to the Market Place.

□ □ □

THERE was a lucky escape in 1771 for a boy playing on the rock behind Shire Hall, overlooking Narrow Marsh. Feeling a wall give way, he jumped and landed in a vat of ale. According to observers, beer splashed in all directions.

□ □ □

IN January 1774, temperatures dropped so low that the River Trent was frozen over for five days.

Nelson's steward writes home

NILE VICTOR: Admiral Nelson

A NOTTS seaman wrote a first-hand account of one of the greatest Royal Navy triumphs of the Napoleonic Wars, the Battle of the Nile, August 1, 1798.

Thomas Spencer, 27, was Nelson's steward in HMS *Vanguard*, and described the action in a letter to his parents in Gotham.

The French ships were moored in Aboukir Bay, expecting an attack from the seaward side. Nelson surprised the enemy by deploying his squadron on both sides of their line.

"It was the hardest battle ever fought," Spencer wrote to his parents.

It took two months for the news to arrive in England. In Nottingham, it was Goose Fair week. Bells were rung and a public subscription was launched for the families of wounded seamen and marines.

Notts also produced a distinguished admiral, Richard Howe of Langar, later Earl Howe.

He commanded the Channel Fleet at the victory of The First of June (1794).

Hero's welcome for 'the Happy Man'

COMMODORE Sir John Warren was created a Knight of the Bath in 1794 for his role in the war against the French.

The Stapleford sailor's squadron had conducted a campaign of harassment along the French coast, and he fought in that year's action known as 'The Glorious First of June'

When Sir John returned on September 19 his coach was met by a crowd at Trent Bridge. The horses were removed, and the townsfolk took over. "The hero was drawn into town amidst the acclamation of thousands," the *Nottingham Date Book* recorded.

The procession included "a company of Light Horse, 12 sergeants, five drummers ... and the Cock o'th'Blue himself in his full-bottomed wig."

In 1796, Sir John received the

HAPPY COUPLE:
The Warrens on the pub sign

thanks of Parliament for his victory off Achile Head. He also received the Freedom of Nottingham. He became a member of the Privy Council and was elected MP for

Nottingham in 1797.

Promoted rear-admiral, he commanded a squadron in the West Indies. In 1812, a full admiral, he became commander-in-chief, North America.

Two pubs are named in his honour — the Sir John Borlase Warren at Canning Circus, and The Happy Man in Stapleford.

The story of the latter is that he took a fancy to general's daughter Caroline Clavering. At a dinner party, he passed a note to her, written in French.

The message said that if his heart was worthy of her, she would make him "the happiest of men." Miss Clavering read it, and said in English: "Then you shall be happy."

The couple married and lived happily together until the admiral's death in 1822.

Tornado smashes through Sneinton

HOUSES were smashed and trees uprooted as a tornado tore through Sneinton and Colwick.

It happened on November 1, 1755, when witnesses in Nottingham saw a dark cloud heading towards the Trent.

"When the cloud crossed the river," reported the *Gentlemen's Magazine*, "it did not seem more than 30 or 40 feet from the surface of the water, which was violently agitated and flew upward.

"Some persons, who saw it from Trent Bridge, described it as a huge black inverted cone, in which they perceived a whirling spiral motion, with a rumbling noise like distant thunder.

"The middle of the column appeared to be nearly 20 feet in diameter."

According to witnesses, the phenomenon moved towards the village of Sneinton, where it ripped thatched roofs from barns and cottages and tore up apple trees by the roots.

The cloud passed over Colwick Hills, accompanied by flashes of lightning.

No serious injuries were recorded, although a boy of 14 was blown from one field, over a hedge, and into the next.

Several witnesses complained of severe headaches which lasted for several hours.

Town and Government clash in 1802 election Page 18

'UNHAPPY WHITE': Kirke White, and his birthplace as shown on a plaque

Condemned, then gallows were stolen

TWO men sentenced to death in Nottingham in 1800 on a charge of forgery.

Abraham Whitaker, 45, and John Atkinson, 35, worked as hawkers all over the country, the court heard, "principally for the purpose of passing spurious Bank of England notes."

A Stapleford man, John Greasley, became suspicious when the pair passed some of them to him, and they were arrested in Eastwood.

Both men went to considerable lengths to try to escape. Their execution was delayed when some young men-about-town stole the gallows.

But it seems that the convicts were reprieved at the last minute. Whitaker accepted transportation to New South Wales.

Menagerie joins Goose Fair

ATTRACTIONS at the 1805 Goose Fair included a lion, a Bengal tiger and tigress, two leopards, panthers, wolves and kangaroos.

It was the first year that Wombwells Menagerie made its appearance at the Nottingham fair, starting a tradition that would last for 100 years.

Clifton Grove inspired poet

NOTTINGHAM-born poet Henry Kirke White died on October 19, 1806, aged just 21.

He was a butcher's son, born in a house overlooking The Poultry. He was baptised at the Independent Chapel in Castle Gate, and was educated at the Nottingham Academy in Parliament Street.

In spite of Henry's budding literary talents, his father apprenticed him to a stocking-frame knitter.

White later entered the solicitor's office of town clerk George Coldham. While studying for his articles, he also taught himself Latin, Greek, Spanish and science.

His first volume of verse was entitled Clifton Grove and Other Poems (1803). The title reflected his love of the countryside south of the Trent.

The generosity of family friends enabled White to go up to St John's College, Cambridge, where his intensive studies undermined his already delicate health.

His admirers included Robert Southey, and Lord Byron, who wrote:

Unhappy White! While life was in its spring

And thy joyous muse just waved her joyous wing,

The spoiler swept that soaring lyre away...

STAGE STAR: Sarah Siddons (by Gainsborough, right) played Lady Macbeth in Nottingham in 1807.

Later in the year, her brother Charles Kemble played Hamlet.

Five years later, Siddons retired from full-time acting.

The story goes that in her final performance as Lady Macbeth the audience would not allow the play to continue after her climactic sleepwalking scene.

SNEINTON-born Mary Voce was hanged in 1802 for poisoning one of her children.

Voce, 24, who lived in Fisher Gate, seems to have enjoyed male company a little too much. Her husband, a bricklayer, left her.

It is recorded that: "Finding her youngest child a obstacle in the way of her improper connections, she poisoned it."

Voce appears to have undergone conversion to Christianity while she awaited sentence to be carried out.

She went to the gallows "amidst the greatest concourse of spectators ever witnessed in this town; about 100 voices singing penitential hymns on the way to, and at, the gallows."

□ □ □

THE death occurred in Nottingham in 1805 of a highly eccentric man called George Wright.

He was a pedlar broker, which meant that he toured auctions buying job lots of anything he could, repaired his purchases and sold them.

He called his house Little Paradise. In the middle of the parlour was a highly polished mahogany coffin which he kept for years in readiness for his death.

□ □ □

TWO men were sentenced to death in 1802 for highway robbery.

Henry Palmer and Ferdinando Davis were charged with stealing a silver watch, leather pocket book and money from a butcher's apprentice at Lenton.

Davis was hanged in Nottingham. Palmer was reprieved and sent to a prison hulk.

□ □ □

THE architect Jeffry Wyatt (also known as Wyatville) was commissioned in 1801 to modernise Wollaton Hall.

His internal alterations continued throughout the early part of the century.

□ □ □

THE population of Nottingham in 1801 was recorded as 28,801.

Hosiers under attack as the Luddites run riot Page 19

THE town's reputation as a hotbed of radicalism prompted the arrival of Bow Street Runners in 1800.

They reported that nightly meetings were held in the Masons Arms, where sentiments were loudly voiced opposing the monarchy and supporting the French Revolution.

In the event, the Government responded by sending in extra troops.

□ □ □

THOMAS Hawkesley, future engineer, was born in Arnold in 1807.

□ □ □

JOHN Heathcoat perfected his bobbinet machine in 1808, using moving bobbins. A revised version, patented in 1809, allowed for lace to be made of greater width.

□ □ □

A VISITOR to the County Gaol in Nottingham recorded that both debtors and felons received 1lb of bread per day. Felons were also given a penny a day, and an extra penny a week for buying soap.

□ □ □

SCOTSMAN Robert Calvin was ordered into the stocks in 1808 for assaulting two girls. Large crowds witnessed what was claimed to be the first public pillorying in two generations.

□ □ □

WHEN the war with France resumed in 1803, prompting renewed invasion fears, 750 Nottingham men volunteered for the local militia.

□ □ □

THE last of 13 windmills to be constructed on the Forest was built in 1807. It burned down in 1858, and was commemorated by The Windmill pub on Alfreton Road.

□ □ □

CHARLES Sutton founded the radical *Nottingham Review* in 1808 to fill what he saw as a niche in the political market.

□ □ □

THE corporation changed its stance on the war with France when hostilities resumed in 1803 (see right). The city gave 400

Goodacre's academy

TEACHER Robert Goodacre, who ran a successful school at the turn of the century, bought land from the Duke of Newcastle in 1806 and built the Standard Hill Academy. It had 28 pupils and a rooftop observatory.

One of its earliest pupils was George Green, future mathematician, whose baker father bought land in the village of Sneinton in 1807. Green Snr built the brick windmill known as Green's Mill.

As well as the 50ft windmill, the property included a miller's house, stabling for eight horses and a granary. The Green family built a home nearby about ten years later.

Officer shot in duel

A 17-year-old soldier, Lieut Brown, was killed in a duel in Basford in 1806.

He had been drinking in a pub called the Fox and Crown and became involved in an argument with an older man, Ensign Butler, from another regiment. Both men were on recruiting duties.

The argument became more heated, and it was agreed to settle the matter at a secluded spot nearby. There, Brown was shot dead.

Witnesses took the young soldier's body to Basford parish church. Butler and his associates fled and a coroner's jury later returned a verdict of wilful murder.

Art world admires Bonington, Sandby

THE PAINTER Richard Parkes Bonington was born at Arnold in 1801.

He studied in Calais, and in Paris made friends with the great French romantic painter Eugene Delacroix.

Continuing his studies at the Ecole des Beaux-Arts, Bonington made a name for himself with his watercolour landscapes.

Bonington returned to England with Delacroix in 1825 and added historical scenes to his portfolio.

His reputation in Britain grew with his exhibitions at the British Institution in 1826 and the Royal Academy in 1828. He died in London that year.

Paul Sandby, the Nottingham-born artist who was a founder member of the Royal Academy, died in 1809.

Born in 1730, he began his professional life as a draughtsman. Employed by the Military Drawing Office in London, he worked on the highways survey of the Scottish Highlands in 1746.

His brother Thomas became deputy ranger of Windsor Forest, providing Paul with access to his favourite water colour subject, Windsor Castle.

He painted several Windsor scenes over the next half-century, although he continued to pursue his career as a draughtsman.

Gainsborough referred to him as "the only man of genius who has painted real views from nature in the country."

ARNOLD ARTIST: Richard Parkes Bonington

Insults, stones and acid fly in Nottingham election

THE 1802 General Election saw intimidation and rioting.

The two initial candidates were Daniel Parker Coke and Admiral Sir John Warren — and it seems the corporation did not approve of Coke.

The council had opposed Britain's war with France — in 1798 refusing to make a donation — and believed Coke had not voiced his opposition enough.

A third candidate, John Birch, was brought in on behalf of the corporation.

The crowd stoned Coke, and electors complained that they had been prevented from voting for him.

Birch was elected, but a parliamentary committee investigated in March 1803, declared the result void, and enacted a law compelling magistrates to keep order while ensuring free elections.

Coke then beat Birch by 195 votes, but there were still violent incidents and complaints that acid was thrown at the hustings.

1813-14 freeze: 'Ice in June'

A PERIOD of exceptionally cold weather began on Christmas Eve, 1813. According to the *Nottingham Date Book*: "The frost ... continued without any thaw until January 26 when it partially broke up, but gathering renewed intensity, extended its frigid dominion with little variation, eight weeks longer."

On the night of January 28, the mail coach left Nottingham at 7pm, but eight miles out the horses could no longer pull it through the snow. The coachmen ordered an overnight stop, then noticed what they took to be a dead body. It was an elderly man, who was unconscious.

When revived, he told them that he was 70, and had walked the 16 miles from Mansfield into Nottingham that day, and was walking home when he collapsed.

One source reported snow so heavy, and temperatures so low, that ice remained on the ground until June.

Second time lucky

NOTTINGHAM people turned out in their hundreds on November 1, 1813, when the town saw its second balloon ascent.

The first, in 1785, could hardly have been described as successful. On that occasion, thousands gathered on the Forest to watch a Mr Cracknell take off in his hydrogen balloon.

Only, he didn't. For seven hours he tried to inflate his balloon. Finally, the crowd made a bonfire of his equipment and cut the ropes that held his balloon down. It drifted off and was later found at Horncastle.

By contrast, Mr Sadler did take off in 1813, from Canal Wharf.

In 1826 a man called Green secured a balloon in the market place. Wisely, he inflated it the night before ascent, then the following day charged the public 10s 6d [about 52p] per ride.

He soared off to Edwalton with just one passenger.

Disease amid the dungheaps

THE fear of smallpox or cholera outbreaks led to several public health prosecutions in the early 19th Century.

In January, 1813, Sarah Parker was prosecuted at the Quarter Sessions for skinning a dead horse at Park Row.

Defendants named Toone and Dutton were in court following complaints from Back Lane residents about the stench from dead horses.

Horses were the primary means of long-distance travel, so hundreds would have been stabled around the town and hundreds more would have been ridden through the streets every week — creating an obvious problem.

In 1808, Nottingham justices ordered that dung, once collected into heaps, should not be moved through the town between 10am and 9pm.

The corporation was already taking a leading role in street cleaning, contracting the Parish of St Mary at £60 a year to clear refuse from the several markets which operated from the Shambles, across the town centre, to Beastmarket Hill.

● A city and county lunatic asylum was built at Sneinton in 1810. Designed for 60 patients, it was later extended to accommodate 312.

Hosiers face Luddite fury

LUDDITE activists cut loose in Nottingham in 1811 amid growing anger over the pay and conditions of frame knitters and the loss of work caused by machinery.

First they broke into workshops in Arnold and disabled knitting machines.

Then a demonstration in Nottingham's market place drew knitters from all over the county. The crowd was dispersed by the militia, but that night they again targeted Arnold, smashing 63 machines.

Dragoons were called out, but during the next three weeks, 200 frames were vandalised in Notts.

Arnold remained a centre for protest. Feelings had been running high since the closure in 1810 of the Worsted Mill at Arnot Hill Park, which threw 400 adults and several hundred children out of work.

Later in 1811 a gang of 70 armed men marched on the house of Bulwell hosier Edward Hollingsworth.

A rioter, John Westley, was

CHAMPION: Lord Byron

shot dead. The mob entered the house and destroyed both furniture and knitting frames.

However, the Luddites had a champion in Lord Byron, who told the House of Lords that the rioters had been driven by "unparalleled distress".

In spite of a Government crackdown, machine breaking continued throughout the East Midlands for several years.

Premier's murder: Nottingham 'rabble' rejoice

PRO-Luddite sentiment was behind reaction in Nottingham to the assassination in 1812 of the prime minister, Spencer Perceval.

Perceval was shot dead by John Bellingham in the lobby of the House of Commons on May 11. News of his death reached Nottingham the following day.

The Nottingham *Journal* was outraged by the response.

"A few deluded men and ignorant boys had been taught to believe that that gentleman was the prime cause of all our commercial distresses and sufferings among the people," the newspaper reported.

"They assembled in the neighbourhood of Fisher Gate

and proceeded with a band of music all through the principal streets.

"They were soon joined by a rabble who, in the most indecent and reprehensible manner, testified their joy at the horrid catastrophe by repeated shouts, the firing of guns and every species of exaltation."

NOTTINGHAM faced a bleak recession in 1812, especially badly felt by people employed in the clothing trade.

Napoleon's actions in Europe had ensured that almost all European trade had been cut off, severely curtailing exports.

The war effort demanded increased public expenditure, and income tax at ten per cent was rigorously imposed.

To add to the problems of Nottingham people, large numbers of troops were billeted on them.

❑❑❑

MARY Saxelby of Arnold was transported to the colonies for seven years for stealing a bottle of liquor. The value of the goods was ten pence [about 4p].

❑❑❑

THOMAS Chambers Hine, the architect whose buildings remain landmarks in Nottingham, was born in Southampton Street, Covent Garden, on May 31, 1813.

❑❑❑

THE authorities in Nottingham banned merry-go-rounds from the 1813 Goose Fair, insisting they were "disgraceful and dangerous machines."

❑❑❑

EDMUND Hart, of Poplar Place, was presented with the freedom of the town "for having vaccinated upwards of 1,500 poor children, gratis, in Nottingham and its vicinity."

Debts force abbey sale

FACING mounting debts, the poet Lord Byron sold Newstead Abbey, *right*, in 1817 to his old schoolfriend, the Corunna and Waterloo veteran Colonel Wildman. The price: £94,000.

Wildman began restoring the abbey buildings in 1818, employing the fashionable architect John Shaw. Most of the work was completed by 1829.

THE town's fast-growing rag trade was hit by a nine-week strike by framework knitters in 1817. Almost 10,000 stopped work, protesting that they earned less than seven shillings a week [35p] while working up to 16 hours a day.

ACTOR Edmund Kean visited Nottingham in 1817 to play Richard III and Macbeth.

MADAME Tussaud's life-sized wax models were shown at Goose Fair in 1819. Visitors were charged one shilling [5p] to see the display.

THOMAS Forman, who was to found the company which published the Nottingham *Evening Post*, was born in Louth, Lincolnshire, in 1819.

JOHN Boot, father of businessman and philanthropist Jesse Boot, was born at Radcliffe-on-Trent in 1815.

A PUBLIC subscription fund for families of Nottingham soldiers killed at Waterloo raised £1,200.

AN earthquake shook Nottingham just after midday on Sunday, March 17, 1816. Services at St Peter's and St Nicholas's were interrupted.

BASFORD Workhouse opened in 1816. It had cost £8,500 and was intended to accommodate 240 inmates.

Ten killed in canal blast

TRAGEDY: Scene of the explosion (early 20th Century picture)

TEN people were killed in 1818 in a huge gunpowder explosion. Property was also extensively damaged in the canalside blast near what is now Carrington Road.

A vessel had arrived from Gainsborough laden with flagstones, cotton wool, molasses, soap and 21 barrels of gunpowder.

During the transfer of the cargo to a warehouse, several pounds of powder escaped from a barrel being rolled by the boat's captain. As he tried to plug the leak, one of his crew accidentally dropped hot coals on the exposed powder.

The crewman was blown across the canal. Nine others perished, including an 11-year-old who was fishing nearby.

According to Bailey's *Annals of Nottingham*, "the loss of property, though secondary to that of life, was immense.

"The concussion was so tremendous that it was not only heard throughout the town, but also in Loughborough, Alfreton and even at Newark. At Castle Donington it was even considered to be a clap of thunder."

The account continued: "Numbers of people entered the yard where a scene of devastation presented itself such as they had never seen.

"Bricks, slates, tiles, human bodies, huge masses of timber and all kind of goods lay smoking on the ground in all kinds of disorder.

"Many women were running about distracted, anxiously inquiring about the fate of husbands or relatives.

"The noble range of warehouses was found to be completely destroyed, not a vestige of the building remaining in its former position."

A public subscription fund was launched for the relief of families who had lost bread-winners.

Spy traps dupes

THE Luddite riots had put the Government on its guard against more civil insurrection.

In 1817, the Nottingham home of Gravener Henson was searched for "treasonable and seditious papers" on the orders of the Home Secretary, Viscount Sidmouth.

The town was also the stamping ground of a Government spy known as "Oliver". Acting as an *agent provocateur*, he held meetings in the Three Salmons pub and interested the disaffected in a Midlands uprising.

The authorities had been alerted to the possibility of disorder, and 481 special constables were recruited.

The rebels marched on Nottingham, but broke up in the driving rain. Hussars captured about 30. Four were hanged.

"Oliver" was rewarded with an administrative job in the Cape Colony, where he was convicted of theft.

Gaslight firm founded in 1818

NIGHT lighting was revolutionised by legislation in 1818 which allowed the formation of the Gas-Light and Coke Company.

The private enterprise was licensed to light the streets within the town boundaries, but was not granted a monopoly.

Land for a gas plant was acquired near the Nottingham Navigation Canal. A holder — 18ft deep with a diameter of 29ft — was built in 1819 to store 12,000 cubic feet of gas.

Streets and some houses were lit by gas for the first time on April 13, 1819.

The ghost of Harlow Wood

THE ghost of a 17-year-old girl, brutally murdered in 1817, was said to haunt a spot near Harlow Wood. Elizabeth Sheppard was battered by Charles Rotherham, who took her shoes and umbrella.

He was caught after he tried to sell them at the Three Crowns Inn, Redhill.

According to legend, his victim's ghost appears whenever her memorial stone is moved.

IMAGES OF A LEGEND: Contrasting portraits of Byron. Left, in tartan. Right, in costume brought home from Albania

Farewell to Byron, crusader for liberty

LORD Byron, romantic poet, traveller and champion of liberty, died in Greece in 1824.

He was born in January 1788 in cheap furnished rooms off Oxford Street. His mother was the Scottish heiress Catherine Gordon, and his father Captain 'Mad' Jack Byron, nephew of the fifth Lord Byron.

When the boy was four, his father died, and when the fifth baron died, he inherited the title and Newstead Abbey estate in Nottinghamshire.

Byron was educated at Harrow and Cambridge, and his early verse was published

RESTING PLACE:
Hucknall Church

in Newark. *Hours of Idleness* followed, and enjoyed some success, then came *English Bards and Scottish Reviewers.*

His travels took him to the Mediterranean, and on his return, publication of *Childe*

Harold's Pilgrimage made him a sensation in London.

And he was a sensation for other reasons, attracting notoriety for his affair with Lady Caroline Lamb — who described the poet as "mad, bad and dangerous to know."

He married Annabella Millbank, but he was dogged by scandal over another relationship — with his half sister Augusta. There were also financial problems, which led to the sale of Newstead estate.

Byron's other great works included *Don Juan, Beppo, Manfred* and *The Prisoner of Chillon.*

On his last venture abroad, he campaigned for the Greeks in their war of independence against the Turks. He died of fever at Missolonghi. His body was returned to Notts, where it was buried at Hucknall Torkard Church.

The following year, Sophia Hyatt, the mysterious 'White Lady of Newstead', was run over by a delivery man in Maypole Yard in 1825.

She was knocked down by a horse, fell under the cart wheel and was killed.

An avid admirer of Byron, she had spent many years "in pensive solitude" wandering in the abbey gardens.

She rests near her idol at St Mary's, Hucknall.

'Model' workhouse opens

THE Thurgarton Incorporated Workhouse opened at Upton, near Southwell, in 1824. It was a model for all deterrent workhouses.

The forbidding three-story brick building was just the sort Charles Dickens had in mind when he wrote *Oliver Twist.* Families were split up. Men lived separately from their wives, and mothers handed over children to be housed in another part of the building.

Humiliation was a daily part of life for inmates, who worked for no money and lived on an unremittingly dreary diet based on gruel.

The building later became a hospital, and more recently was the subject of a £1 million museum project.

Both Thurgarton and its sister workhouse in Bingham, demolished in the 1950s to make way for council housing, were influential in the framing of the 1834 Poor Law Amendment Act which established similar workhouses all over the country.

THE 1820s saw a building boom in Nottingham, with developers filling in any available land. Enclosure restrictions limited the outward spread of the town.

Speculative builders even built over open drains, so that families were separated from sewers only by their floorboards.

THE Nottingham Horticultural and Botanical Society, formed in 1761, became the Nottingham Floral and Horticultural Society in 1825. It held flower shows which, later in the century, were an annual attraction at the Arboretum.

THE corporation received complaints in 1824 of rowdiness at a public house at St Ann's Well. Council members heard of "great disorder, riot, drunkenness and fighting very frequently."

A BRIEF boom in the lace trade ended in the mid 1820s, with hosiers counting the cost of speculation, over-investment and over-production. With an over-satisfied market, prices fell, and in 1825 some 300 skilled Nottingham lace workers lost their jobs.

NOTTS cricketers looked on in horror as temporary grandstands collapsed during a match at Darnal, Sheffield, in 1822. Two spectators were killed, and 23 were taken to hospital.

FUTURE engineer Thomas Hawksley left Nottingham Old Grammar School in 1822. He was articled to Edward Staveley, aged 15, before embarking on an international career that included positions with Nottingham's gas and water companies.

JAMES Gandon, architect of Shire Hall, Nottingham, died in 1823. He spent most of his career in Dublin, where he designed several public buildings in the neo-classical style.

Castle torched as vote angers reform rioters  Page 23

Bromley House move for library

THE Nottingham Subscription Library, founded five years earlier, bought new premises in 1821 at Bromley House, on Beastmarket Hill, for £2,750.

The exclusive private library was instrumental in promoting the work of one of its members, the mathematician George Green.

His first major essay, on electricity and magnetism, was published in 1928.

It was privately sold to subscribers who were attracted by an advertisement in the Nottingham *Review* of December 14, 1827.

The 51 sponsors each paid 7s 6d [about 37p] for their copy. Half were fellow members of library.

The work was unusual in that the author had not studied at university, nor even at a grammar school. It was dedicated to the Duke of Newcastle, owner of Nottingham Castle.

Green's father, Sneinton-based baker and miller George Snr, died in 1829, aged 70. He left the business to his son, and property in Nottingham town centre to his daughter Ann.

New look for market place

IN 1826 work began on the renovation of Nottingham's Great Market Place.

The area was levelled and repaved, and a new 24ft wide carriage road was created on the north side of the square.

Some of the costs were passed on to market traders, and in 1829 there were disputes about the new stall rents.

Trader John Kennedy, who had withheld his rent, complained that his stall had been seized by the mayor's sergeant.

During the early 19th Century, the cattle and hide markets were moved out of the square to new sites in the Sherwood Street area.

LEARNING PROCESS: A reading room at the subscription library

Early years of 'the General'

BUILDER'S son William Booth, who was to found the Salvation Army, was born in Notintone Place, Sneinton, on April 10, 1829.

He was two days old when baptised at nearby St Stephen's Church.

Young William was educated at Sampson Biddulph's Academy in a chapel building in Halifax Place (the site is now the Lace Market Theatre).

At the age of 13 he was apprenticed to Francis Eames, whose pawnbroker's shop and silver dealership was in Hockley. Up the hill in Goose Gate, Booth's widowed mother ran a small shop dealing in toys, tape, cotton and needles.

Booth drifted away from the Church of England and into Wesleyan circles.

He had been moved by the plight of Nottingham's ragged children as they begged for food in the streets, and in 1844 he converted to Methodism.

He soon found himself an evangelist, reputedly preaching his first sermon in 1845 at a house in Kid Street (off Lower Parliament Street).

The following year he led his gang of ragged children through the main entrance of Broad Street Wesleyan Chapel where

FOUNDER: William Booth

they occupied the best pews for a Sunday morning service.

The party was banished to benches out of sight of the congregation.

His apprenticeship completed, 19-year-old Booth went to London and worked for a pawnbroker at Kennington Common. In 1854 he became a full-time Methodist preacher in Islington.

Breaking with Methodism in the 1860s, and supported by his wife Catherine, he started the Christian Mission in Whitechapel. It became the Salvation Army in 1878.

NOTTINGHAM audiences wanted to be entertained, and weren't bothered how unusual the entertainment was, so long as it was performed well and generally kept them amused.

There can't, however, have been many more unusual feats than the one an unemployed baker performed in 1821 on the Forest.

His task was to pick up 100 stones with his mouth, and drop them in a basket.

❏ ❏ ❏

RICHARD Birkin founded his Nottingham-based lace-making empire in 1827.

❏ ❏ ❏

THE last criminal to be hanged at Gallows Hill, near the junction of Mansfield Road and Forest Road East, was executed on April 2, 1827.

❏ ❏ ❏

THE town council invested in the new London University in 1929, acquiring the right to send two local scholars to the capital to further their education.

❏ ❏ ❏

THE George Hotel was built on the newly constructed George Street in 1822. It was originally named the King George the Fourth.

1839: The railway age comes to Nottingham ➡ Page 24

Robert Millhouse, poet

RIGHT: The poet Robert Millhouse, born in Nottingham in 1788, the second of ten children, and brought up in considerable poverty. He died in 1839 at his home in Walker Street, Sneinton, leaving a widow and three children.

Reform stalemate: Mob torches castle

THE Duke of Newcastle's mansion at Nottingham Castle was set alight by rioters in 1831 in a violent protest against opponents of the Reform Bill.

Lord Grey's government was committed to reform — the extension of the vote to middle-class men, and better representation for rapidly growing industrial towns like Nottingham.

Nottingham had elected pro-reform MPs, and supporters claimed to have gathered 12,000 local signatures in support of the Bill.

Trouble flared in several towns when the legislation was rejected by the Lords, on October 8. News arrived by mail coach next morning — and spread rapidly across Nottingham, where the population had been swollen by Goose Fair.

Rioters attacked the homes of anti-reform citizens. Shops were looted and the mayor was injured. The Riot Act was read, and the 15th Hussars were deployed to keep order.

Next day, October 10, a pro-reform meeting was scheduled for the market place. Some 20,000 attended, and the meeting ended peacefully, with an appeal to King William IV to support the cause.

Hours later, though, the window breaking was resumed.

ABLAZE: Nottingham Castle burns following the riot in 1831

The mob marched through Sneinton to Colwick Hall. The occupier was absent, and his wife hid in the gardens while their home was looted.

The rioters returned to the town and tried to break open the house of correction.

Some 600 people then marched on the castle. It was unoccupied at the time, but was a symbol of the power of the reactionary duke.

The gates of the lodge were smashed, mansion windows were broken and the mob made a pile of furniture, tapestry and fittings — then set fire to it.

By the time fire gripped the building, it was dark. Flames leapt out of windows and roof. In spite of hours of rain, all but the walls were destroyed.

Next day the rioters headed west to Beeston. A silk mill owned by reform opponent William Lowe was set ablaze.

Returning to Nottingham, the mob caused more mayhem in Lenton and Wollaton. Several were arrested after clashing with the yeomanry, and imprisoned at the county gaol.

October rioting in Nottingham, Bristol and other towns concentrated minds in Parliament. The Reform Bill was enacted in 1832.

● Three Nottingham men paid with their lives for their involvement in the rioting. On February 1, 1832, Armstrong, Beck and Hearson, convicted of arson at the Beeston silk mill, were publicly hanged at Shire Hall.

A FIGHTER died during a bare-knuckle scrap at Mapperley Plains in May, 1835. His first name is not recorded, only his surname, Lupton.

He was fighting Austin in the culmination of rivalry for the attentions of a servant girl at a public house in Woolpack Lane.

It is recorded that the fight lasted two hours, by which time "Lupton was rendered insensible, and died soon afterwards."

❑ ❑ ❑

TWO youths were sentenced to death and a third to transportation in 1831 after being found guilty of rape.

There were suggestions that the woman had consented, and the judge delayed execution for 14 days to allow inquiries to be made.

The *Nottingham Date Book* records that 15,000 came to watch the public execution of Reynolds and Marshall.

❑ ❑ ❑

JOANNE Ledwich, convicted of robbery and awaiting transportation, made a daring escape from the County Gaol at Shire Hall on March 14, 1831.

She created a rope from a clothes line and strips of sheeting, secured it to a window and began to descend the 70ft to the Narrow Marsh.

The rope broke and Ledwich fell to the ground, but she was not seriously hurt.

❑ ❑ ❑

ENGINEER Thomas Hawksley built a cholera hospital in Nottingham to help doctors counter the epidemic of 1832. The outbreak claimed 330 lives.

❑ ❑ ❑

SAMUEL Robinson rented an old bakehouse in Kimberley and converted it into a brewery in 1832. It was the start of the enterprise which became Hardys and Hansons Ltd.

❑ ❑ ❑

GEORGE Green, the Sneinton miller's son who became a mathematician, went up to Cambridge University at the age of 40. He arrived at Gonville and Caius College on October 1833.

Death of George Green, miller-mathematician Page 25

POLICE inspector Isaac Phelps died of rabies in 1839 after being bitten by the dog he was trying to rescue.

Phelps was on duty in the Carter Gate area when he heard a dog whining from a hole. As soon as he got within reach, the pointer bit his nose and escaped.

The wound healed, but Phelps began to show signs of hydrophobia. Taken ill in Mansfield Road, he told a pub landlord: "I am going mad, but I shall not hurt you."

A subscription raised more than £500 for his widow and their nine children.

□ □ □

AUTHOR William Howitt described Goose Fair in the 1830s in his *Rural Life of England*.

He wrote of "cages of wild beasts, theatricals, dwarfs, giants and other prodigies and wonders, all manner of wild and peculiar looking people, strollers, beggars, gypsies, singers, dancers, players on harps, Indian jugglers ... and similar wonderful artists."

□ □ □

THE actor William Charles Macready visited Nottingham in 1834 to play Hamlet.

□ □ □

THE eccentric John Wheatley died in 1838 after years of keeping a coffin in his bedroom, which he kept well stocked with fine wines and liqueurs.

□ □ □

BY 1837, Nottingham had six fire engines. The oldest was 70 years old.

□ □ □

A MAN was killed by lightning at Basford during a thunderstorm in 1835.

□ □ □

TRENT Bridge cricket ground was laid out in 1838 by William Clarke, who married the landlady of what is now the Trent Bridge Hotel.

□ □ □

THE year 1839 ended in economic depression, with 3,481 people on parish relief and 541 in the Poor House.

GREAT MARKET PLACE: Nottingham town centre in the early 19th Century, painted by John Tarlton. The Exchange is at the back of the square

Livestock alarmed by 'the new racer'

THE railway age came to Nottingham on May 30, 1839. On that day, the first special trains ran on the new line to Derby.

It might have been later were it not for the fears of Erewash Valley colliery owners, whose markets had been hit by the opening of the Leicester and Swannington Railway in 1832.

The result was the creation of the Midland Counties Railway.

Charles Vignoles was appointed engineer for a scheme that would link Nottingham and Derby.

Permission for the line was secured by Act of Parliament in 1836.

The MCR station, engine house and goods sheds were built on a meadow formerly owned by Nottingham town

STEAM AGE: The first Nottingham Station

council. A new access road was created for the 11-acre site, which lay to the west of the current Nottingham Station.

The Band of the 5th Dragoons played and soldiers paraded for the opening ceremony on May 30. Thousands watched from Castle Rock and the hillside overlooking the canal.

Four engines — Sunbeam, Ariel, Mersey and Hawk — hauled trains of between two and six carriages westwards towards Derby.

The first left at 12.30pm. When the second left three minutes later, the dragoons played the national anthem.

"The road was lined in many places with admiring crowds," a passenger wrote. "Ever and anon, a dog tried his powers of speed by running by the side this new racer, which left the astonished animal in the distance.

"The cows generally remained quiescent; the horses seemed alarmed, and retreated to the farthest hedge; the calves and sheep also ran away affrighted."

The outward journey took 46 minutes, including a water top-up at Breaston, and the return journey 42 minutes.

On June 4, the 7am departure from Nottingham inaugurated the timetabled service. Trains left Nottingham at 7 and 10.30am, 1.30, 3 and 7.30pm. Fares settled down at 3s 6d first class [about 17p], 2s second class [10p], 1s third class [5p].

Bendigo takes on bare-knuckle champ

TWO of the giants of bare-knuckle fighting met at Appleby House in Nottingham in 1835. It was a brutal encounter lasting 22 rounds.

The rivals were Ben Caunt, Hucknall-based Champion of All England, and William Thompson of Nottingham, better known as Bendigo.

Caunt had long tried for a match against Bendigo, and resorted to taunts to lure him to the ring.

Caunt punched Bendigo to his knees. But he then dealt an illegal blow and was disqualified.

The rematch took place at Shelby — and this time it lasted 75 rounds, with rival fans joining a free-for-all. This time Bendigo was disqualified.

Their final encounter was the longest — 93 rounds in front of 10,000 spectators in Oxford. Caunt was disqualified for a low blow.

Family poverty in Arnold shocks observers ➡ Page 26

Election riot at market

THOUSANDS witnessed a clash between election speakers in Nottingham market place in 1842.

Standing for election to Westminster were the Tory democrat John Walter, editor of *The Times*, and Chartist campaigner Joseph Sturge, champion of the working classes.

Supporters of both parties drew open wagons into the square and 16,000 citizens waited to hear two of the finest orators of the day — The Rev J. R. Stephens (representing Walter) and Feargus O'Connor (for the Sturge cause).

The wagons were just 15 yards apart and the two men spoke simultaneously.

Suddenly the crowd roared when O'Connor jumped from his wagon and cleared a path to Stephens, arms flailing. The latter retired to The Bell Inn.

ORATOR: The Feargus O'Connor Memorial, Arboretum

Birth of Watson Fothergill

The architect Watson Fothergill was born in Mansfield in 1841, and christened Fothergill Watson (he changed his name in middle age).

He was responsible for some of Nottingham's most striking buildings: Queen's Chambers, the Express Building, the former Baptist Chapel in Woodborough Road, the Black Boy Hotel and the brewery pub in Mansfield Road.

Maths genius Green dies aged 47

GEORGE Green, the Nottingham miller's son who became a pioneering mathematician, died aged 47 on May 31, 1841.

He died of influenza at the Notintone Place home of his common-law wife, who had given birth to her seventh child the previous year.

On June 11, the *Nottingham Review* published a modest obituary: "Had his life been prolonged, he might have stood eminently high as a mathematician."

Events were to prove that he was a mathematician and physicist of enduring eminence, and his techniques were still being used in the sciences and technology in the late 20th Century.

Green, Fellow of Gonville and Caius College, Cambridge, was buried at St Stephen's Churchyard in Sneinton, alongside the remains of his parents.

RESTING PLACE: St Stephen's Church, Sneinton

Royal couple travel by rail

QUEEN Victoria and the Prince Consort travelled by train from Chesterfield to Nottingham on December 4, 1843.

Guns on Castle Rock sounded a royal salute as their train was sited — and crowds in specially constructed platforms strained for a few of the couple.

When the train drew into the station, still a terminus, soldiers of the 64th Regiment of Foot presented arms, and the national anthem was played by the Band of the Iniskilling Dragoons.

The Queen and Prince Albert were greeted by the Lord Lieutenant. He presented the mayor, who welcomed them to Nottingham.

The royal party stepped into horse-drawn carriages for their journey to Belvoir Castle, home of the Duke of Rutland.

They left Nottingham by a new highway which was later named in honour of her visit. It is Queen's Road.

However, Queen Victoria was not the first royal passenger to use Nottingham Station.

On July 22, 1840, just a year after the Nottingham-Derby line opened, Queen Adelaide, widow

TRAVELLER: Queen Victoria in the 1840s, painted by Winterhalter

of King William IV, passed through Nottingham with her sister, Duchess Ida of Saxe-Weimar.

They arrived by road from Belton House in Lincolnshire, and caught a train of three carriages and four trucks for the journey to Harewood House.

In 1846, the railway extension to Lincoln was opened, and two years later, a new Nottingham Station was built.

THE threat of a 'gas war' loomed in 1840 and 1841 when Bills were presented to Parliament for the formation of the Nottingham New Gas Company.

Street and domestic gas lighting in the town had been provided since 1819 by the Gas-Light and Coke Company, but they were not allowed a monopoly.

When competition was proposed, the company did not mount a formal objection, although behind the scenes, sympathisers campaigned against it.

The debates before a Commons committee concerned the unreliability of the old company's supply to outlying areas, and its excessive profits.

Both Bills failed, but supporters of the New Gas Company presented another in 1842. Compromise was reached when its stakeholders were given shares in the old company.

Radford gasworks was built in 1844 at a cost of £15,000.

◻ ◻ ◻

IN 1842 a restaurant was established in Nottingham which later became The Mikado cafe and dance room.

◻ ◻ ◻

PROMINENT baker and grocer Samuel Fox founded Nottingham Building Society in 1849.

Arboretum prompts outburst of civic pride Page 27

THE foundation stone was laid in 1840 for Holy Trinity Church, in what became Trinity Square, now the site of the multi-storey car park. In the mid-19th Century, it was said to have the largest congregation in Nottingham — the parish included high-density housing in the area later levelled for the Victoria Station.

□ □ □

IN 1847 architect T.C. Hine, 34, moved into the home he designed at 25 Regent Street. It contained one of the first purpose-built WCs in Nottingham.

□ □ □

THE Nottingham Mechanics Institute, inaugurated in 1837, opened in January 1845. It featured two large halls, reading rooms, a library and coffee and billiard rooms, and would welcome speakers including Charles Dickens, Sir Henry Wood and Arthur Conan Doyle.

□ □ □

SEVEN prisoners escaped from the county gaol on New Year's Eve, 1843, after overpowering a warder.

□ □ □

HORSE-drawn omnibuses, run by private operators, were licensed in 1848 to run services in Nottingham town centre.

□ □ □

REAR-Admiral Sir Nesbitt Willoughby died in 1849. He was a member of the Willoughby family of Wollaton Hall, and bathed regularly in a naturally-filling cistern which became known as 'The Admiral's Bath'.

□ □ □

A GENERAL Post Office was opened in Albert Street in 1848 to cope with an upsurge in mail following the introduction of the penny post in 1840. The site is now occupied by Marks & Spencer.

□ □ □

FORMER farm manager Stephen Hanson opened a brewery in Kimberley in 1847 — competition for the brewery opened by Samuel Robinson in nearby Cuckold Alley.

WALTER FOUNTAIN: The death of John Walter MP in 1847 prompted his son to build a public drinking fountain in Lister Gate (pictured in the 1890s). The 50ft monument was removed in 1950

Misery of the Arnold poor

ATTENTION focused in 1846 on deplorable conditions in the village of Arnold — which had all of the poverty of inner Nottingham, but none of the public facilities.

"The agricultural worker earns between eight and 13 shillings a week [40-65p]," a Nottingham newspaper correspondent observed.

"Half fed, half clothed, with no furniture or bedding, the whole family works long hours every day.

"The framework knitter works 70 hours for six to eight shillings [30-40p] a week. The average life span is 27 years.

"There was no magistrate, one constable, no sanitary arrangements and all filth was thrown out into the village stream.

"Water, carried by half-naked children up to half a mile, contained its full quota of pollution from putrified sheep, kittens, dogs, rats and human waste.

"The inevitable destiny of the workers was that of a pauper which rendered them first hopeless, then reckless, then dissolute until the men were without honour and the women without virtue ..."

Bentinck, the 'First Lord of the Turf'

LORD George Bentinck died in 1848, aged 46. Although he is remembered chiefly as a horse racing reformer, he was one of the most prominent politicians of the day.

He was born at Welbeck, Notts, second son of the 4th Duke of Portland, and entered the Commons in 1828 as a moderate Whig. He later argued for more conservative policies, including protectionism. This led to a political and personal feud with Sir Robert Peel.

His political associates included a future prime minister, the young Benjamin Disraeli.

Bentinck's racing interests caused him to be nicknamed 'the first Lord of the Turf' — possibly the inspiration for the Turf Tavern, a Nottingham pub renamed in the 1990s.

12 perish in crush at execution

TWELVE people were killed (13, in some accounts) and 50 others were injured in the crush to witness an execution outside Shire Hall on August 8, 1844.

The condemned man was William Savile, convicted of murdering his wife and three children.

Nottingham was so scandalised by the crime that a huge crowd packed into High Pavement to see Savile hanged.

Most of the injuries happened as the crowd dispersed and several were forced down the steep Garners Hill. So concerned were the county justices that a crowd control expert was contracted for the next public execution, in 1860.

Park estate for middle classes

IN 1844 the town map of Nottingham showed how The Park was beginning to emerge as an estate for the prosperous middle classes.

But it also showed the emergence of back-to-back slums that were to be home for 80% of the population.

'Model' factory includes chapel for workers ➡ Page 28

'Newgate of the Midlands'

THE philanthropist Hepworth Dixon delivered a withering indictment of the county gaol at High Pavement.

"It is the 'Newgate' of the Midland counties," he wrote, referring to the notorious London prison.

"For its persistency in retaining all the good, sound, solid abuses of the past, it refuses to yield the palm. Few better specimens of the horrid dungeon-like prisons can now be found.

"The invasion of a spirit of reform, of economy, of humanity, has been successfully repulsed."

Attempts to expand the prison and improve conditions in the 1820s and 1830s had been slowed by rock falls on the south face.

In 1841, alterations costing £2,928 were proposed — but spending was halted until the authorities learned more about methods being tried at the New Model Prison at Pentonville in London.

☐ ☐ ☐

T.C. HINE designed his first factory in 1851 — a five-story building in Station Street which was the first to incorporate steam-operated stocking frames.

The building was destroyed by fire in 1859. A later factory became part of the Boots complex.

Also in the 1850s, Hine designed new premises for Bluecoat School.

☐ ☐ ☐

HARVEY Hadden was born in The Park in 1851. He later ran the family hosiery business, J. and H. Hadden, until 1896, when he went to Canada to make his fortune in real estate.

ABOVE: Gates to the Arboretum, which opened in 1852.
RIGHT: Charles Dickens, who visited Nottingham the same year

Civic pride in Arboretum

VISITORS from Birmingham, the Potteries and Yorkshire joined thousands of Nottingham citizens for the biggest civic party in memory — the opening of the Arboretum.

The town's new park, which cost £6,554 to create, was opened on May 11, 1852.

At 2pm, a crowd gathered in the market place, marched up Mansfield Road, and turned into the land set aside under the Enclosure Act of 1845.

The 18-acre site had been landscaped by Samuel Curtis of London, briefed by the council to create a peaceful haven for the relief of town dwellers. The plan included flowerbeds and a lake stocked with aquatic birds.

One of England's first inner-city parks, the opening was deemed important enough for coverage in the *Illustrated London News*.

After three cheers for Queen Victoria, and more for the mayor, 25,000 people celebrated long into the evening. In the market place, a firework display was enjoyed by thousands more people.

In its first years, there was a charge for admission to the Arboretum — £1 bought a family ticket valid for one year.

CHARLES Dickens and his touring theatre company visited Nottingham in 1852, staying at the George Hotel. His business partner W.W. Wills signed a cheque for £37 17s [£37.85].

☐ ☐ ☐

MARY Thompson, pipe-smoking mother of Nottingham prizefighter Bendigo, died late in 1850, aged 83. Some said she was his toughest opponent.

☐ ☐ ☐

JESSE Boot, founder of the Nottingham-based pharmaceutical and retail empire, was born on June 2, 1850. His father was John Boot, a fervent Methodist who was interested in herbal remedies.

☐ ☐ ☐

PUBLISHER Thomas Forman added more titles to the Nottingham Guardian group. First came the *Midland Sporting Chronicle*, a racing paper launched in 1852, then the *Midland Counties Observer*, filled mainly with cricket news.

Second main station opens at London Road

THE town's second major station, the London Road terminus, opened in October 1857. Built for the Ambergate Company, it became part of the Great Northern Railway.

The 'Low Level' declined in importance after the opening of Nottingham Victoria in 1900.

Notts County FC, the oldest league club of all Page 29

Launch of enduring book trade

IN 1854 a small bookselling business was started at 3, Lister Gate, at an annual rent of £40.

It later moved to Albert Street. Charles James Sisson was manager.

He was succeeded by his widow Eliza, who ran the business with Joseph Parker — hence the name Sisson and Parker, now part of Dillons.

❑ ❑ ❑

IN 1855 a man sold his wife in St Peter's Square, Nottingham ... for a shilling [5p] and a pint of ale.

❑ ❑ ❑

DERBYSHIRE businessman Joseph Burton moved his grocery shop from St Ann's Well Road to Smithy Row in 1858.

❑ ❑ ❑

ARTHUR Shrewsbury was born on April 11, 1856, at Kyte Street, New Lenton. He grew up to play cricket for Notts and England, and in the 1890s was reckoned to be the finest professional batsman of the day.

❑ ❑ ❑

A SPORTS club called The Lings was founded — the forerunner of Nottingham Forest FC. It took the name Forest because early matches were played on the Forest recreation ground.

❑ ❑ ❑

ST George's Hall opened in Upper Parliament Street in 1854. It was a music hall built in the Elizabethan style, and the first entertainment was a concert in aid of families of soldiers serving in the Crimea. The hall was demolished in 1902.

❑ ❑ ❑

PREACHER William Booth returned to his home town to speak at Broad Street Wesleyan Chapel, where he had worshipped as a young man. During six weeks of meetings in 1856, 740 people were converted.

Bell memorial for Mayor Birkin

LEFT: The Chinese Bell was installed at the Arboretum in 1859 to commemorate Richard Birkin's four years as Mayor of Nottingham.

It had been captured at Canton during the Anglo-Chinese war and was presented to the borough by Lt Col Burnester and soldiers of the 59th Foot (Nottinghamshire) Regiment.

The guns at the site were captured at Sebastopol, and the fountain was given in 1859 by Mr and Mrs W. Enfield.

Chapel for workers in 'model' factory

ONE of Nottingham's most important buildings opened in 1855 — the Lace Market warehouse designed by T.C. Hine for Adams Page and Company.

The E-shaped building was built in Hine's Anglo-Italian style, and benevolent employers provided a chapel for the workforce, for which a chaplain was employed.

The factory was noted for its light and roomy working conditions. The workforce was also provided with a bathroom and tea rooms.

On the strength of his work in the Lace Market, and his criticism of Nottingham's public buildings, Hine was invited by the town council's improvement committee to redesign the market place.

Hine's drawings show an Italianate replacement for the Exchange (where the Council House now stands) and a sunken square with permanent market stalls built into arches under Long Row and South Parade.

At the centre was an ornamental fountain.

Backers were found for the scheme, the pay-off being a 99-year lease on the covered stalls

FINE HINE: The Adams Building, now a college campus

— but Hine's project was to remain only a vision.

However the architect was to make his mark just a few hundred yards to the west, at the Duke of Newcastle's Park Estate.

In 1854 he was appointed the 5th Duke's agent, and was briefed to develop The Park.

His office designed almost a third of the houses created on the estate. The first, in Castle Grove, were completed in 1856.

Hardy brothers buy Robinson's Kimberley brewery

AMBITIOUS young brothers William and Thomas Hardy, Heanor-based beer merchants, bought the Kimberley brewing business of Samuel Robinson in 1857.

It was the first involvement of the Hardy family in the brewing enterprise which later became Hardys and Hansons Ltd.

The brothers bought the goodwill and brewing equipment, and rented the building from Thomas Godber, who had leased it to Robinson in 1832.

The Hardys built up profits from a maximum output of 30 barrels per brew. William managed production while Thomas, travelling five days a week, concentrated on sales.

By 1861 they had saved enough to buy nearby land called Spring Flatt. Architect Robert Grace was commissioned to design a brewery on the site, with maltings, brewhouse, bottling and cask-filling cellars, cooperage, offices and stables for up to 40 horses.

Oldest League club founded

NOTTINGHAM Football Club met for the first time at Cremorne Gardens, an open space in The Meadows, in November, 1862.

The Nottingham *Guardian* reported that a side was chosen by W. Arkwright and Charles Deakin — and Notts County FC, the oldest League club in England, dated their history from that moment.

Headed notepaper used in the 1880s suggested 1860 as the inaugural year, although some sticklers prefer 1864 when, on December 7, a meeting at the George Hotel elected Frederick Smith president and authorised a five shilling [25p] subscription.

A 20-a-side kickabout against Trent Valley was played next day, but the club's first big game was in January 1865, when Sheffield were entertained in a 18-a-side match at the Meadows.

The Forest club was founded in 1865, and the following year the two local teams opposed each other for the first two times. Both matches were goalless.

In 1870, Notts players won what were thought to be the club's first representative honours. Charles Rothera and E.H. Greenhalgh played in the North team which lost 1-0 to the South at Kennington Oval.

Prizefighting legend dies

BARE-knuckle prizefighter Ben Caunt died of pneumonia in 1861 and was buried at St Mary's Churchyard in Hucknall.

His brutal fights in the 1830s with local rival, William Thompson of Nottingham, better known as Bendigo, were epics of fighting history.

They would square up for purses of £300 and more, a fortune for an ordinary working man.

Hundreds more would be wagered on the outcome of the matches, which were seen by up to 10,000 people.

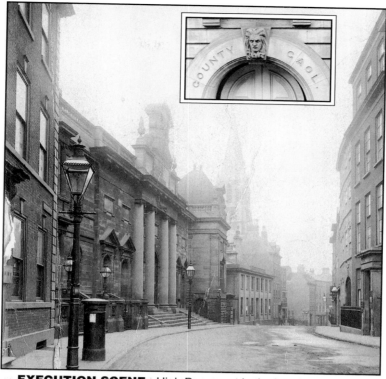

EXECUTION SCENE: High Pavement in the late 19th Century,

Crowd fears at hangings

RADFORD architect Richard Charles Sutton was contracted to supervise crowd safety for the public execution in 1860 of the murderer Fenton.

The county justices, responsible for executions at Shire Hall, were anxious to avoid a repetition of the incident in 1844 when 12 spectators died and 50 were injured after the hanging of William Savile.

Sutton ordered traffic restrictions, and had anti-crush barriers erected in the High Pavement area.

The event passed without incident, and Sutton was engaged for Nottingham's next public hanging — of Richard Thomas Parker in 1864.

Again, there was no trouble, thanks to Sutton's precautions.

"The greater proportion of the crowd were evidently possessed of very low mental organisation," according to the *Nottingham Review* reporter.

"The dull, morose expression of countenance, which usually characterises a great portion of such crowds, was on this occasion especially observable."

Viscount Allenby, victor of Megiddo

EDMUND Allenby, *right*, was born at Southwell in 1861. He became one of Britain's finest Great War generals, victor over the Turks at Megiddo.

He had Western Front experience before taking command of the Egyptian Expeditionary Force. From 1919 to 1922 he was the British High Commissioner in Egypt.

Field Marshal Viscount Allenby died in 1936 and his ashes are interred at Westminster Abbey.

Plight of factory children

A COMMISSION of inquiry heard damning evidence in 1863 about working conditions for children in Nottingham lace and clothing factories.

The commissioners heard that youngsters' growth was stunted, and that some were deformed or sickly.

Even though many children of needy families were required to work from early in the morning until late at night, there were no beds — they slept where they could find a quiet corner.

"Children begin very young," a witness from Bulwell explained about a glove factory. "My little sister, now five and a half years old ... has been at it for two years.

"Parents are not particular about the age. If they have to work, they must do it. Mothers will pin them on their knee to keep them to their work, and if they are sleepy give them a slap on the head ..."

The mothers were also vulnerable to ailments. Curvature of the spine and anaemia were common — so was miscarriage.

By 1864, the town had 250 lace manufacturers.

□□□

MARKET Street was created in 1865 by the widening of Sheep Lane, allowing R. and E. Dickinson and Fazackerley to extend their Long Row shop.

The store was later known as Fazackerley, Griffin and Spalding, and is now the Nottingham branch of Debenhams.

□□□

AN Act of 1864 confirmed Nottingham Gas-Light and Coke Company as England's biggest geographical supplier of gas, to 137 square miles.

□□□

A NEW Nottingham House of Correction, designed with medieval-style turrets, was completed in 1860. It stood at the junction of Parliament Street and King Edward Street.

JOHN Boot died in 1860, leaving his widow Mary to run the family herbal remedy business in Goose Gate.

She was also left with two children to bring up — ten-year-old Jesse and his baby sister. At the age of 13 Jesse left school to help his mother in the shop.

John Boot had been a fervent Methodist, and would have been influenced by John Wesley's interest in herbal medicine.

He founded the business, known first as the British and American Botanical Establishment, with help from his father-in-law.

As well as preparing remedies for his customers, many of whom would have been worshippers at the town's Methodist chapels, John Boot lectured extensively on herbal remedies, and organised a medical botany exhibition in Nottingham.

THE foundation stone for the new Trent Bridge was laid by the Mayor of Nottingham, Alderman Barber, on July 15, 1869.

The bridge was opened two years later.

THE town's first steam fire engine was demonstrated in Great Market Place in 1864. Spectators saw a 1in diameter hose project water 130ft.

Four years later a new £650 Shand & Mason engine pumped 400 gallons of water a minute to a height of 180 feet.

WISDEN cricketers' almanack praised the art of Notts batsman Richard Daft, whose 1869 innings included an unbeaten 103 against MCC and 93 not out against Surrey.

Daft was admired especially for his defensive technique.

GREEN'S Mill at Sneinton was abandoned in the 1860s after tenant miller William Oakland was involved in disputes over its upkeep.

SIGNATURE: The initials of T.C. Hine, with architect's setsquare and compasses, as left on the Birkin Building in the Lace Market

St Pancras rebuff

THE partnership of Hine and Evans was invited to compete for the design of St Pancras Station and the Grand Midland Hotel in London. They lost out to George Gilbert Scott, whose much more expensive Gothic design was accepted.

T.C. Hine was more successful in his home town. In 1864-5 he designed the £3,000 borough reservoir at the summit of Robin Hood Chase. It stored up to 2.5 million gallons of water.

More importantly, the architect began work in 1867 on the wreckage of the mansion at Nottingham Castle.

Player packs are winners

ESSEX lawyer's son John Player arrived in Nottingham in 1862 and learned the business skills that were to help him launch his tobacco empire.

He worked initially as a draper's assistant and later launched an agency in Beastmarket Hill for an agricultural supplier.

But it was an inspired sideline that was to create his fortune.

Smokers bought tobacco loose, from jars, often mixing two or more blends.

Player decided to pre-pack popular mixtures — offering the customer consistency while saving him time. Soon the sideline became the business.

He bought a tobacco factory in the Broad Marsh, where 150 people produced pipe tobacco as well as hand-made cigarettes.

His branding and marketing were so successful that he invested in a site at Radford.

Castle Tobacco Factory, with machinery driven by a 300hp engine, opened in 1884. A few months later, John Player became ill and died in Bournemouth, aged 45.

RIGHT MIXTURE: John Player (1839-1884), founder of the Nottingham tobacco giants

Builders' chorus for new Royal

THE 'new' Theatre Royal was constructed in just six months during 1865 — and the workforce had the honour of giving the first performance on the stage.

At the opening night, on September 25, the builders and actors formed a chorus as Madge Robertson sang the national anthem.

An audience including the Duke of St Albans then saw productions of *The School for Scandal,* and *The Rendezvous.*

The building, designed by the architect Phipps, could accommodate 2,200.

The builders were brothers John and William Lambert and patrons admired internal detail which included cameos of Shakespeare, Jonson, Webster and other English playwrights.

Above the proscenium arch was a painting by the fashionable artist Henry Holiday, showing Shakespeare and several of his characters.

"We hope ... to add to the number of those who seek a healthful pleasure in intellectual recreation," said manager Walter Montgomery on the opening night.

"With a well-conducted theatre and with a company of ladies and gentlemen, what is to prevent the drama from becoming a teacher of the highest morality, nay, even the gentle handmaiden of religion?"

The old Theatre Royal in St Mary's Gate had been turned into a music hall — Middleton's Alhambra Palace of Varieties.

Morley under fire in election rioting

RIOTING broke out during the 1865 election campaign when thousands of rural citizens arrived by rail for a rally in Nottingham.

Charles Paget and Samuel Morley *(his bust is pictured)* were due to address a meeting in the market place on June 26. Supporters of Morley fought their way from the Midland Station to the square, but they were constantly stoned by opponents.

The speakers' platform was set on fire and Morley and his supporters were "set upon by a violent rabble". Troopers were called.

FOUNDER: Thomas Forman and his Sherwood Street headquarters

Town buys gas firm

THE corporation took the town's gas supply into public ownership in 1874 — acquiring the Gas-Light and Coke Company for £463,000.

Shareholders met at the George Hotel and accepted £75 for each £50 share.

It was a blow for the company's chief engineer, Thomas Hawksley, who was convinced the corporation did not have the expertise.

Coun D.W. Heath was appointed chairman of the Nottingham gas committee. Marriott Ogle Tarbotton and John Wilson were appointed, respectively, chief engineer and general manager.

During the 1870s, when cooking by gas became more popular and prices were progressively lowered, sales of gas doubled to 890 million cubic feet.

First Evening Post rolls off the presses

WILFORD toll bridge was opened on June 16, 1870 — seven years after work began. The bridge closed to traffic in 1974.

❏ ❏ ❏

THE Wesleyan Chapel in Mansfield Road was opened in 1874. It was used by several denominations before closing in 1973.

❏ ❏ ❏

WILLIAM Hardy, 46, retired from Hardy's Kimberley Brewery, selling his half-share to his brother Thomas.

❏ ❏ ❏

WALTER Montgomery, former manager of the new Theatre Royal, committed suicide while on honeymoon in 1871.

❏ ❏ ❏

WATCHED by almost 3,000 at Trent Bridge, the Royal Engineers beat Nottingham Forest by two goals to one.

THE first edition of the Nottingham *Evening Post* appeared on the streets on May 1, 1878.

It was printed on a Victory press at the Sherwood Street headquarters of its sister paper, the *Daily Guardian*. It consisted of four broadsheet pages, and sold for a halfpenny.

The launch crowned the career of founder Thomas Forman, who had taken over the ailing *Guardian* in the 1840s.

A respected figure in the rapidly expanding town, Forman was a JP and lived in a turreted house in The Park.

He would be driven to the Sherwood Street works each day by his coachman John Langsdale, who was liveried in navy blue tunic with silver buttons and cream knee breeches.

The first editor of the *Post* was Forman's son Jesse, who moved from the *Daily Guardian*.

The Sherwood Street site had been the home of the group since earlier in the decade, when the *Daily Guardian* and its sister publications outgrew their offices at the junction of Long Row and Greyhound Street.

When a plot at the corner of Sherwood Street and North Street became available in 1870, Forman bought it for £4,047.

A new office and works were built at a cost of £10,000. In 1871 the jobbing department moved from Long Row, followed in 1872 by the editorial department.

'WG': Centurion

Grace hits 116, but Notts win

GLOUCESTERSHIRE'S match at Trent Bridge in 1871 gave many their first sight of W.G. Grace.

Notts supporters got the perfect result — a ten-wicket win, but innings of 79 and 116 from Grace.

Notts players Alfred Shaw and J. Selby were in the team which in 1877 played Victoria and New South Wales at Melbourne — in what is regarded as the first Test match.

Boot ideas for family herbal business

IN 1871, Jesse Boot, 21, became a partner in the family herbal medicines business in Goose Gate.

Throughout the 1870s the range of stock was broadened to include proprietary medicines, toiletries, beauty treatments and other household essentials.

There were soon 2,000 lines, with emphasis on low prices. In 1877, Jesse took day-to-day control, effectively founding his pharmaceutical and retail empire.

Birth of D.H. Lawrence, novelist and poet ▶ Page 33

IN 1879 the MCC arranged a North v South match in honour of Notts bowler Alfred Shaw's feats both for and against the Marylebone club.

His record had included a 13-wicket haul for Colts of England in 1864; another 13 for MCC against Knickerbockers the following season; 71 maidens in 104 overs for MCC against Cantabs in 1870; 18 wickets for MCC against Thorndon Hall the same year; and seven for seven in 41.2 overs for Notts in 1874.

In a Middlesex v Notts match at Prince's Club in the 1870s, play was abandoned in unusual circumstances.

Mr Box, the groundsman, fell off a chair and died.

Notts, with one wicket down and time in hand, had needed just 45 runs to win.

THE Prisons Act of 1877 transferred control of local jails to the Government.

Nottingham's county gaol in High Pavement was among 113 transferred to the Home Office in 1878. It was immediately closed down.

The last escape from the jail happened on February 4, 1877, when four prisoners climbed on to the infirmary roof, then down into an adjoining yard.

FOREST enjoyed a good FA Cup run in 1878-9, starting with the 3-1 defeat of Notts County at Beeston.

In subsequent rounds, Sheffield and Old Harrovians were both beaten 2-0. But after the 2-1 defeat of Oxford University, Forest were knocked out by Old Etonians.

A.G. SAVILE opened his new school at Grosvenor Villas, Forest Road West, in January, 1876. It was later known as Grosvenor School.

JANE Green of Sneinton, common-law wife of the late mathematician George Green, died in 1877, aged 75.

NEW USE: Nottingham Castle became provincial England's first civic museum in 1878

Castle gallery opens but radicals object

THE town was brought to a standstill by the visit of the Prince and Princess of Wales to open the Midland Counties Museum and Art Gallery — the first municipal project of its kind outside London.

It had been created in the rebuilt mansion at Nottingham Castle, and date for the opening was set for July 3, 1878.

At 10am, the royal party left Bestwood Lodge, home of the Duke of St Albans.

Bunting lined the route through Daybrook and Sherwood. Respectful of the princess's Danish birth, an archway bore the greeting *Willkomen*.

At the market place, an estimated 45,000 were gathered. Choirs of children sang *God Bless the Prince of Wales*.

At the Castle, the prince was presented with a gold and silver key for ceremonially opening an

'SELFISH': The Prince of Wales

elaborate lock made by Messrs Chubb.

The prince said the museum set "an example which, I trust, will speedily be followed by other municipal bodies."

A crowd of 50,000 saw a £300 firework display created by Mr Brock.

THERE were dissenting voices about the museum and the royal visit — reflecting concern for social conditions and criticism of the Royal Family.

Anti-royalist sentiment had grown during Queen Victoria's prolonged mourning for the Prince Consort — and her heir's racy reputation also excited the editor of the satirical magazine *The Owl*.

Previewing the royal visit, he wrote: "He will gain in our affections in the measure in which he seeks to modify a surface of character which seems to many selfishly sensuous."

The Owl also attacked the expenditure of £50,000 on the museum and civic junketing.

VC for Rorke's Drift hero

NOTTS-educated Lt Gonville Bromhead was awarded the VC for his role in the defence of Rorke's Drift, South Africa, in 1879.

The 150 defenders of the outpost, mainly Welshmen of the 24th Foot, held out for 12 hours. Twenty-seven died during the action, during which 500 Zulus were killed.

Bromhead died of fever in India in 1891.

Final Shire Hall execution

THOMAS Gray was the last man to be hanged at Shire Hall, on November 21, 1877. It took place at the rear, because public executions had been abolished.

Tarpaulins were used to shield the execution from the eyes of workmen, who were engaged on repairs following the Shire Hall fire of 1876.

Cured by cycling, Bowden invests in Raleigh  Page 34

Booze inquiry at General Hospital

THE General Hospital and its wealthy benefactors were criticised in 1880 for allowing patients to drink too much alcohol.

An article in the magazine *The Hospital* suggested that too much money was reserved for wines, beers and spirits.

An investigation showed that expenditure on wine was £52.

However, the hospital management hit back, pointing out that if all that year's patients had consumed every drop, they would still have imbibed less than sixpence worth [about 2p].

Not enough, the authorities believed, to retard their recoveries from illness.

The hospital matron and secretary were commended for their management.

Stapleford blaze throws 200 on dole

STAPLEFORD was stunned by a £50,000 fire which destroyed Joseph Fearfield's lace factory.

About 200 men and women were thrown out of work, and the parish feared for the local economy.

The parish manual fire engine was sent, and a messenger rode to Nottingham, where Supt Knight sent the Imperial fire engine and another pump.

Forty-four lengths of hose were joined together to pump water from the River Erewash, 400 yards from the factory — but it was too late.

Mr Fearfield was insured for only part of the damage.

☐☐☐

IN 1881, Jesse Boot moved to larger premises in Goose Gate. Two years later, Boot & Co was established as a private company. Jesse was chairman and managing director.

Fight fans hoodwink town police

PROMOTERS fooled the police when Jim Rowbotham met William Halfred for an illegal prize fight. It was deliberately rumoured that the £20 purse would be contested in Gedling. The fight was at Beeston.

According to the *Evening Post*, scores of observers were expecting "an exhibition of fistic skill" — but it soon became clear that Rowbotham was not in prime condition. It was Halfred who collected the money.

Trader shoots at ex-lover

A MARKET trader shot at his former lover in Nottingham market place.

It happened on a May afternoon when a Mrs Thompson was on duty at her fruit and vegetable stall.

The *Daily Guardian* reported that a man with whom she had once "found an intimacy with", Harker Pratt, obtained a licence for a similar stall near Mrs Thompson's pitch.

At 3.50pm he visited her stall and "words were exchanged ... which ripened into more decided proof of hostility."

Folk gathered, and a police officer told Pratt to leave.

He obeyed and the crowd dispersed. However he soon returned, drew a revolver, fired twice at Mrs Thompson, but missed. A third shot injured his cheek and he was overcome by another policeman.

Pratt was later under guard at hospital.

LITERARY LEGEND:

David Herbert Lawrence, *right*, was born into a miner's family at Eastwood on September 11, 1885.

After an education in Nottingham, he would write poems, short stories and novels including *The Rainbow, Sons and Lovers* and *Lady Chatterley's Lover*.

First phones connected

THE first telephone exchange in Nottingham was opened in Bottle Lane in 1881.

The National Telephone Company's system began with just two local subscribers — but this was only three years after the first telephone had been introduced to the town.

It linked Nottingham Castle with the police and fire headquarters in St John's Street. Because there was no bell mechanism, the user had to whistle into the instrument or tap it — and hope that a constable was within earshot.

Competition for NTC arrived in 1888, when the General Post Office opened a rival exchange in Nottingham. The GPO took over completely when services were nationalised in 1912.

The city's first automatic exchange was commissioned in 1928, enabling Nottingham subscribers to self-dial most local numbers.

However, most long-distance calls still depended on operator connection — until 1962, when Subscriber Trunk Dialling (STD) was introduced.

By the mid-Eighties, British Telecom (newly separated from the Post Office) served 500,000 lines in a Nottingham area of 1,200 square miles.

ONE of the last known survivors of the Battle of Waterloo died at his home in Mount Street. James Davey, 91, had served in the 61st Foot in 1815.

☐☐☐

SEAL brown and olive green were the colours for the spring and summer of 1881, according to the Nottingham *Guardian* fashion correspondent.

☐☐☐

THE congregation of St Ann's Church was addressed by the Rev H. Pahtahquahong Chase, hereditary chief of the Ojibway tribe. He explained how Christian missionaries had helped end the enmity between his own tribe and the Sioux Indians.

☐☐☐

A DINNER was held in honour of Nottingham Forest player C.J. Caborn, who was emigrating to Canada. He was presented with a silver revolver, a supply of cartridges and a purse of sovereigns.

☐☐☐

TWO great actresses made their first appearances in Nottingham in 1882 — Sarah Bernhardt and Lily Langtry.

☐☐☐

NOTTINGHAM Band of Hope temperance union agreed to petition Parliament against a clause in the Inland Revenue Bill which would allow the sale of alcohol and tobacco in railway carriages.

☐☐☐

TRAM driver Thomas Johnson was charged with reckless driving — after his vehicle scattered a troop of the Yeomanry Cavalry in Mansfield Road.

☐☐☐

THE town council endorsed an application by the chief constable for 11 new officers, taking the strength of Nottingham police to 200. Crime had risen following the borough extension and the building of 5,000 new homes — the population had increased from 137,000 in 1871 to about 155,000.

Diamond Jubilee: Victoria grants city charter ▶ Page 35

DOUBLE murderer Henry Westby, 18, was cornered in Lenton Sands in 1881.

Westby, a Nottingham solicitor's clerk, beat a young colleague to death with an iron bar.

The same day he bought a revolver and returned to the family home in St Ann's Well Road, where his father was a tobacconist.

In the early hours of the morning, Westby shot him twice. He collapsed and died in front of his wife.

□□□

DOCTOR'S son Eric Coates, who became one of Britain's most popular composers of light music, was born in Hucknall on August 27, 1886.

His hits were to include *Sleepy Lagoon* and *The Dambusters' March*.

□□□

THE 16th Trades Union Congress was held in Nottingham in 1883.

Delegates debated training for steam engine drivers, and the right of the relatives of dead miners to be represented at coroners' inquests.

□□□

NOTTS bowler Alfred Shaw's XI beat Eleven of New South Wales at Sydney, with the touring captain putting up an astonishing bowling performance.

In the first innings Shaw's 26 overs went for just 24 runs; in the second, he took three wickets for five runs in 29 overs, 25 of which were maidens.

□□□

AN audit of Nottingham Town Council salaries in 1888 showed the town clerk to be receiving £1,100 a year, with extra responsibility payments of £800. The chief constable received £550.

□□□

A MAN convicted of travelling by rail without a ticket told Nottingham magistrates he was unable to pay the 10s fine [50p]. He was sentenced to 14 days' hard labour.

□□□

FOREST began the 1884-5 season at their new ground in Lenton in front of what the Nottingham *Daily Express* described as "a tolerably large gate". Smallheath Alliance were beaten 3-2.

FOUNDER MEMBER:
Robert Mellors

New county council elected

THE first meeting of the new Notts County Council took place on April 1, 1889. Following the first county elections that January, 68 councillors took their places at Shire Hall.

Reform of local government had been on the political agenda throughout the 1880s amid increasing concern about housing conditions endured by the poor.

The first elections caught the imagination of voters. Hucknall pitmen were allowed time off to vote, and in Kimberley and Gotham, the turn-out was more than 90 per cent.

The first chairman was Lord Belper, who held office for 25 years.

Viscount Galway succeeded him in 1914 — and during the First World War, at the age of 70, he volunteered as a special constable. He was one of four founder members of the council who were to serve at least 35 years. The others were Robert Mellors, the Duke of Portland, and Colonel Robert Mellish.

One of the most important responsibilities for the new council was highways. It took charge of 370 miles of main roads outside Nottingham, with an annual maintenance cost of almost £14,000.

Cure inspires bike investor

CYCLING enthusiast Frank Bowden founded the Raleigh Cycle Company in 1888, based on the two-year-old Woodhead, Angois and Ellis workshop in Raleigh Street.

Bowden had taken up cycling to improve his health after working in Hong Kong. He bought a 'Raleigh' for a European tour and was so impressed that he decided to invest.

The workshop had been making only three bikes a week. Bowden switched production to a five-storey factory in nearby Russell Street. The workforce rose to 200 as production expanded to 60 machines a week.

In 1889 the business was floated, with capital of £20,000. Determined to appeal to all sectors of the market, the firm sent 23 different models to an exhibition in London in 1890 — half of them new products.

In the 1890s a purpose-built factory opened in Lenton.

Sales were boosted by the success of Raleigh bicycles in international sporting competitions.

In the early 1890s, riders using

ENTHUSIAST: Sir Frank Bowden, painted later in life

Raleighs held the world quarter-mile record, and European titles for distances of up to 100km.

The company's greatest 'salesman' was American world champion 'Zimmy' Zimmerman, whom Bowden persuaded to try Raleigh's racers.

He rode Raleighs to success in British amateur championships, winning the one, five and 50-mile races. He also broke the world sprint record.

Blaze at tannery

THE Nottingham sky was lit by a huge blaze which destroyed Turney's Tannery at Basford.

The cause of the fire was a mystery, but damage to the 25-year-old factory was estimated at £15,000, and 100 employees were thrown temporarily out of work.

"A portion of men engaged on the premises left off work at 7.30pm, and two of the engine drivers on the hour," the Nottingham Daily Express reported in January, 1888. "There was not a single light burning."

A man named Bannerman saw flames shooting from a ventilator, and the alarm was raised at the Central Fire Station in St John Street. Crews attended but the building was wrecked by 11.30pm.

Apathy over Byron centenary

THE literary world celebrated the centenary in 1888 of the birth of Byron, but it was a low-key affair in Nottingham.

"There seems to be a deep sleep over the Literary Club in taking no public steps to celebrate the centenary of the natal day of the most powerful and famous of modern poets," complained the Nottingham *Daily Express*.

"There is no reason why we should not join the intellectual millions in putting a red mark against January 22, 1888."

Sneinton drunkard sets fire to wife

NOTTINGHAM was shocked in May 1885 by one of the most cynical crimes ever recorded in the town.

Drunkard Joseph Tucker, 37, battered his common law wife Elizabeth Williamson, emptied the contents of a paraffin lamp on to her clothes and set fire to her.

Neighbours in Sneinton tried to douse the flames, but the culprit said: "Let the beast burn." The victim died a week later, and Tucker was hanged in August.

Nottingham rider wins National on Manifesto ➡ Page 36

JPs pity abandoned mum

ABANDONED mother Priscilla Richards, a lace-hand from Byron Street, was in court for sending her children out to steal. She was charged with receiving a pair of boots valued at 2s 11d [about 15p], knowing them to have been stolen. Also in court were her son and daughter, and another boy.

The justices said Mrs Richards' remand in custody had been punishment enough. She was freed, her children sent to the workhouse, and the other boy ordered to an industrial school.

Turpin 'reborn' in circus

GEORGE Gilbert's Circus came to town, featuring a re-enactment of Dick Turpin's ride to York — "The Death of Bonny Black Bess." A reviewer was impressed.

"It was rather touching," he wrote, "to witness the apparent reality of the death throes of Black Bess.

"It is most certain that the horse had been under clever training to imitate the struggle as it did." One of the performances was a benefit for circus clown Sam Watson.

£80,000 for tram fleet

CITY Transport was founded in 1897 when Nottingham and District Tramways agreed a take-over by the corporation.

The decision was taken at the George Hotel, where shareholders accepted a £80,000 offer, plus £1,500 fees for the retention of directors until the end of 1898.

Horse-drawn trams had run in Nottingham since the 1870s. Under city ownership they were liveried in maroon and cream.

The first all-electric trams were introduced on the Sherwood and Bulwell routes in 1901, and the last horse-drawn services were sold the following year to private operators.

The first motor omnibuses were trialled in the Carlton area in 1906, but were unreliable and unpopular — and phased out.

By 1929, City Transport employed 1,339 people. The fleet included almost 300 vehicles of various types — covering 7.6 million miles a year and taking 84 million fares.

In 1936, the last electric trams, to Arnold, were phased out. By that time City Transport had Britain's largest fleet of trolley-buses. By 1953, there were 155 of them.

□□□

GLAZIER Frank Garvican, from Narrow Marsh, was fined ten shillings [50p] for stealing a gallon of ale from a pub cellar in Red Lion Street.

The landlord heard a noise and found Garvican next to a barrel.

The defendant, who disputed the amount of beer he had drunk, told the court: "When he first saw me I had my mouth under the tap. Could I have drunk a gallon in that way?"

Queen grants city charter

NOTTINGHAM, for centuries a town, became a city in 1897.

The charter was a Diamond Jubilee gift from Queen Victoria and was confirmed in a letter to the mayor by the Prime Minister, Lord Salisbury.

According to records, the news "sent a flutter of excitement through the town and gave evident satisfaction to all classes."

The *Evening Post* thought the charter "a fitting recognition of the position and influence of the town which justly assumes the title Queen of the Midlands."

Celebrations included a party for 46,000 children at the Forest.

In 1897, Nottingham was a town of about 250,000 people. It might have received city status in 1884, when a new Anglican diocese for Nottinghamshire was created — but it was decided that Southwell should be the bishop's seat.

The Midland Railway

DIAMOND JUBILEE:
Queen Victoria

Company marked the jubilee by giving 1,000 guineas (£1,050) to the Prince of Wales's Hospitals Appeal.

Bizarre end of Notts FA Cup hero

TRAGIC END:
Jimmy Logan at Notts County

JIMMY Logan, hat-trick hero of Notts County's FA Cup win in 1894, died after a bizarre incident.

The Ayrshire-born centre-forward had left Notts and was playing in 1896 for Loughborough.

They travelled by train to Newton Heath, Manchester. Loughborough's kit was lost en route, and they played in their travelling clothes. It rained heavily throughout, and the players returned to Leicestershire in sodden clothes.

Logan caught a chill, and died of pneumonia on May 25. He was buried in a pauper's grave in Loughborough.

NOTTINGHAM Racecourse was established at Colwick Park.

The city's previous course, in use since at least the 18th Century, had been on the Forest recreation ground, now the home of Goose Fair.

□□□

A YOUNG horse slid on ice while hauling a Nottingham Corporation cart in Sherwood Rise, and careered through the front window of Mrs Dunn's shop.

The horse was cut, and several pork pies were destroyed.

□□□

TWO cabbies were fined 15 shillings [75p] for being drunk in charge of hackney carriages, and both had their licences revoked by the justices.

One of the drivers said he had been given whisky as a tip.

□□□

NEW Basford and Hyson Green branch of the British Women's Temperance Association heard Father Hayes ask for tolerance for older imbibers.

He said society should concentrate on ensuring that children grew up to be total abstainers.

□□□

THE Great Northern Railway launched an inquiry after a runaway engine rolled away from Netherfield depot and ploughed into the ground alongside a footbridge.

Several children had been playing nearby just before the crash.

□□□

MINERS at Bestwood went on strike in 1897 to back claims for better pay. The most experienced and productive men were earning 5s a day [25p], but some lads were getting just 1s 3d [7p].

Manifesto wins the National

NOTTINGHAM jockey George Williamson rode Manifesto to victory in the 1899 Grand National.

The horse had a huge heart — twice the normal size, which helped him repeatedly defy the handicapper.

Manifesto ran in eight Nationals, the last when he was 16. His first win, with Tommy Kavanagh aboard, came in 1897.

In 1899, with Williamson in the saddle, he carried the huge burden of 12st 7lb.

At Canal Turn on the first circuit, the field encountered a blanket of straw which had been put down to protect the ground from frost. It should have been removed before the race, but had been overlooked.

When Manifesto landed on the loose straw, he slipped, his belly touching the ground.

The jockey allowed his horse to recover in his own time and he went on to win as the 5-1 second favourite and collect the £1,975 prize.

Owned by J. Crocker Bulteel, Manifesto was trained by Willie Moore.

The race was the first to be shown by means of the Biograph, that same evening at the London Palace, after a swift journey by rail from Liverpool.

Williamson began racing on the old Forest racecourse in Nottingham, just a few hundred yards from his home in the Grosvenor Hotel.

On the day he won the Grand National, he set off for Prague, changing in the train. On reaching Prague he won the Austrian national steeplechase. On the same tour he won the Hungarian Grand Steeplechase and a flat race in Turkey.

Such was his popularity in Austria that he caught the eye of Baroness Buren. Their brief marriage ended in divorce.

Williamson hunted with the Quorn and South Notts, and was also a billiards player of considerable ability.

He died in 1937 at his home in Loughborough Road, West Bridgford, at the age of 69

NEW LOCATION: Workers at Island Street

New look for the 'Royal'

Boots expands works

JESSE Boot began expanding the industrial side of his business from 1892 by acquiring sites in the Island Street and Station Street areas, south of the city centre.

The firm's manufacturing chemist H.B. Holthouse and his assistants were transferred from the firm's Goose Gate headquarters.

It was an inspired choice of site. Island Street was so named because the district was almost surrounded by the Nottingham Canal and its basin — and waterways were still cost-effective for shipping fuel if industrial plants were close enough.

It was also convenient for the stations of the two major railway companies — the Midland Railway, based at Carrington Street, and the Great Northern, based at London Road.

The retail side of the business was also flourishing.

In the seven years from 1893, the chain expanded from 33 shops — seven in Nottingham — to 250.

SHOW GOES ON: The renovated Theatre Royal

THE Nineties saw the city's entertainment quarter transformed, with the renovation of the Theatre Royal, and the building of The Empire — a variety hall — next door.

The developments were the idea of Robert Arthur, who had taken over the failing Theatre Royal in the mid-Nineties, and the impresario Henry Moss.

They contracted the architect Frank Matcham, who had built or refurbished several theatres for the Moss organisation.

Matcham went to work from the winter of 1896-7, and the Empire opened on February 28, 1898. It accommodated 2,500 patrons in stalls and two tiers.

The new-look Royal had re-opened in 1897. The first show, from September 6, was *The Taming of the Shrew*, performed by Augustin Daly's Company.

In October, 1897, the Royal was visited by two legends of the stage — Henry Irving and Ellen Terry, with the London Lyceum Company.

They played Shylock and Portia in two performances of *The Merchant of Venice*, and appeared as Napoleon and a washerwoman in the French comedy *Madame Sans-Gene*.

Nottingham architect Hine dies at 86

ARCHITECT T.C. Hine, creator of some of Nottingham's most important buildings, died aged 86 in February 1899. He was buried at Rock Cemetery, Mansfield Road.

His legacy included the Adams Building and the Broadway warehouses in the Lace Market, part of the Debenhams building, Coppice Hospital, the Corn Exchange and houses in Regent Street, where he lived, and The Park.

FOREST won the FA Cup in 1898 after knocking out Grimsby Town (4-0), Gainsborough Trinity (4-0), West Bromwich Albion (3-2) and beating Southampton 2-0 in the semi-final replay.

In the final at Crystal Palace, Forest beat Derby County 3-1 with two goals from Capes and one from McPherson. The match was seen by 62,017, who paid £2,312 in receipts.

☐☐☐

FORMER Notts cricket captain George Parr died in June, 1891, aged 65. With the wreaths was placed a branch from 'George Parr's Tree' at Trent Bridge.

Parr toured America with an English team in 1859, and captained an English XI in Australia four years later.

☐☐☐

JESSE Forman, first editor of the Nottingham *Evening Post*, died aged 43 in December 1892. He was succeeded by William Kerr.

☐☐☐

THE talking point at the 1899 Goose Fair was Pat Collins' attraction — the Channel Tunnel Railway. It allowed young couples to spend most of the ride unseen and in darkness.

☐☐☐

MUNDELLA Higher Grade School opened in The Meadows in 1899. It was named in honour of the late Nottingham MP A.J. Mundella, who had been president of the Board of Education.

2d ticket heralds the age of the electric tram ➡ Page 39

Hysteria and parades for relief of Mafeking

NEWS of the relief of Mafeking reached Nottingham on the night of May 18, prompting what the *Post* described as "an outburst which has had no parallel for many years."

As word spread that British columns in South Africa had come to the rescue of Col Baden-Powell's garrison, citizens crowded around the *Post* offices for further news.

By coincidence, the travelling entertainment at the Forest was Mr Fillis and Company's *Savage South Africa*, which told of the valour of British troops in Transvaal. An announcement was made to the audience at 10pm, resulting in hysterical cheering.

By 11pm, streets were crowded with revellers, and bunting was flying. Crowds broke into spontaneous choruses of the national anthem and *Rule, Britannia*.

Next day, the *Post* reported, patriotic displays were to be found "even in the dismal tenements and squalid slums."

The stars of *Savage South Africa* paraded in the market place with Maxim guns, followed by students of University College. The mayor, Alderman Pratt, announced a half-day holiday for schools.

At the Navigation Inn in Wilford Street, the licensee — a Crimea War veteran — organised a concert at which Miss May Watson sang *Red Cross Heroine*.

Extra donations took *The Daily Guardian* Shilling Fund for the dependents of soldiers to £9,400.

'Victoria' opens on Queen's birthday

NOTTINGHAM'S Victoria Station opened on May 24, on the birthday of the queen whose name it honoured.

The choice of name solved a dispute between the Great Central Railway and their joint-investors, the Great Northern.

GCR favoured 'Nottingham Central' — but the GNR, who would be transferring passenger services from London Road Low Level Station, felt left out.

Noting that the opening had been scheduled for Queen Victoria's birthday, the town clerk suggested Victoria — and that is what it was called.

The station was a showpiece on the GCR's line from the North to its new London terminus, Marylebone.

It was part of company chairman Sir Edward Watkin's vision of express trains running to the Continent, via London and a Channel tunnel.

Logan & Hemmingway built the line through the city. The station was designed and built by Henry Lovatt, supervised by Edward Parry.

More than half a million cubic yards of sandstone were excavated to create a huge cutting off Mansfield Road and tunnels at either end.

The frontage was dominated by the 100ft clock tower — all that remains. Access to the two main platform islands, each 1,270ft long, was via the oak-panelled booking hall and overhead bridge and staircases.

MANSFIELD ROAD: Nottingham's new station, the summer after opening (the adjoining hotel, far right, was completed in 1901)

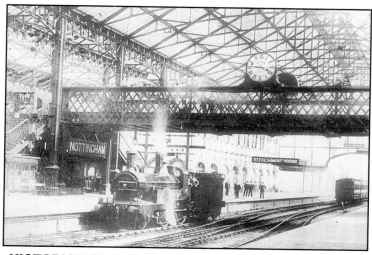

VICTORIAN GLORY: Station staff look on from Platform 7 as a 2-4-0 locomotive steams into Nottingham Victoria

THE Rector of Linby was at Shire Hall to answer a charge of threatening behaviour following a dispute with a neighbour over a gate.

It was alleged that he produced a knife and flashed it menacingly.

According to the prosecution, the clergyman said: "I have thrashed better men than you ... if you want any, I am prepared to give it to you now."

The allegations were denied. The chairman of the magistrates said he had heard enough and the case was dismissed.

❑❑❑

JESSE Boot's wife Florence inaugurated the Boots Book Lovers' Library at the turn of the century.

Customers could borrow books at 6d a time [about 2p], and volumes with racy content were given a red warning label on the spine.

By 1903, there were libraries in 193 Boots branches, usually at the back of stores. By the 1930s, there were 450.

Florence also developed an idea from London department stores — customer cafes. The second Boots cafe was at the Pelham Street outlet.

❑❑❑

ARSENIC was found in Notts beer supplies in 1900. Analysis showed the poison was derived from kilning malt and hops with coal or coke.

"There is not a brewer in the county who can guarantee that his beer is free from arsenic," the analyst wrote.

A brewer was fined £29, and his company directors were fined £10 each.

❑❑❑

MORE than 450 Boys' Brigade lads, escorted by 39 officers, travelled by special train to Whitsun camp at Skegness.

❑❑❑

NOTTINGHAM'S first electric tram was assembled at the Corporation depot in Sherwood. It was given the number 4, and was trialled on the new rails in Mansfield Road on November 17, filled with three tons of sand to represent a full load.

Mrs Milne, last of the Crimea camp-followers ▷ Page 39

Goose Fair under fire

GOOSE Fair faced criticism on two fronts — from townsfolk who believed its attractions were waning, and from city traders concerned about its impact on business.

Both causes were taken up by the *Evening Post*, which on October 3 — the first day of the 1901 fair — argued: "The cherished institution is but the framework of a fair compared with the carnival of a few years ago.

"Even schoolchildren can remember when it was of more imposing proportions. Many former elements have been eliminated, and the general character of the fair is fast passing away."

In spite of that, Goose Fair was no longer contained in the market place. There was overspill in Parliament Street and Sneinton Market.

The *Post* continued: "The central portion of a great city cannot be upset for three days for the purpose of an event which is calculated to do little substantial good to the real trade of the town."

❑ ❑ ❑

THE Lord Chancellor upheld a complaint by John Player that a Leeds businessman was selling inferior cigarettes in packaging similar to the firm's own.

❑ ❑ ❑

A GROCER from St Ann's Street was fined £1 by Nottingham magistrates for allowing his eight-year-old son to beg in the city centre.

❑ ❑ ❑

HUCKNALL Temperance Society began a series of weekly meetings in October. The 200 members sat down to tea and were entertained by the Nottingham Alberta Glee Singers.

❑ ❑ ❑

THE great American musician-composer John Philip Sousa brought his band to the Albert Hall. The programme included arrangements of Wagner, Lizst and Donizetti, and Sousa's own march *Invincible Eagle*.

QUIET TRADE: A Nottingham market scene in the early years of the century

2d ticket heralds age of the tram

SIX weeks after its successful trial, Nottingham's first electric tram went into service on New Year's Day, 1901. The fare on the market place to Sherwood route was 2d [about 1p].

Later in the year a depot was built at Trent Bridge to accommodate the growing fleet — the initial order for 12 vehicles was supplemented with three further orders for 32 trams. Anticipating further growth, the depot was built for 80.

During the first year, services from Trent Bridge to the city operated every two or three minutes. In the summer, the Bulwell route was electrified.

In 1901 a driver earned £1 8s [£1.40] for a 62-hour week. A conductor received about £1. Both had five days' holiday a year, with every other Sunday off.

Destination plates were colour-coded according to route. Services between Station Street and Sherwood had red and white plates; trams between Mapperley and Trent Bridge had yellow and blue.

SHERWOOD-BOUND: A tram in Mansfield Road

Roberts honours veterans as Foresters hold firm

THE Commander-in-Chief, Field Marshal Lord Roberts, was cheered by Crimean War and Indian Mutiny veterans as he arrived at Victoria Station for a day of charity and military duties.

In the market place he presented Boer War medals to officers and men of local regular and volunteer battalions.

He opened a bazaar at the Victoria Hall in aid of Nottingham Children's Hospital, which he also visited.

After travelling to Lenton Parish Church to see a new stained glass window dedicated to seven local soldiers who had died in South Africa, he attended an army veterans' dinner at the Albert Hall.

● The war was continuing, and the Sherwood Foresters distinguished themselves at Moedwill. They were part of a unit surrounded by 1,000 Boers.

After a bloody battle, Lord Kitchener reported: "The whole force behaved with great gallantry, the Sherwood Foresters doing particularly well."

Tragedy of Notts batsman Arthur Shewsbury ➡ Page 40

Survivor Ann, last of a gallant band

ANN Milne, 71, was feted as possibly Nottingham's last survivor of a gallant band — the British women who in the 1850s were allowed to accompany their soldier husbands to the Crimean War.

She was married to Sgt-Major C.T. Milne of the 8th Hussars, who was posted to Yunybuzzar in Bulgaria and appointed to a military hospital.

He was struck down with fever, and his wife patiently nursed him back to health.

The Milnes then travelled via the Bulgarian port of Varna to Scutari, Turkey — the main medical centre for British soldiers injured in the Crimea. While there, Mrs Milne met Florence Nightingale.

Sgt-Major Milne was sent across the Black Sea to the war zone, and served on Lord Raglan's staff at Inkerman. Promoted to Troop Sergeant-Major, he and his wife were then posted to Ismitt, Turkey.

But his fever returned, and he was invalided to Scutari.

In later life, Ann Milne became a lady member of the Veterans' Association, which paraded in 1906 at Derby where King Edward VII took the salute.

She presented the king with a rose, and he said he was delighted to meet someone who who had served the nation so faithfully.

Ann Milne died in March, 1908. Her pall-bearers were non-commissioned officers of the Robin Hood Rifles. She was buried at the General Cemetery.

Return of the heroes

GRATEFUL: Kitchener

HEROES of the Boer War were beginning to return home, with men of the Notts and Derbys Regiment among them.

Nottingham welcomed back 2nd Lt Herbert Millward who had received special mention from Lord Kitchener for his conduct at Vlakfontein.

The return of Pte Herbert Chapman of the Notts Regiment and Driver George Higgs of the Royal Artillery was also given coverage in the *Post*.

Four men would not be returning home: Cpl Richardson and Ptes Richards, Lewis and Taylor of the Robin Hood Rifles. But they would not be forgotten after General Sir H. J. T. Hildyard visited Nottingham to unveil a memorial in St Mary's Church.

Two battalions of the Rifles turned out, making a grand sight as they marched in South Parade.

DECAYING: The Marsh Farmhouse in the old Narrow Marsh

City hygiene 'behind the age'

THE hygiene of city areas like the Narrow Marsh came under intense scrutiny.

Not for the first time, the public health officer called on the corporation to tackle the vexed problem of wooden pail closets.

They were blamed for the high incidence of typhoid in the city. "In regard to drainage, Nottingham is altogether behind the age," it was reported, "with the result that typhoid is endemic."

In fact, Nottingham had the highest rate of typhoid in the country, but it was several years before problem was controlled.

SIR Charles Wyndham, third member of the triumvirate of theatrical knights along with Sir Henry Irving and Sir Squire Bancroft, made his long awaited debut in Nottingham. This was made possible by a system of 'flying matinees' allowing top performers to depart from the normal provincial tour route for towns not normally visited by top London actors.

A NEW tram route was introduced from Canal Street to Wilford Bridge — with a very specific timetable, the first tram leaving at 7.27½am and the last at 11.02½pm.

THE Nottingham *Evening Post*, four pages since its launch in 1878, was increased in size to six pages a day.

THE Nottingham telephone exchange was handling 27,000 calls a day.

THE 1902 Education Act transferred responsibility for Nottingham schools from an independent local board to the city council.

LADY Elinor Denison officially opened the new county lunatic asylum at an isolated site near Radcliffe-on-Trent. Saxondale Hospital was built for £110,000 to accommodate 452 patients.

EASTWOOD miner's son David Herbert Lawrence, 16, contracted pneumonia and spent the spring convalescing at his aunt Nellie Staynes' boarding house in Skegness.

LORD Willoughby, owner of Wollaton Hall, opened a new institute in the village, built on a cricket pitch. He had given the land for the institute in memory of a local JP and it was named the William Wright Institute.

SCHOOLBOY Walter Walker had a lucky escape when he stumbled in front of a tram. The quick-thinking driver, not having enough time to stop, lowered the life guard and lifted the boy clear.

Barrie and Peter Pan: The Notts connection  Page 41

125 Notts motors registered

THE registration of motor vehicles became compulsory, under the Motor Car Act, on November 26.

There were 125 registrations in Notts — including nine steam engines and 40 powered bicycles and tricycles.

The rest were cars, and the first to be registered was vehicle AL1, owned by Robert Millington Knowles of Colston Bassett Hall.

Owners paid £1 for a car registration, five shillings [25p] for a motorcycle, and a further five shillings was charged for a driving licence.

Under the Act, a limit of 20mph was introduced, with 10mph in towns.

THE first meeting of Notts education committee was held in May under the chairmanship of Henry Mellish. It became responsible for 319 elementary schools and several voluntary schools.

Children were allowed to be withdrawn from school aged 12 if they had not reached a certain standard, although the 1918 Education Act raised the universal school leaving age to 14.

Mellish was chairman until 1927.

THE International Exhibition Pavilion was built on the banks of the river at Trent Bridge and opened in 1903.

It contained exhibits from around the world and incorporated a concert hall and roller-coaster.

The building was damaged by fire and closed the following year — replaced by a new public building called The Pavilion, later a cinema.

THE first edition of Nottingham's *Football Post* was published on September 5, 1903. A sister paper of the *Evening Post*, it was edited by Harry Hild.

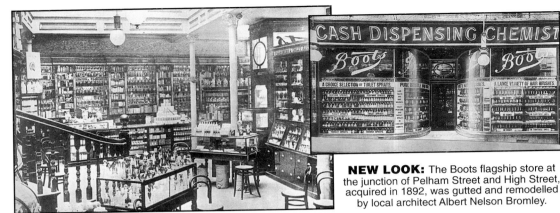

NEW LOOK: The Boots flagship store at the junction of Pelham Street and High Street, acquired in 1892, was gutted and remodelled by local architect Albert Nelson Bromley.

Cricket hero dies in shooting tragedy

MASTER batsman Arthur Shrewsbury, 47, committed suicide — convinced he was suffering from an incurable disease.

The incident happened at a house in Gedling. After hearing a gunshot, Shewsbury's girlfriend Gertrude Scott found him in a bedroom. By the time a doctor arrived, the Notts and England cricketer was dead.

Shrewsbury had complained of pain in his kidneys in 1902, but London specialists could find no sign of serious illness.

He told Notts he was unlikely to play in the 1903 season, and on May 12 he bought a revolver and bullets, which turned out to be wrong for the gun. The next week he bought the right bullets. Later that day he was dead.

At an inquest at the Chesterfield Arms in Gedling, the coroner concluded that Shrewsbury was disturbed by the thought that he was fatally ill, even though there was no evidence of disease.

Arthur Shrewsbury, buried in Gedling churchyard, played in almost 500 first-class matches and hit 26,505 runs at an average of 36.65. He was the first to score 1,000 runs in test cricket.

W.G. Grace, asked who would be his ideal choice as an opening partner for the England XI, replied: "Give me Arthur!"

OBELISK: The memorial framed by buildings in King Street

LORD Methuen, who commanded the British 1st Division during the Boer War, arrived in Nottingham to unveil a memorial the fallen.

The 25ft red granite obelisk, presented by Mr T. I. Birkin, was erected at the junction of King Street and Queen Street.

A dense crowd filled the space between the Exchange and King Street, cheering Lord Methuen as he emerged to inspect 150

Monument to the fallen

members of the Boys' Brigade. He spoke about the service and sacrifice of regiments such as the Sherwood Rangers, South Notts Hussars and Robin Hoods.

The memorial bore the names of 80 officers and men. It was later moved to the Forest.

Buffalo Bill thrills thousands ... but no Sitting Bull

COLONEL William F. Cody, Buffalo Bill, brought his Wild West Show to Nottingham.

Thousands went to Radcliffe Road, West Bridgford, to see his company of 1,300 men, women and horses which had travelled by four special trains. They included 100 American Indians, many of them captured by the US Cavalry in the previous century.

There were also Cossacks, Bedouins, Arabs, Cubans and Mexicans, plus a re-enactment of the Battle of San Juan during which Teddy Roosevelt's 'Rough Riders' earned their colours.

On Cody's previous visit, in 1891, he was accompanied by Annie Oakley. He no longer had the services of Sitting Bull, killed at the battle of Wounded Knee a few months earlier.

Duchess unveils Nottingham's Victoria statue  Page 42

'Quiet, ordinary' Chaplin takes a bow

SUPERSTAR: The Charlie Chaplin the world came to know

CHARLIE Chaplin, destined to become the greatest comic actor of the silent movies, made one of the earliest of several appearances at the Empire Theatre in Nottingham.

He first appeared in the city, at the age of ten, as member of a troupe of clog dancers called the Eight Lancashire Lads — even though he was born in Walworth, London.

In his teens he became a member of Fred Karno's travelling comedy troupe and appeared at the Empire near the bottom of the bill as Chas. Chaplin.

A messenger boy of the time, Harry Dawes of Sneinton, years later recalled that one of his favourite tricks was to pretend to be a member of the audience and fall out of a box.

"I did not think much of him," Mr Dawes said. "He was just a fool. I did not expect him to become what he became later.

"Off stage, he was quiet and ordinary. It was my job to call the artistes ten minutes before curtain-up and he was not very polite."

During his visits to Nottingham he always stated in a boarding house in Bilbie Street kept by a Mrs Lomas.

It is also believed that around the same time, Chaplin took part in a 20-mile championship walk round Nottingham. A researcher in the 1970s discovered that he not only competed but also won a £25 prize.

Chaplin also appeared at the Grand Theatre, Radford Road, which opened in 1886 and became renowned for pantomime and later, when it was owned by Sir Albert Ball, father of the VC hero, for repertory theatre.

'Curious village lad' inspired Peter Pan

J. M. BARRIE'S most famous play, *Peter Pan*, opened in London — and legend continues to this day crediting Nottingham with the inspiration for his story.

The great man arrived in Nottingham from his native Scotland in 1883, in answer to an advertisement by the Nottingham *Journal*: "Wanted on a Liberal morning paper. Gentleman, conversant with politics and social matters to undertake the writing of articles and assist in general literary work."

He gained lodgings with a Mrs Gilding in Birkland Avenue off Peel Street and remained on the staff of the newspaper for two years, turning out between 10,000 and 20,000 words a week for the princely sum of three guineas — without the aid of a typewriter.

It was during this time that he shared an alfresco lunch by the Trent with a journalist colleague named G. Basil Barham, who later told the following story.

He and Barrie were strolling through Clifton Grove when "a village lad came by and he was a curious sight.

"Someone had pinned a handkerchief or something of the kind to his trousers and he seemed very brave as he cut down the thistles and dandelions that grew in his path.

"Barrie stopped and said: 'See that lad. His name is Peter and he's lost his shadow.

J.M. BARRIE: Lodged in Birkland Avenue while writing for the *Nottingham Journal*

His sister's pinned that rag on him for a shadow...' I took little notice of what he said and neither of us could have guessed that those words would lead to a title of Sir James M. Barrie, nor that the name of Peter Pan, thus coined by Barrie and dubbed to a Clifton Grove urchin, would one day echo around the English-speaking world."

Sir James never forgot his associations with Nottingham and regularly corresponded with his old landlady Mrs Gilding, and other notable citizens.

He was moved to be made an honorary member of the strangely titled Nottingham Odd Volumes Society. When he died in 1937, he bequeathed royalties from *Peter Pan* to the Hospital for Sick Children in Great Ormond Street.

THE city council ordered that all new houses should be equipped with a WC.

Nottingham had a bad record for enteric fever, something the Medical Officer of Health had highlighted in 1902.

The majority of working men's homes relied on pail closets — there were 38,000 of them in 1904.

◻◻◻

TWO of Nottingham's open-top trams were fitted with hard tops, at £85 each.

The experiment was popular with passengers used to braving wind and rain on the top deck, and the corporation authorised the conversion of the rest of the fleet.

◻◻◻

THE new attractions at the 1904 Goose Fair in Nottingham market place were four-abreast Galloping Horse roundabouts.

An early Bioscope show was also open. Tickets for the best seats cost 2d [about 1p].

◻◻◻

THE last of the caves of Sneinton Hermitage were removed for road widening in 1904.

Most had been destroyed by the Great Northern Railway in 1897.

◻◻◻

ALFRED Martin founded the Savoy Cafe in St James's Street — Nottingham's first vegetarian restaurant. Mr Martin had been advised by his doctor not to eat red meat. He and his family converted to vegetarianism.

◻◻◻

THE number of motor vehicles registered in Notts rose from 125 to 413.

Crowds gather as blaze destroys Albert Hall ➡ Page 43

1905

Statue signifies end of Victorian chapter

THE marble statue of the late Queen Victoria was unveiled by the Duchess of Portland on July 28 in Nottingham's market place.

It was situated at the west end of the square, and the queen looked eastwards towards the Exchange and The Poultry.

The occasion was described as "the last words of the final chapter of Nottingham's association with Victorian times."

The statue was carved from a single block of flawless Carrara marble, selected by the sculptor Albert Toft from the Sicilian quarry and worked in his London studio.

The finished figure stood 11 feet high and depicted the queen in her latter years, holding the sceptre in her right hand, the orb in her left hand and wearing a small crown.

The statue was placed on a granite base which held four bronze panels. On the front was a shield inscribed Victoria Queen Empress 1837-1901,

MARBLE EMPRESS: Crowds witness the unveiling at the western end of the market place

surmounted by the arms of Nottingham and symbols of the empire.

The side panels depicted the mercies of Victoria's reign — feeding the hungry and clothing the naked.

The rear panel showed Maternity with outstreched arms, each supporting a child, representing shipping and engineering, the two key industries which had advanced

the prosperity of the Victorian era.

The officers involved in siting the statue could not agree and had a wooden copy made which was moved around the market place until a point between Angel Row and Long Row, anciently called The Stones, was selected. The statue remained there until the 1950s, when it was removed to Trent Embankment.

GENERAL HONOURS:

William Booth, Sneinton-born founder of the Salvation Army, received the Freedom of Nottingham in November. Booth, 76, was also awarded the Freedom of the City of London that autumn.

□ □ □

FOREST handed out a football lesson to the clubs of Argentina and Uruguay, returning in August with eight wins in eight games. The story of the tour is told in the goals for and against columns: Forest scored 57 times in official matches, but conceded only four goals.

□ □ □

WHITEHALL'S factory on the corner of Wollaton Street was gutted by fire on August 5, affecting the businesses of a motor car manufacturer, jam maker and hosiery company. Great crowds gathered in Theatre Square, outside the Rutland Hotel, as flames gripped the building.

□ □ □

NOTTINGHAM'S favourite holiday resort, Skegness, reported its best-ever summer season in 1905. By early August, the number of visitors for the year was 23,000 up on the equivalent period of 1904. "Boarding houses are full almost to the last room", the Evening Post reported, "and only one house is unlet."

□ □ □

NORTH Street, off Sherwood Street, was renamed Forman Street to honour the late Thomas Forman, founder of the Nottingham Evening Post, whose offices faced the road.

BACK-SEAT DRIVING: Bike makers Raleigh diversified into motor-powered vehicles with the launch of the Raleighette cycle-car (left). The 3.5-horsepower machine had a passenger chair seat mounted between two front wheels, and was steered by a rider mounted in a saddle over the rear wheel. It was road-tested by The Motor Cycle, whose writers recorded a top speed of 30mph, and average fuel consumption of 65 miles per gallon.

Not very much future in a visit to the fortune-teller's

A WOMAN visited a professional palmist to have her fortune told ... but died while waiting for the consultation.

Miss Annie Sharp, 32, had been an occasional visitor to palmist Annie Sansom's home in Hyson Green, a Nottingham inquest was told.

Miss Sansom finished a reading at 6.05pm and found Miss Sharp waiting in the hall. She told her client she would see her after she had taken tea.

Miss Sharp told her: "I feel rather queer in the head just now."

The palmist said the woman looked ill and called for help. Another client asked: "Has she had a shock?"

Miss Sansom, suspecting a heart attack, replied: "No, it's the engine that is passing."

Her diagnosis was wrong. After hearing medical evidence, the jury concluded that Miss Sharp had suffered a stroke.

City gas supply: Inquiry clears chief officer   ➡ Page 44

King's chauffeur gets lost

KING Edward VII paid a flying visit to Nottingham, motoring from Rufford Abbey to take tea at Wollaton Hll with Lord Middleton.

The visit was supposed to be totally secret, but word leaked from the hall and a large crowd gathered to watch the vehicle containing the king, who was heavily cloaked and goggled, sweep through the arch of Lenton Lodge.

He stayed for about an hour but when his chauffeur began the return journey, he took a right turn into Lenton Boulevard and drove through the city until they reached Carrington Street.

The driver had to stop for directions to Mansfield Road, passers-by having no idea his back seat passenger was the reigning monarch.

New clubhouse for golf 'Artisans'

LARGE crowds gathered at Bulwell Forest golf course to witness the opening of the new clubhouse.

The decision to rebuild was taken after the Notts Golf Club moved its headquarters to Hollinwell, the Bulwell Artisans Club moving into the new premises.

A number of matches were held to mark the occasion including a professional fourball involving Tom Williamson (Hollinwell) and W. Tedder (Bulwell Forest) against J. Sherlock (Oxford) and B. Hutchings (Derbys).

At a celebration lunch Bishop Baynes commented on the number of women and clergy taking up the game. He urged the golfers to heed the words of St Paul: "Blaspheme and curse not."

Post projects news as Liberals win

SIR Henry Campbell-Bannerman's Liberal Party had a landslide victory in the 1906 General Election.

News was relayed to crowds by means of projections on to a screen mounted over the main entrance to the *Evening Post* offices in Forman Street.

TRENT BRIDGED: Wilford suspension bridge was opened on September 12, built to carry water pipes from Wilford Hill Reservoir to The Meadows, and to provide a footbridge over the Trent

Blaze wrecks Albert Hall

AT 4.35pm on April 23, the alarm was sounded on one of the most spectacular fires seen in the city.

In less than two hours, the Albert Hall, whose 120ft tower dominated the Nottingham skyline, was all but destroyed.

News of the fire spread almost as quickly as the flames and vast crowds gathered at every vantage point to watch the drama unfold.

The first tender and horse-drawn carriage charged towards the scene but at the junction of Upper Parliament Street, Chapel Bar and Derby Road they were almost blinded by smoke.

As they neared the 20-year-old Albert Hall they could see flames roaring through every window and door and commanding officer Supt Broakes telephoned for every available firemen.

"With the utmost expedition the five steamers, Trent, Sherwood, Clumber, Little John and Robin Hood, were despatched with full complements of men," reported the *Daily Guardian*.

"Pending their arrival, seven jets were got to work but from the very outset the Albert Hall was hopelessly doomed."

The hall's construction, lined with pitch pine, only served to

OLD GLORY: Crowds at the fire. The tower roof has already fallen through

feed the flames and soon the roof had collapsed, the floors were gone and only the walls remained.

Speculation about the cause of the £25,000 fire surrounded a new electrical system for the giant organ.

The Good Templars of Nottingham in 1873 laid the foundations of what they hoped would be a temperance hall.

But they ran out of money and a limited company took over, opening it in 1876 as a concert and meeting venue. It was taken over by the Wesleyans for £8,500, the limit of their insurance, which left them with a debt after the fire.

Problems for city's new buses

FIVE years after electric trams were introduced, the corporation bought its first motor buses.

The three Thorneycroft double-deckers were intended to replace the horse-drawn trams operated on the Carlton route by local contractor W. Bamford.

However the new service proved to be unreliable.

Delays were caused by blocked petrol pipes and the vibration caused by solid tyres running over cobbled streets.

After two disappointing years the service was withdrawn in 1908.

Mr Bamford and his horses were re-engaged at 9d [about 2p] per mile. To be sure the city didn't lose out, fares were collected by a corporation conductor.

▢ ▢ ▢

ON the site now occupied by Rivermead flats, Jesse Boot built a pavilion with tennis courts and children's amusements.

This followed a bout of illness when he felt compelled to take more time from his business duties.

He regularly visited the place, as did many of his employees.

In 1910 the pavilion was swamped when the River Trent broke its banks.

▢ ▢ ▢

D.H. LAWRENCE, 21, enrolled on a two-year teacher training course at University College, Nottingham.

The miner's son from Eastwood had attended Nottingham High School, where his subjects included French and German.

He left aged 15 to work as a clerk-translator at a dealership in surgical appliances, based in Carter Gate.

While at University College he met his future wife Frieda, then married to Prof Ernest Weekley.

PRODUCTION of Raleigh bicycles rose to 30,000 in 1907, a 200% increase in four years. Orders were boosted by the introduction of hire-purchase deals.

❏ ❏ ❏

FOREST spent a season in the Second Division, but were promoted back to the first in 1907. The championship was secured with a 2-1 win over Leicester Fosse.

❏ ❏ ❏

THE thickest fog in memory descended on central Nottingham on the night of October 31. According to the *Evening Post*, at 8pm pedestrians could not see more than a yard ahead.

❏ ❏ ❏

AFTER 60 years out of power in Nottingham, the Conservatives narrowly failed to take overall control of the corporation. The 1907 election result: Liberals 24, Conservatives 23, Labour 1.

❏ ❏ ❏

KING Alfonso of Spain and Queen Victoria Eugenie were guests at Welbeck Abbey of the Duke and Duchess of Portland. The entertainment included a ball in the Picture Gallery, and a partridge shoot.

❏ ❏ ❏

VESTA Tilley appeared at the Empire, singing three songs including *Jolly Good Luck to the Girls who Love the Soldiers*. Also on the bill were Irish ballad singer Joe O'Gorman and fox terrier trainer Ida Kessanly.

❏ ❏ ❏

THE corporation extended the electric tram network with routes to Colwick Road and London Road. From 1907, all new trams were ordered with covered top decks.

❏ ❏ ❏

THE corporation markets manager, Joseph Radford, presided over organisation of the last of his 34 consecutive Goose Fairs.

❏ ❏ ❏

A TRAFFIC survey on the Great North Road in Notts (now the A1) showed 28 cars passing in a single hour.

Topsy bowls Notts to the county title

NOTTS were county cricket champions, winning the official title for the first time since the sequence of seven unofficial championships in the 1880s.

The hero of the season was Tom 'Topsy' Wass, who took 163 wickets at an average of 14.28.

However the Notts cricket community went into mourning for the death of master bowler Alfred Shaw, who died that year in Gedling.

He made his debut for Notts in 1864, and played for the county for 24 seasons. After seven years in retirement he played two seasons for Sussex, retiring again at the age of 53.

"He was the leading slow bowler of cricket history," recorded *The Times*.

CHAMPIONS: The 1907 team, with Topsy Wass on the left of the middle row and Ted Alletson (see Page 48) second from left, back row

Gas problems: City inquiry clears chief

A LONG-running political row over the management of Nottingham Gas Undertaking resulted in an inquiry which in 1907 exonerated J.H. Brown, the chief executive.

Brown had been appointed engineer and manager in 1902, and identified serious flaws in the city's gas operation.

There were problems with the carbonisation plant, the Basford Gasworks retorts, the Giltbrook chemical plant — and even in the city's mains, where pressure was variable.

Brown was honoured by the Institution of Gas Engineers for his experiments with blue-water gas.

But a faction on the corporation argued that he was too concerned with awards and outside consultancy work.

There was criticism of executive decisions made by Brown and the gas committee chairman which were not referred to other councillors, and he also had management problems at Giltbrook and the undertaking's Eastcroft station.

A demand for Brown's resignation was rejected by the gas committee, and three members resigned.

They were not to give evidence at the subsequent inquiry, which concluded that the gas operation had been badly managed until 1902.

The report also noted that the committee had failed to follow Brown's advice on crucial issues.

In November 1907 the gas committee had a new chairman, Coun Albert Ball (later Alderman Sir Albert Ball, father of the flying ace). Brown departed in 1911.

❏ ❏ ❏

THE United States ambassador paid glowing tribute to Nottingham at the Chamber of Commerce annual dinner at The Exchange.

The Hon Whitelaw Reid praised local industry and made a florid reference to Lord Byron ... "one of the most brilliant poets of the great Georgian choir".

He urged more trade between Britain and the US. At the time, British Empire countries sold goods worth £75 million to the States.

Pankhurst riles 'vulgar' youths

SUFFRAGETTE leader **Emmeline Pankhurst**, *pictured*, was heckled as she addressed a 'votes for women' meeting at Nottingham Mechanics Hall.

Youths sang, stamped and, according to one witness, "shouted vulgar epithets from the rear of the room."

The deputy mayor, Alderman J.A.H. Green, stepped on to the platform to quiten the young men, reminding them of Nottingham's tradition for free speech.

But there was uproar when Mrs Pankhurst continued: "Don't you think we are capable of using the vote wisely? I dare say we can teach some men a lesson."

Several men rushed at the platform, and sympathisers like the Rev Lloyd Thomas barred the way.

Pankhurst had founded the Women's Social and Political Party in 1903.

Tonics sold as flu bug hits city

WINTER returned to Nottingham in March, driven by a biting north wind. The heavy snowfall drew tobogganists to the southern slopes of The Forest.

The freeze coincided with an influenza bug. A London remedies manufacturer took advantage by advertising discounted Hall's Wine in Nottingham.

"Practically every person who has been taking Hall's has avoided the epidemic," the advertisement boasted. "It makes blood — new, rich, red blood — creating the power to resist the deadly germ."

● The city council authorised the purchase of 48 acres at Wilford Hill for the creation of a cemetery. Proposals for a crematorium were shelved.

'Let them wash in the Trent!'

THE corporation heard arguments for providing public bathing facilities in The Meadows, where most of the 30,000 residents relied on buckets and sinks for washing.

One proposal was to convert the old horse-drawn tram stables in Muskham Street — but City Transport said the site was still needed. Councillors agreed to look for alternative locations ...

But not before one member said Meadows people could always bathe in the River Trent!

RAVE REVIEW: Actor Johnston Forbes-Robertson, appeared as Hamlet at the Theatre Royal. "A tour de force," said the *Post* critic

Arthur Mee, the children's instructor

PROLIFIC WRITER: Arthur Mee, by Frank Salisbury

THE *Children's Encyclopaedia* was founded in London by a former Nottingham journalist who became one of the century's most prolific writers for young people.

Arthur Mee was born in Stapleford in 1875 and at 16 became an apprentice reporter on the Nottingham *Daily Express*; at 20 he was editor of the Nottingham *Evening News*.

Mee moved to London and launched the *Children's Encyclopaedia* in 1908. It was released in 50 fortnightly instalments, each costing 7d [about 3p].

His other ventures included the *Children's Newspaper*, which was founded in 1919 and continued until 1965, the *Children's Shakespeare*, the *Book of Everlasting Things* and the *World's Great Books*.

Mee is best remembered for his King's England series — a 41-volume pre-war guide to the shires, with notes on 10,000 towns and villages.

The books, in eye-catching navy blue dustjackets, were still being reprinted in the 1990s.

Mee died in London in 1943, aged 67. He left a £200 bequest to his school in Stapleford to provide an annual prize for the best boy pupil.

Motor taxis join the rank

THE first motor taxi to ply for trade on the streets of Nottingham made its appearance on February 17.

Observers of the time doubted whether the new addition to the city transport scene would last, and the old cabbies were less than impressed as it parked alongside the 'growlers' and hansoms in the market place.

Made by Humber Ltd at Beeston and painted red, it looked a grand sight.

But it was greeted with contempt by rival drivers: "It can't pay. Look how long we have to wait for a job. Trams go everywhere, there is no room for cabs in Nottingham."

In fact, the new cabbie, a Mr Harold Lees, would later recount tales of how the irate hansom drivers would force him with their whips from his car to seek shelter under the vehicle, keeping him there until the square filled with people and they were required to set him free.

The Humbers came with two bodies — covered saloon and open sports — which could be changed simply by removing four bolts and sliding them on and off built-in rollers.

Despite the city cabbies'

THE "call office cabinet" outside the Theatre Royal was one of the city's first six public telephone kiosks, installed in 1908.

Nottingham's boxes were three feet square with a pitched roof and three glass sides.

It was agreed that the city police force would have free use of the phones. A coloured signal indicated that beat bobbies were required to call headquarters.

pessimism, Renault and Rover were both expected to introduce motor taxis on to the ranks, and soon afterwards a list of licensed cabs included makes such as Gladiator, Fiat, Napier and Darracq.

JESSE Boot gave funds for the rebuilding of Albert Hall, which had been destroyed by fire.

He also gave £5,000 for the Binns organ and paid the organist's salary for three years — on condition that recitals were given every Sunday, with a maximum ticket price of threepence.

Boot also stipulated that Saturday evening concerts be given "for the purpose of promoting the love of high class music especially among the working classes."

□ □ □

SUPERFIT cyclist Harry Green, riding Nottingham-built Raleighs, smashed the Land's End to John o'Groats cycling record — in spite of persistent stomach and knee pains.

He arrived at Scotland's northernmost point after two days, 19 hours and 50 minutes, breaking the record by almost three hours. Raleigh later launched 'Harry Green' special models.

□ □ □

THE Hippodrome variety theatre opened in Wollaton Street in 1908. In the 1920s it was renamed the Gaumont Cinema. It closed in 1971 and was demolished in 1973.

□ □ □

SARAH Bernhardt appeared in Nottingham as Marguerite Gaultier in *La Dame aux Camellias*. The single performance on July 15 was seen by D.H. Lawrence.

Municipal factories plan for ailing lace trade  Page 47

MISS Green, daughter of the town clerk of Nottingham, executed a citizen's arrest when a man tried to steal her front doormat.

It happened in The Park, where several well-to-do residents had complained of doormat thefts.

Miss Green, watching from a front window, saw the man take the mat, roll it up and place it under his arm. But before he could walk off she went outside and detained him until police arrived.

THE Great Central Railway claimed to have broken all records for Whitsun bank holiday excursions from Nottingham.

GCR figures were not published, but the Midland Railway sent 2,850 passengers on special excursions to London, Scotland, the Isle of Man and nine other destinations. The only reported problem came when a woman fell down the Midland Station staircase — she returned home in a cab.

The Great Northern claimed 3,400 excursion fares, including 1,030 on day trips to Skegness.

KEIR Hardie, founder of the Independent Labour Party addressed local supporters at the Victoria Hall, Burton Street, after first talking to hundreds of people outside who were unable to gain access to the meeting.

JESSE Boot, founder of the Nottingham-based pharmaceutical and retail business, was knighted for his philanthropy and services to the Liberals.

FARMERS welcomed torrential rain in June after a drought in May. But the cloudbursts coincided with Nottingham Agricultural Show at Colwick Park — organisers admitted attendance was sparse.

CAPT J.A. Morrison, parliamentary candidate for Nottingham East, inherited £1.3 million on the death of his uncle, the city financier Charles

EXPLORERS: Captain R.F. Scott (left) and Lieutenant Evans planning their South Pole expedition. Scott was a hero of boys at Mundella Higher Elementary School in The Meadows. The 900 pupils raised funds to buy a husky for the venture, which Scott named Mundella

Votes: Girl on hunger strike

LENTON vicar's daughter Helen Watts, 28, became a heroine of the suffragette movement when she staged a 90-hour hunger strike in prison.

She was the daughter of the Rev Allan Watts, who encouraged her involvement in the movement to secure the vote for women.

Her first prison sentence, in 1909, followed an attempt by suffragette marchers to enter the Houses of Parliament.

She was given a month in Holloway Prison, and returned to Nottingham to a heroine's welcome.

Later that year she was jailed in Leicester for trying to disrupt a meeting at which the rising Liberal politician Winston Churchill was speaker.

A women's gathering was arranged to coincide with the meeting, and supporters took to the streets of Leicester on horseback to rally more support.

Helen Watts was one of seven people charged with a breach of the peace.

She told the court: "I stood still when the police tried to make me move — if you can call that disorderly."

The defendants received short jail sentences, and responded by refusing to wear prison clothes and staging a 90-hour fast.

Helen was again feted when

TARGET: Winston Churchill, pictured in 1912 — targeted by suffragettes

she returned to Nottingham and was treated to supper at Morley's Cafe, a meeting place for members of the Women's Social and Political Party.

The WSPP honoured her with a special silver medal bearing the words 'For Valour'.

Helen worked in the War Office and later the Ministry of Labour and retired to Sussex. In 1965, at the age of 84, she boarded an aircraft for the first time and emigrated to Canada.

● Her medal was sold at auction in London in 1999 for £5,400 — £4,000 above its reserve price.

Skate craze on a roll at Empress

ROLLER skating fever came to Nottingham with the opening of the Empress Skating Rink on the corner of Lower Parliament Street and Glasshouse Street, site of the former House of Correction.

It was built by an American company called Rinking Ltd which was cashing in on the skating craze, opening similar venues in 20 towns and cities across Britain following the success of roller skating in the United States.

The Empress was an instant success, with hundreds of people flocking to the new facility

But one week after temporary summer closure on May 22, it was destroyed by fire.

The blaze was spotted by a tramcar passenger who raised the alarm, but despite the attendance of the city fire brigade, nothing could be done to save the rink.

Within 20 minutes the wood, glass and steel structure was reduced to a skeleton of twisted girders.

Worship bonus for constables

TWO councillors caused problems for corporation staff when they demanded a pay and hours breakdown of every council employee paid less than £2 a week.

It emerged that 4,026 people received less than £2, including clerks, scavengers, constables, meter inspectors and cricket groundsmen.

The hardest working were housemaids at Bagthorpe Hospital (81 hours a week).

City constables, entitled to 21 days' holiday, were otherwise required to work eight hours a day, seven days a week — but with some flexibility on Sundays "to enable them to attend public worship".

A Home Office inspection in 1909 showed the Nottingham police force to comprise a chief (£800 a year, plus a house and £25 expense allowance), six superintendents, 15 inspectors, 50 sergeants and 254 constables.

Heavy-hitter Alletson flays the Sussex attack  Page 48

NEW HOME: Notts County and reserves, 1909-10. After sharing with Forest at Trent Bridge, Notts moved to a new ground in Meadow Lane in 1910 ... when a fan complained to the *Post* about foul language at both grounds: "I wonder if those who swear have any regard for children and ladies?"

Council factories for ailing lace industry?

CIVIC leaders debated a plan to bolster Nottingham's flagging lace-making fortunes — the creation of municipal factories, possibly with corporation-owned homes for workers.

But the idea was criticised in a trade publication, the *Textile Mercury*. It said employers should unite to do the job themselves.

"Municipal administration is far more wasteful and inefficient than private control," the editor wrote.

"Municipal control should be a last resort, to be taken only when private enterprise breaks down. Proof that private enterprise has failed, however, is lacking.

"Nottingham is on the verge of creating a precedent which will be worked on Socialistic platforms for all it is worth.

"It is the way of the apostles of universal municipalisation to fasten upon each new departure in municipal ownership and proclaim them all over the land.

"The first town to have a municipal tramway, the first to have a municipal milk depot, and a municipal flagstone manufacturing process, have all had notoriety in turn.

"The town that is first to provide municipal factories will be heralded as the forerunner of the municipal provision of textile machines, or even of textile fabrics!"

The *Mercury* acknowledged the conditions under which Nottingham's lace workers toiled. They needed more room, more cleanliness, more light ... "but these are as easy for private enterprise to achieve, singly or in concert."

Authorities which had built artisans' cottages, the editor continued, had found them uneconomical. Notts and Derbyshire Traders' Association also objected.

EDWARDIAN HUSTINGS: A candidate addresses voters from his automobile during a pre-Great War election in Nottingham

JAMES Bywater made his 102nd court appearance, which Nottingham police believed was a record.

For once, it wasn't for drunkenness — although drink may have explained why he was found in the Guildhall, soaking wet, at 4am. He said he had fallen into the Trent.

On hearing that Bywater had no money and nowhere to stay, magistrates remanded him for what the police superintendent described as "a wash-up".

□ □ □

A MAN nicknamed 'Buffalo Bill' was sentenced to three months' hard labour for allowing his rented property to be used as "a disorderly house" — the usual term for a brothel.

William Burdett rented a house in Union Street, paying 4s 6d a week [about 22p] per room. Three rooms were sub-let to women, who each paid 15 shillings [75p] a week.

A police officer said two of the women had been fined £2 each. But their activities had continued, as Burdett knew full well.

□ □ □

ADELE Pankhurst, of the campaigning 'votes for women' family, was pelted with missiles in Nottingham market place. The *Evening Post* reporter described her assailants as "stunted slips of invertebrate humanity."

□ □ □

MAGISTRATES made an example of two of the youths who scrumped apples in a Bulwell garden. The owner said children had broken his fence and plundered his produce, and he had even been hit with a stick of his own rhubarb. The lads were both fined 10s [50p].

□ □ □

EVENING Post photographer Charles Shaw took what is considered to be England's first aerial picture — a shot of the River Trent at Burton.

□ □ □

CITY police took charge of their first motorcycle — a second-hand machine used by PC 103 Dench. They also recruited what was believed to be Nottingham's first police dog.

Aviation pioneer touches down in home city ➡ Page 49

A LACE manufacturer appealed to leaders of British fashion to reject the latest Paris styles and support Nottingham's major industry.

French creations including the hobble skirt and the harem skirt were affecting sales of more traditional garments using Nottingham-made lace, B.F. Stiebel complained.

"The interests of the fancy and other textile trades are greatly injured by the sometimes extravagant and · grotesque vagaries of Paris fashions," he told the Chamber of Commerce.

He urged "legitimate ladies of English society to set the fashion for English ladies' dresses."

● The *Post* reported that in Belfast, an Italian woman accepted a trader's offer of £5 to anyone who would wear a harem skirt in public for two hours. After half an hour of jeering, she fled into an ice cream shop.

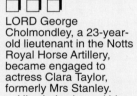

LORD George Cholmondley, a 23-year-old lieutenant in the Notts Royal Horse Artillery, became engaged to actress Clara Taylor, formerly Mrs Stanley.

His choice barred him from a £3,000 bequest which was dependant on his marrying "a lady in society".

Lord George and his fiancee, the *Evening Post* noted, were members of the Sunday Skating Club at Olympia, London.

Clara's divorce in 1909 had caused a sensation. Both she and Mr Stanley alleged the other to be guilty of misconduct with other parties.

AT the Sacred Harmonic Society's concert at the Albert Hall in March, the soloist in Max Bruch's Ave Maria was the soprano Carrie Tubb.

According to the *Post* critic, she sang "with somewhat more power than sympathy".

FOREST were relegated from the First Division after a miserable 1910-11 season in which they were also knocked out of the FA Cup in the first round — West Ham winning 2-1.

LOVER'S WALK: Willie Jones, 17, dived into the Trent here in 1911 to rescue a child of five

Alletson's innings smashes records

NOTTS cricketer Ted Alletson indulged in the most sustained feat of heavy hitting ever seen in the first-class game.

In the match against Sussex at Hove in May, he scored 189 out of 227 in 90 minutes — the last 89 coming in just 15 minutes.

Notts began their second innings 176 runs in arrears. When Alletson walked to the crease, the Notts XI was nine runs ahead — but with only three wickets in hand.

He began his innings steadily, scoring 47 in the final 50 minutes before lunch.

Forty minutes after lunch, he was out — after slaughtering the Sussex bowling for 142 out of 152. Observers said they had never seen anything like it.

Alletson hit E.H. Killick for 22 in one over, then for 34 in an over containing two no-balls.

The match was drawn.

It was Alletson's only first-class century.

Edwin Boaler Alletson played in 100 matches for Notts from 1906, but did not return to the first-class game after the Great War.

He worked for several years as an official at Manton Colliery, for whom he still played when he was 50. The bat with which he made his famous innings was displayed in a glass-fronted case at his home in Worksop.

FIREFIGHTERS: A Nottingham Fire Brigade crew in the years before the Great War. In 1911 the city took delivery of two six-cylinder Dennis motor fire engines. They were equipped with 75bhp turbine pumps capable of delivering up to 800 gallons of water a minute

Teapot handle became money

COUNTLESS bogus coins were in circulation, the product of backstreet counterfeiting.

Two cases were brought before Nottingham Assizes in the spring of 1911.

Labourer James Harris was sentenced to three months' hard labour for trying to pass counterfeit shilling pieces to two city tobacconists.

Detectives were tipped off, and raided the Eldon Street lodgings Harris shared with another man, Williams. They confiscated a galvanic battery, a coil of copper wire, a blow lamp, plaster of Paris and a metal teapot.

Asked what had happened to the teapot handle, Harris said Williams "was handy at making things".

Plaster of Paris, used to create moulds, figured in a case against warehouseman Frederick Thompson.

He had made the acquaintance of a widow in a Nottingham pub. They "lodged together" and next morning she discovered him melting metal in a saucepan. Police were called.

Bishop urges miners to adopt purer lifestyles  Page 50

1912

Pioneer on a flying visit to home city

AVIATION pioneer Bob Slack touched down in his home city — piloting his Bleriot biplane on a 25-minute flight from Leicester to Woolley's Meadow, near Clifton Grove.

It was part of a round-Britain flying expedition in which Slack was to fly almost 2,000 miles, averaging about 65mph.

Slack was born in 1886, lived at Edwalton and trained as a motor engineer at Cripps Garage in Nottingham.

He saved enough money to pay for flying lessons at Hendon and enrol as a student at ICS (International Correspondence Schools) in London.

Spotted by flying exhibition sponsor Graham White, Slack was engaged to fly Bleriot biplanes at displays around the country.

On June 23, 1912, he took off from Thurmaston at 4.30am and flew north through clear skies, followed on the ground by a team of supporters in a car.

Thousands of Nottingham people turned out to see the Bleriot aircraft and witness Slack's departure.

The following year, the pilot flew a Morane-Saulniers monoplane from Paris to London. He reached the height of 6,000ft when a pressure gauge exploded, soaking him with fuel.

Slack touched down near Folkestone, and resumed his flight. The standard time from the Channel to London would have been an hour — but because of violent cross-winds, it took more than seven hours.

He was killed later in 1913 — not in an air accident, but on the road. On December 21, he was at the wheel of his car

TOUCHED DOWN:
Bob Slack

at Radlett in Hertfordshire when a tyre burst and the vehicle overturned.

Slack, 27, left a wife and two children. He was buried at the General Cemetery in Derby Road.

Numbers up

A NEW numbering system replaced coloured destination boards on the city's electric trams.

Routes were: 1, Sherwood to Mapperley; 2, Mapperley to Trent Bridge; 3, Bulwell to Trent Bridge; 4, Basford to Colwick Road; 5, Nottingham Road to Radford and Lenton; 6, St Ann's Well Road to Lenton and Radford; 7, Wilford Road to London Road; 8, Carlton to Market Place. Route 9 was added in 1915 — Arnold to Market Place and Derby Road.

SWANNING IN:
Ballerina Anna Pavlova was the main attraction at the Theatre Royal in December. Billed as "the Sarah Bernhardt of dance", Pavlova was praised by the *Evening Post* for displaying "the highest charms of the corybantic art." She performed *The Passing of the Swan* to music by Saint-Saens. With Laurent Novikoff she danced Rubinstein's *Valse Caprice* and Glazunov's *Bacchanale*.

THE GLOBE: A new picture house opened in London Road in 1912. The Globe, shown here on a foggy day in the 1920s, survived until 1962

A LOVE story touched hearts in the public gallery of Birmingham Assizes, but not those of jury and judge.

Nottingham bandleader John Guy, 25, stayed at a hotel in Birmingham and fell for the proprietor's young sister-in-law, Dorothy.

He was frank with her. He was married with two children, but intended to divorce.

A love letter was read to the court: "Come to Nottingham ... I cannot live without you."

Dorothy's family tried to end the relationship. The girl was allowed to see him off at New Street Station, where Guy asked: "Will you go with me?" She said yes.

There was only one problem. She was under 18. Guy was later arrested for abduction, which he denied.

Dorothy, giving evidence, said nothing had occurred beyond "ordinary love-making" [which at that time meant there had been no sexual relationship]. She said she was happy with Guy in Nottingham.

His counsel concluded: "Events had simply gone love's way". There was then a burst of applause from the gallery.

The jury found Guy guilty and he was sentenced to six months' hard labour.

CITY market traders reported brisk business on Christmas Eve, 1912, with turkeys selling fast at a shilling [5p] per lb.

But they caught a cold with the traditional decorations, holly and mistletoe. Heaps of the greenery remained unsold, prompting a Boxing Day lament from the *Post* ...

"Holly was never more plentiful and never in better condition, but there was no demand. It would appear that the old-fashioned custom of decorating the home is falling out of favour."

GENERAL William Booth, Sneinton-born founder of the Salvation Army, died aged 83. The final entry in the Salvation Army's official diary of his life recorded: "The Founder promoted to Glory."

A PUPIL at Mundella School wrote in an essay: "England in 2000AD will have no navy, no colonies, no Ireland, no churches, no pubs — only Germans, socialists, suffragettes, chapels and lemonade."

1914: The summer the world changed for ever Page 51

FORMER Nottingham East MP Captain James Archibald Morrison was sued for divorce in a high-profile undefended case in which his wife alleged desertion and adultery.

The court reporter noted that the Hon Mary Morrison, giving evidence, was "attired neatly, but fashionably, in black."

She said she and Morrison married in 1901. They had three children.

In 1911, her husband travelled to America, and she had not seen him since. She won a decree for the restoration of conjugal rights, but he had not returned.

Statements were submitted from staff at the Hotel Palais d'Orsay in Paris, confirming that Morrison and a lady had been guests, staying in communicating rooms.

The court also heard of a divorce obtained by a M. Morand on the grounds of his wife's misconduct with Morrison.

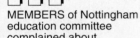

MEMBERS of Nottingham education committee complained about standards in 'the three Rs'.

R.H. Swain, applauded by other councillors, said reading, writing and arithmetic had declined among the 42,495 children being educated in city schools at a cost of £106,000 a year.

The chairman doubted the claim. He said the committee was under increasing financial pressure because of teachers' salaries, the need for new schools and Government pressure for smaller class sizes.

THE *Evening Post* employed a motoring correspondent, C.W. Brown, to advise readers on the perils of the road.

On July 5, his 'Hum of the Wheel' column included a rather obvious tip ... not to go round corners on the wrong side of the road.

However Brown offered sound advice at a time when traffic law was in its infancy, and signs were few and far between. He argued for a junction rule requiring drivers on a minor road always to give way to main road traffic.

TOOLED UP: The Raleigh workshop in Nottingham, pictured in 1913

Clean it up, says bishop

CHARACTER PLEA: Notts miners, pictured in 1910 by the Rev F.W. Cobb

THE Bishop of Southwell, Dr Hoskyns, appealed to Notts miners to adopt a purer lifestyle.

"The thing required in the great colliery districts is the strengthening of the manhood of the population," he told Notts Federation of the Church of England Men's Society.

"In these days we ought not to turn towards the law to put down drinking clubs and to raise the tone of working men's clubs. It would be much more healthy for the men to do it themselves.

"If we could get a higher tone among the men in the pits with regard to their conduct towards, and in the presence of, boys, it would be much more wholesome than laws or rules.

"At some of the pits it has had the effect of stopping many of those things which are very deleterious to the character of the boys."

Dr Hoskyns said he was astonished by the latest gambling craze ... "a coupon system in connection with Association football."

MPs probe phone delay

A FIRE at Jacoby's Factory at Daybrook prompted questions in the Commons and a row about the efficiency of the telephone service.

After the blaze in May, it was discovered that half an hour elapsed between the attempt to raise the alarm by phone and a response from Nottingham Fire Brigade.

During that time, flames gripped the upper storey of the factory, causing thousands of pounds worth of damage.

Questioned by local MPs at Westminster, the Postmaster-General, Herbert Samuel, admitted the blunder was down to inattention by a night telephone operator — who had been "suitably punished".

He promised "special measures" to ensure it did not happen again.

Mr Samuel defended the efficiency of the General Post Office and its stewardship of the telephone network.

Local calls were usually picked up by the operator within five seconds, he added.

Suffragettes turn to vandalism

SUPPORTERS of the Women's Social and Political Union were responsible for several acts of vandalism in 1913, including the smashing of windows in Goldsmith Street .

Suffragettes were also blamed for a fire at Nottingham Boat Club which caused £2,000 damage.

VC for Gallipoli hero; tobacco at the front line  Page 52

Tram rage: 'Blackguard' fined £3

DESCRIBED by the chief constable as "a low racing man and a perfect blackguard", James Humphreys, 45, of Elgin Street, appeared before the court after an incident of tram rage.

Much the worse for drink, he attempted to board a Sherwood car at Victoria Station but when he was refused by the conductor, he kicked him in the stomach.

As the car left him behind, he ran after it all the way to Milton Street where he again violently assaulted the conductor.

He was fined £2 for the assault, £1 for being drunk and told the court he remembered nothing about the incident.

Bolting cart wrecks store

CHAOS reigned in Peas Hill Road when a runaway horse and cart, loaded with one and a half tons of asphalt, crashed into a general store.

The cart driver had stopped on the steep road, fixing a thick piece of wood to the cross-trees for a brake. It did not work and the horse, pushed by the weight of his load, was forced at ever-increasing speed down the hill.

The nag charged straight through the door of the shop, suffering nothing worse than a cut on the head. But the cart demolished the shop.

POLISHED ACT: With more men disappearing to the front, city women were called upon to work. Window cleaners in Nottingham during the Great War

The lady window cleaners of Nottingham.

War blows the summer away

THE *Evening Post* of August 3, 1914, told of the typical summer events: Sutton Bonington flower show; a record-equalling 65 at Bulwell Forest Gold Club; first-class batting averages which had Jack Hobbs third with 50.17.

But early editions carried news from the Continent, scattered over several pages. German Army corps were marching into France, Luxembourg and Belgium.

The news was consolidated in a special final edition with the *Post*'s first all-news front page, dominated by a map of Europe.

On August 4 the paper published reassuring pictures of Grand Fleet battle squadrons at full steam. On August 5, it reported the declaration of war on the German Empire, with effect from 11pm the previous night.

The *Post* drama critic, straining for a topical angle, wrote from the Theatre Royal:

"The European death grapple is the one topic of conversation just now, and by an interesting coincidence the relations of Britain, Russia and Germany come under notice in the first act of the play *Diplomacy*..."

Of more immediate concern to ordinary Nottingham people was the effect of the war on food prices — there had been protests in Glasgow about a 200% rise in sugar prices in just two days.

Following a 30% increase in the price of flour, Nottingham Master Bakers' and Confectioners' Association debated whether to add a farthing or a halfpenny to a 2lb loaf.

Spokesman C.F. Collins appealed to the public not to panic-buy, for fear of driving up prices still further.

The *Post* reported that well-to-do citizens with motor cars had been driving from shop to shop buying provisions at £10 to £15 a time.

NOTTS Territorial Army units were immediately mobilised on the declaration of war.

They included the 7th (Robin Hood) Bn, Sherwood Foresters; the South Notts Hussars Imperial Yeomanry; and the Nottingham Royal Horse Artillery Battery.

Army and naval reservists received 3s [15p] for expenses, plus railway passes — but with the loss of their civilian incomes, scores of city families struggled.

A War Relief Office was set up in South Parade, managed by A. Durose and staffed by clerks with experience of running a similar operation during the Boer War.

Miners at Clifton Colliery did their bit for colleagues who had joined TA and RNR units. They pledged 10s per week [50p] for their families.

❏❏❏

FIRST-HAND news from Belgium came from a Nottingham nurse working near Brussels. The *Evening Post* did not name her, but published a letter received by her family.

"The heroism of the Belgian soldiers contrasts most forcibly with the machine-like dispirited Germans, who have to be pushed to fight by their officers," the nurse wrote.

"The Germans are not fighting fairly. Their spies are using Red Cross badges and flags to get into towns.

"Near Antwerp, a well-known German gentleman who had lived there many years was caught putting a bomb on the railway line over which Belgian troops were being sent. He was tried and shot."

❏❏❏

THE celebrated Russian composer-pianist Rachmaninov arrived in Nottingham to perform at the Mechanics Institute in a concert sponsored by Wilson, Peck and Co.

❏❏❏

A YEAR after relegation, Notts County returned to the First Division — Peart and Richards scoring 49 goals between them. The Second Division championship was secured with a win at Barnsley.

Bunting is out for long-overdue royal visit

KING George V and Queen Mary visited Nottingham in June, two months before the outbreak of war.

They were welcomed in the market place by the mayor.

Flags were unfurled, bunting was strung between lamp posts and thousands of Union Jacks were waved by citizens in the streets.

It was the first *official* royal visit to Nottingham since the reign of Charles I and no one wanted to miss it.

Official secret as Zeppelin bombs Nottingham ➡ Page 53

THE weekend of November 13-14 saw a freak run of accidents in Nottingham — four fatal.

An errand boy was knocked down by a taxi in Gregory Boulevard, a confectioner was hit by a car in Arkwright Street, and a 44-year-old woman broke her skull falling downstairs at the County Club in Bridlesmith Gate. All three died in hospital. The fourth death happened when a window cleaner fell from a window in Union Street.

There was more. A nightwatchman was found dead in his hut of Alfreton Road — natural causes were suspected; a hosiery worker was injured by a lorry in Highbury Vale, and a woman was severely hurt when falling from a tram in Arkwright Street.

LEWIS Waller, one of England's most popular romantic actors, died at the Rufford Hotel while staying in Nottingham following a week's performances at the Theatre Royal.

He was suffering from a cold when he arrived in the city, in mid-October, but was well enough to play a round of golf with comedian Harry Lauder, and honoured a promise to recite to wounded soldiers at Bagthorpe Military Hospital. He collapsed at the end of his hospital performance.

Waller first appeared at the Theatre Royal in 1907 in a play about Robin Hood. He returned in 1910 in *The Three Musketeers*.

THE Chamber of Commerce voted £20 to the Notts Soldiers and Sailors Christmas Gift Fund, which stood in mid-1915 at £5,423.

Another contribution was expected from a concert featuring Robert Radford, "England's greatest living bass", and Hucknall-born composer and musician Eric Coates.

RALEIGH boss Frank Bowden received a baronetcy in the King's Birthday Honours following his offer of part of his Nottingham factory for munitions manufacture.

FLEET ALERT: HMS *Sherwood*. A Nottingham sailor serving on another destroyer wrote in 1915 of his frustration that the German High Seas Fleet made only occasional sorties: "We are all disappointed that 'Willie' [the Kaiser] should have allowed Trafalgar Day to pass without a bump"

Gallipoli VC for rescuer

WALTER Parker was awarded the Victoria Cross for his heroism at Gallipoli in 1915.

Grantham-born Lance-Corporal Parker, who settled in Stapleford, joined the Royal Marines in Nottingham in 1914 and served in the Royal Naval Division in the campaign against the Turks.

On the night of April 30, 1915, he was working with a stretcher party and volunteered to help wounded men in an isolated trench.

Braving Turkish fire, he covered 400 yards of exposed ground, reached the trench and tended the injured men — even though he had been shot.

During the Marines' withdrawal, he continued to care for the wounded in spite of his injuries.

Parker, who received his VC from King George V, appeared to have recovered and served in Ireland. But in 1916 he was invalided out of the Marines.

He died in the 1930s and was buried at Stapleford.

Another who was wounded at Gallipoli, Private H. Butler of the 9th Sherwood Foresters, wrote to praise the *Football Post* Tobacco Fund.

Pledge forms appeared in both the *Football Post* and *Evening Post*, allowing civilians to have packets of cigarettes sent to relatives or friends in the services.

"I am recovering from the effects of a 'Turkish Delight'," wrote Pte Butler, coining Gallipoli slang for an enemy bullet. "The Cigarette Fund is admirable, for the boys don't have too many comforts."

Vickers leads spirited stand

ACTING Captain Charles Geoffrey Vickers, 7th Sherwood Foresters, was awarded the VC for his role in the battalion's heroic defence of Hohenzollern Redoubt.

Under fire on two sides, and when nearly all his men had been killed or wounded, he directed the repair of their trench barriers while keeping the Germans at bay with bombs.

"Finally he was severely wounded," the citation recorded. "But not before his magnificent courage and determination had enabled the barrier to be completed. A critical situation was saved."

Capt Vickers, son of a lace manufacturer, was later recovering from his wounds at a London hospital.

● Conscription had yet to be introduced, but in October Nottingham recorded its biggest monthly total of volunteers since August 1914: 1,596 men.

EXECUTED HEROINE:
Nurse Edith Cavell

Cavell: Judge hits out at German justice

RECORDER Sir Ryland Adkins compared British justice with the German version — at a time of shock over news that British nurse Edith Cavell had been executed by the enemy.

"Everyone must be struck by the fact that the judicial proceedings of the Germans, even when technically correct, appear to be actuated not by a spirit of justice, but of murder," he said. "We must deepen our resolve to discharge our own judicial duties in a spirit of subordination to the true equity of mercy ..."

Sir Ryland was speaking at the Quarter Sessions at Guildhall, where six prisoners appeared for offences of burglary, deception and theft.

Posthumous VC for fighter ace Albert Ball  Page 54

Hush-hush Zeppelin strike is talk of city

A GERMAN Zeppelin attacked Nottingham on September 23-24, dropping bombs which damaged buildings in the city centre.

The airship was one of six which crossed the North Sea to Cromer, then split up to raid various parts of England.

Zeppelin L17 made for Nottingham, where eight explosive and 11 incendiary bombs were dropped.

They fell on the city centre, and buildings were damaged in Lister Gate, Castle Gate, Greyfriar Gate and Broad Marsh.

Wartime reporting restrictions meant newspaper readers had to put two and two together. The *Evening Post* published a rare Sunday edition on September 24. But even though the bombing was the talk of the city, readers were told only that ...

"An air raid took place in a Midland town between 12.45 and 1am this morning. There was no damage of military importance." Next day, September 25, news broke that one of the Zeppelins had been shot down in Essex while flying back to Germany.

The crew — described in newspapers as "baby-killers" and "arrogant Prussians" — were arrested by a special constable.

A communique from Berlin confirmed the raiders had dropped bombs on outer London, Hull, Sheffield and Nottingham.

BY 1916, the war was having an effect on both the national and city economies.

Family incomes were lowered when men left civilian jobs to join up — and Nottingham firms in non-essential manufacture struggled for materials.

Signs warning "No more ale until Saturday" were commonplace outside pubs, many of which brewed their own ale. There were shortages of both hops and malt.

A city firm licensed to bottle Guinness became a victim of the glass shortage, and production was cut by 80%.

There was evidence of domestic economies, with the corporation gas undertaking facing rising demand for pre-payment slot machines.

Another 1,049 were fitted in Nottingham homes in 1916, bringing the total to 44,402.

More women became tram conductors — and some male passengers complained that they were too bossy.

The Sheriff told the council: "Some women conductors have acted as if they own the trams, but speaking as a whole they are doing their job well."

There were occasional potato shortages. A 12-year-old girl was put on probation after stealing a purse from a woman waiting in a potato queue in Radford Road.

□□□

MAJOR Roderick Webb, owner of Newstead Estate, died in 1916. He had served in East Africa and had been wounded earlier in the war.

□□□

CITY libraries brought comfort to convalescing servicemen. Once read in local libraries, thousands of magazines and periodicals were distributed to hospitals, and parcels of books were sent to sailors in the cruiser HMS *Nottingham*.

□□□

NAVAL surgeon Blurton, son of a West Bridgford doctor, served in the destroyer HMS *Tipperary* at the Battle of Jutland. His ship was lost, but he was rescued by a Dutch vessel and taken to Holland.

FRONT LINE: British soldiers in the trenches, 1916

PRIVATE Peach of the Sherwood Foresters wrote home ...

"What the Sherwoods did in the great advance was accomplished with valour. We advanced through the wood with little shellfire until we came to a German communication trench.

"During the night we let Fritz know we weren't asleep by keeping up rifle and machine-gun fire until daylight. At 2am an officer said, 'Get ready, my lads — on the top! And don't forget, keep in touch!'

"We advanced towards Fritz's dug-outs, jumped into the trenches and found 700

Sherwood Foresters overcome Germans

Prussians anxious to give themselves up." After a 23km march, Pte Peach complained of pain in his foot. "I took my boot off and found I couldn't get it on again. It turned to septic poisoning and I was sent to hospital, out of the 'scrap'."

Next day, August 4, the *Post* reported casualties, from various dates, among the Foresters: 23 killed, 200 wounded.

More patients, fewer staff at hard-pressed asylum

HEALTH visitors were alarmed at the rising population of the City Asylum. In 1916, 93 men and 125 women were admitted — but only 32 men and 57 women were discharged.

The 950 inmates included 16 soldiers who had been discharged, on mental health grounds.

In 1917, concern was put on the record, under the headline 'Lunacy Not Decreasing'

It was reported that "the admission rate continues to be above average, and is rising, while at hospitals elsewhere, numbers are declining."

Carnage at Chilwell as blast hits shell factory ➡ Page 55

Percy Toplis: Was he the monocled mutineer?

NOTTS soldier Pte Percy Toplis reputedly led the most serious military mutiny of modern times — an incident so embarrassing that it will remain secret until 2017.

The story was told first in the 1978 book *The Monocled Mutineer*, and a decade later in Alan Bleasdale's controversial TV drama of the same name.

The mutiny happened in September 1917 at the 'Bullring' training camp near Etaples in France, where conscripted men suffered appalling conditions and were allegedly humiliated by officers and instructors.

According to some, officers were kept prisoner and even killed, and British troops on active service had to be diverted from the front line to quash the rebellion.

Toplis reputedly deserted, and masqueraded as a captain, wearing a monocle to complete the patrician image. He was captured and sentenced to death, but escaped to England where he became a notorious villain.

However, there are different versions of the story. One suggests that his desertion and impersonation happened before the Etaples mutiny.

And others doubt if he was ever in France, arguing that he served in the Middle East.

FUGITIVE: Percy Toplis

However the known truth was still sensational.

Toplis was the colliery apprentice who ran up a criminal record in the Mansfield and Ashfield areas before the war. He was even jailed for rape.

In 1920 he was the focus of a national police manhunt following the murder of motorist Sidney Spicer on Salisbury Plain.

A suit of clothes belonging to the fugitive were found in Mansfield, along with a monocle. But the hunt was to end in Cumbria where 23-year-old Toplis was shot by police.

The *World's Pictorial News* immediately researched the story, previewing its revelations in a large advertisement taken in the *Evening Post* the previous day.

Readers were promised details on "the mystery man ... fascinator of women ... swindler and swashbuckler."

VC for Albert Ball, 'most daring of all'

CAPTAIN Albert Ball flew his final mission on May 7, 1917. His SE5 fighter plane crashed near the French village of Annoeulin — and the air ace died in the wreckage, aged just 20.

The cause of his death remained a mystery.

Ball, son of Nottingham's Alderman Albert Ball, flew with 56 Squadron, Royal Flying Corps, who were based at Vert Galand, north of Paris. He and ten other SE5 pilots took off at 5.30pm, briefed to make a sweep over German trenches at Cambrai and Douai.

But the squadron was intercepted by Richthofen's 'Flying Circus' — a formation of Albatross Scouts commanded by the Red Baron's brother Lothar.

Ball had been considered a lucky flier. The average life expectancy of a pilot posted to the Western Front was three weeks, but he had survived for 15 months during which he accounted for 44 enemy aircraft.

He was awarded the DSO, the MC, the Freedom of Nottingham (on February 19, 1917) and, posthumously, the Victoria Cross.

Ball was buried by the Germans, with full military honours, in a war cemetery at Annoeulin.

After the war, a memorial statue was paid for by public subscription and erected at Nottingham Castle.

"No bolder lad ever wore wings," said an RFC colleague. Ball's commanding general added: "He was the most daring, skilful and successful pilot the corps ever had."

'NO BOLDER LAD': Capt Albert Ball, VC

Thousands are killed by 'the Hun'

THE *Evening Post*'s daily Roll of Honour told of the continuing slaughter on the Western Front.

On June 1, the roll confirmed 3,676 more officers and men killed, wounded or missing in action. Soldiers serving in East Midlands battalions were mentioned by name.

The tone of reporting had changed from 1914. The enemy was usually referred to in headlines as 'the Hun'.

'Homes for heroes' ... the first council houses  Page 56

DEVASTATION: The scene at Chilwell after the blast

Chaplain of 53 wins VC

A FORMER Nottingham High School teacher became one of the oldest winners of the Victoria Cross. The Rev Theodore Hardy, 53, was an army chaplain attached to the Lincolnshire Regiment.

Mr Hardy, a widower, had already won the DSO and MC. The citation for his VC referred to conspicuous bravery on several occasions, and his fearless devotion to the men of his battalion. He...

● Guarded a wounded officer, under enemy fire, until help arrived.

● Saved at least one life while burrowing for men buried by a shell blast.

● Saved another soldier by protecting him while just ten yards from an enemy pillbox.

During his career at the High School, which ended in 1913, Mr Hardy was a curate at Burton Joyce, then New Basford.

Another remarkable clergyman in the news in 1918 was the Rev Thomas Horne, known at fairgrounds as "the showmen's chaplain".

Mr Horne, who died in Somerset aged 69, had been born in a caravan at Goose Fair. He became the protege of a Leeds clergyman and began theological studies.

He helped persuade the corporation not to cancel the 1914 Goose Fair.

Blast kills 134 shell workers

A HUGE explosion wrecked the National Shell Filling Factory at Chilwell — killing 134 and injuring 250.

The blast happened just after 7pm on July 1. Witnesses reported a massive mushroom cloud and windows were shattered in houses more than two miles away.

"The calm of the evening was broken by the most ear-splitting, paralysing bang we had ever known," said a witness at Attenborough.

"This was followed by the sound of shattering glass as the window of the kitchen blew in.

"We imagined it to be another Zeppelin raid, so we rushed into the cubby hole and waited for the next bomb to fall."

The scene inside the factory was ghastly. Only 32 of the dead could be identified immediately.

However, there was no panic . Workers helped injured mates. Day shift workers rushed back to the factory to help.

The plant was an important element of the munitions industry. With the British and Allied armies preparing for a final push on the Western Front, demand for shells had never been greater — and 10,000 people worked at the factory.

Scotland Yard investigated, and there were several theories about the cause. But later historians reckoned it was a simple industrial accident.

The 134 victims were buried in Attenborough Churchyard.

SCORES of Nottingham people died in the 1918 influenza epidemic.

The flu bug led to the bizarre death of 17-year-old Wilfred Collinson, a dairyman's son from Dalkeith Terrace.

When he complained of a sore throat and head cold, a lodger told his mother that the best cure for flu was Phenol.

A child was sent with the message to a chemist in Radford Road. She returned with a bottle clearly labelled: "Poison: Not to be taken."

An inquest heard that the lodger said Phenol contained only a small amount of poison. "Give him some," he urged the mother, "and take a dose yourself."

A measure was poured into a wine glass and given to Wilfred. Moments later he began moaning.

Phenol was used as a remedy for gastric catarrh, the coroner was told, but only in doses of two to three drops, diluted.

The jury returned a verdict of death by misadventure. They absolved the chemist from blame, but censured the lodger.

❑ ❑ ❑

FOUR boys were rewarded for their honesty when they found a huge number of silver coins scattered in the gutter of Gamble Street. After five months the money was unclaimed, so police gave them the £66.

❑ ❑ ❑

THE War Weapons Week in Nottingham raised £174,975. Attractions included a Joan of Arc pageant involving hundreds of local children.

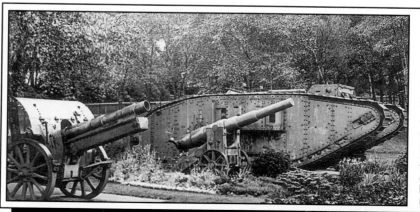

WAR MACHINES: A tank displayed on The Forest after the war. Nottingham civilians first saw the new weapon in the Market Place during the 1918 Tank Week, during which war bonds worth £2.7 million were bought

Boots goes west as American tycoon pays a call  Page 57

Farewell to Belgian refugees

TWO hundred and fifty Belgians gathered at Midland Station in February to begin their journey home.

The refugees had fled after the German advance through Belgium in 1914.

A special train carried them to Hull, where they were to catch a steamer to Antwerp.

On the platform, wellwishers gave them bags of sandwiches.

The mayor said: "We have suffered together, and we have fought together. I hope our hospitality will help create a lasting friendship between our two peoples."

THE first city police woman was a Miss Plumtree. In spite of objections by some members of the watch committee, she began her three-month trial on July 23 at £140 a year.

The trial was extended, but Miss Plumtree caught flu and was off for two weeks. The committee stopped her pay, and later dismissed her.

THE corporation ordered 25 double-decker trams from English Electric.

When the first of them arrived in 1920, they had not been fitted with brakes. A councillor made a quip about "non-stop" services.

NOTTS library service was founded, and book lendings rose steadily to 44,377 in 1920.

SIR Jesse Boot acquired Highfields estate hoping to create a model factory village. The land was to become the campus of University College.

THE city's Boys' Brigade leaders condemned the spread of gaming machines, which had become popular sidelines at tobacco and sweet shops.

MIDLAND CHAMPIONS: In the final season of wartime football, Forest (1919-20 squad pictured) won the Midland Section competition. County were third in a league of 16 teams.

Council invests in 'homes for heroes'

LAND for Nottingham's first council houses was bought in May 1919 — the city's response to the call for improved housing for soldiers returning from the Great War.

"Home fit for heroes" was the cry, and Nottingham was one of the pioneers of council housing.

Government guidelines called for a density of 12 homes to the acre. The density in some of Nottingham's worst slum areas was 50 homes to the acre.

The council decided to hold a competition, which was won by local architect W.A. Kneller. He was engaged in September 1919 to design the Sherwood site.

The second site comprised 31 acres at Stockhill Lane, which the council had bought for £6,115. The design contract was awarded to another Nottingham architect, W.R. Gleave.

His scheme provided 224 houses each costing £850 to build. Contractors included A. Goodchild, W. Marlow & Sons, and F. Evans & Sons.

Keys were handed to the first tenants in 1921. They paid from 7s 6d [about 37p] to 9s 6d [about 47p] a week.

Main roads on the new estates were built 16ft wide, and lesser roads 14ft. Standard width for cul-de-sacs was 8ft.

Councillors were informed: "These compare favourably with the gravel drives to large country houses."

A shortage of building land prompted the corporation to apply in 1919 for an extension to the city boundaries.

Had the extension been approved, Nottingham would have embraced Arnold, Carlton, Beeston, Hucknall, West Bridgford and Ruddington.

MILL SAVED: Green's Mill was bought in 1919 by Nottingham solicitor Oliver Hind. The abandoned mill, pictured dominating the Sneinton skyline, was secured against bad weather and let to a firm of furniture makers

Profit slur: Duke threatens to sue

THE Duke of Portland, *left*, threatened to sue anybody who perpetuated rumours that he had profited from the use of his estates as army camps. His lawyers said the land had been formally offered to the Government. No reward was requested or received.

The point was confirmed in a letter to newspapers from Gen Sir John Maxwell of Northern Command.

Bitterness in Nottingham as pitmen strike  Page 58

Youngest newspaper editor was man of many parts

CECIL Roberts became Britain's youngest morning newspaper editor when he was appointed to the chair of the Nottingham *Journal*, aged just 28.

Born in Nottingham in 1892, he was educated at Mundella School and made an early name for himself as a poet — his first volume of verse merited a foreword from John Masefield.

He entered journalism during the Great War as a special correspondent with the Grand Fleet, Royal Flying Corps and the Army.

During his *Journal* editorship, Roberts' first novel was published. *Scissors* in 1923 was followed by critical acclaim for *Sails at Sunset* and *Spears Against Us*.

He even found time to become the Liberal parliamentary candidate for Nottingham East, although he resigned through ill health.

After five years at the *Journal*, he concentrated on a writing career that was to embrace novels, travel books, poetry and five volumes of autobiography.

He lived much of his later life in Italy, but visited Nottingham whenever he was in England. In 1965 he was awarded the freedom of the city. Roberts died in 1976, aged 84.

ALL ROUNDER: Roberts, an enthusiastic amateur performer, is pictured above (fancy trousers) in a 1920s Playgoers' Club show at East Circus Street Hall. Right: On his 80th birthday

Nottingham MP 'irresponsible'

ALBERT Atkey, MP for Central Nottingham, was described in a national newspaper as "the most irresponsible member of the House of Commons".

His pet grievance, observed the *Morning Post*, was the permanent closure of one of the exits from Nottingham Midland Station.

The paper continued: "Mr Krassin [a Soviet trade envoy] may come to London, Ireland may be reduced to the depths of anarchy, but Mr Atkey has one great object in life — to get that closed exit opened.

"In season and out of season he pesters the Minister of Transport and questions him.

"The other day he brought in a large petition and banged the knees of every member of the Government before he was able to lay it at the feet of the Speaker."

The Minister, said the *Morning Post*, had repeatedly pointed out that he had no legal power to intervene.

❏ ❏ ❏

A THOUSAND ex-soldiers met in Nottingham market place and supported a resolution objecting to the trade blockade of Soviet Russia, and the possibility of another European war.

Going west... Boots & Co

TWO of the most powerful men in world retail pharmacy met in Nottingham in 1920. Their talks resulted in the transfer of Boots to American ownership.

Louis Kroh Liggett was in England hoping to expand the British interests of his United Drug Co. He was tipped off that Boots might be for sale — the firm was rumoured to be having problems with management communications and 'dead' stock.

Liggett made several attempts to contact Sir Jesse Boot, who owned almost 98% of the company. But he was in poor health, and Lady Boot deflected his interest.

But he telephoned again when Lady Boot was away, and Sir Jesse — who was to receive the Freedom of Nottingham in 1920 —invited him for talks. Boots Pure Drug Company and its five subsidiaries were merged into the American company for £2.25 m.

The deal was criticised in the family and among the Nottingham workforce. The city's *Guardian* newspaper insisted the company could

FOUNDER AND VENDOR: Sir Jesse Boot, later 1st Lord Trent

have been kept in British hands. Sir Jesse's son John was devastated by the decision. A condition of the sale was that John be found a suitable job in the new firm and, to his father's surprise, he prospered.

● In 1920, the Boots Company opened its Day Continuation School in Station Street to provide day-release training courses for employees.

Mental patients and nurses scrap with bailiffs ⮕ Page 59

Divorce: The legacy of war

THE Divorce Court reported an "epidemic" of marriage break-ups — 95% of them the result of the Great War, according to the Lord Chancellor.

A typical case concerned the soldier who returned to Nottingham after four years as a German prisoner-of-war.

He discovered his wife had had a child by another man, and sued for divorce ... but not before he began a liaison with another woman, who bore him a child.

The sequence of events was asessed by the court, which heard that the ex-soldier wished to marry the mother of his child. However she gave evidence and said she would not marry him on account of his violence and reluctance to work.

She explained that she had moved on to another man, who had fathered her second child.

In a tangled case, the court granted the ex-soldier a decree because it was in the interest of most of the parties.

□ □ □

NOTTINGHAM sweltered through what was believed to be the longest heatwave since 1863. June temperatures topped 80 degrees for days on end.

□ □ □

FOOT and mouth disease spread to Notts in the summer, but health officials were just as concerned about the faster-spreading disease anthrax.

□ □ □

AN 18-year-old girl from Rancliffe Street threw herself into the canal, off London Road, after a tiff with her young man. She was rescued by a passer-by, checked over at the hospital, and discharged.

□ □ □

RALEIGH founder Sir Frank Bowden died after being taken ill in Lisbon.

□ □ □

THE *Evening Post* launched the morning racing paper *Post Tissue* on March 14.

CART MART: RSPCA-organised horse shows were held in Nottingham market place. This picture dates from the early 1920s

Bitter miners' strike splits public opinion

A BITTER strike by miners divided opinion in Nottingham, where a rising number of industrial workers were laid off because of the stoppage.

"Along with thousands of other innocent sufferers I keep hoping for a settlement," complained an *Evening Post* correspondent who had been laid off because his employer had run short of coal.

"I have been out of a job for three weeks. I have three children, one out of work and two on short time, and three other children still of school age. We are having a desperate struggle.

"At the Clifton miners' meeting in the Wesleyan Hall, speakers said they would rather starve than accept the terms now offered.

"They do not care a straw for the sufferings and privations they are causing others who would be glad to get work, even at a £1 a week reduction.

"They deserve to starve for their unreasonable conduct. All who contribute to feeding their wives and children are making a huge mistake."

One young Notts miner was brave enough to take his views into the "lion's den".

Andrew Clarke was invited to speak at an afternoon tea debate in the drawing room of the Mayfair home of Lady Markham, whose other guests included well-heeled

BREADWINNER: Notts miner and daughter, early 20th Century

opponents of the strike.

"I was asked what wages were required to keep a miner, one wife and three children," Clarke wrote afterwards. "I could not resist asking in return how many wives per husband were customary in Society."

The speaker faced hostile questions, then there was an adjournment for tea.

"A dear old lady assured me they all meant well by the miners, but that we did not realise their difficulty in maintaining social status and educating their children.

"I emerged unscathed at 6pm, popped in [to a pub] and had one to steady me after the excitement."

The *Evening Post* reported that more employers were looking at alternative burning processes that were "not

dependent on the whims of organised labour." Oil-firing conversions started at £5 per furnace, readers were told. While the fuel, at just over £5 per ton, was only marginally cheaper than coal, handling costs were lower.

The newspaper also had a sarcastic dig at the miner who was reported by a reader to have visited a grocers and bought 15s [75p] worth of goods — including cake, tins of fruit and salmon, cream and biscuits ... "It is gratifying to find that he did not forget such necessities as 3d 4d [about 16p] worth of tobacco and cigarettes."

The dispute was resolved in the summer with miners accepting 9s 7d [about 48p] per shift. At that time, four million adults were unemployed.

Construction strike threatens homes crusade  Page 60

Runaway lovers hit headlines

NATIONAL and local newspapers dwelt on the story of teenage sweethearts Jack Betts and Gladys Kerry, who went on the run for a week.

Jack, a young miner, and his girlfriend had just £1 between them when they fled their respective homes in Hucknall, apparently because their parents disapproved of the relationship. They survived on biscuits while making their way to Yorkshire.

When the alarm was raised, the *Evening Post* reported, some locals feared the lovers "had resorted to the waters of the neighbourhood to end their lives." But there were sightings in Arnold and Mansfield before the hunt switched to Wakefield.

There the couple, posing as brother and sister, had been taken in by a sympathetic family. While Jack did odd jobs and considered work with the local brewery, Gladys helped with the housework.

By then their descriptions had been circulated widely, and somebody noticed the label inside Jack's cap: Wass & Co, Hucknall.

The sweethearts were taken into sympathetic custody by Wakefield police. Their fathers journeyed north in a car provided by the *Evening Post*, and there was a tearful reunion.

Captain orders off team-mate

THE Hampshire bowler Newman was ordered off the field by his captain, Major Tennyson, during the match against Notts at Trent Bridge.

Newman had been barracked by the crowd as he painstakingly rearranged his field. Then Tennyson ordered him to the pavilion, and the bowler kicked down the wicket as he went.

Afterwards, the captain said Newman had used objectionable language.

Hospital war over pay cuts

MENTAL patients and their nurses scrapped with police and bailiffs at the climax of a pay and conditions dispute at Saxondale Hospital.

Management wanted to cut nursing and domestic staff pay by 4s [20p] a week for men, and 3s 4d [about 17p] for women, yet ask them to work an extra half-day.

On February 23, the news was posted on noticeboards at the hospital near the village of Radcliffe-on-Trent.

Members of the National Asylum Workers' Union were unimpressed by the sweetener, the scrapping of a limit on overtime.

Two union representatives, Mr Gibson and Mr Shaw, warned the medical superintendent on March 4 that staff would not carry out management orders until the new conditions were cancelled.

The dispute worsened on March 6 when the night staff refused to go on duty. Managers and volunteers worked the shift instead.

On March 11, all officials except medical staff were locked

SAXONDALE HOSPITAL: The site was turned into a private housing estate in the 1990s

out of the hospital wards — and laundry and kitchen staff were persuaded to join the dispute.

That week, the strikers were sacked for indiscipline and insubordination.

One hundred police officers and bailiffs forced their way in using crowbars.

According to reports in local newspapers, patients and staff fought side by side.

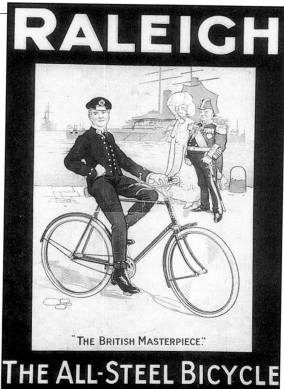

PATRIOTIC CHOICE:

A Raleigh advertisement from the early 20th Century, showing a midshipman whose choice of bicycle meets the approval of an admiral.

In 1922, extensions to the city factory enabled the cheapest model to be reduced in price from ten guineas to £8 10s [£8.50]

RALEIGH

"THE BRITISH MASTERPIECE."

THE ALL-STEEL BICYCLE

City workers join throng to see prince

FLORENCE Lupino, 19, a member of the famous showbiz family, was married at St Ann's Church to Sydney Poole of Nottingham.

The bride, representing the 11th generation of a family of entertainers which had settled in Britain in the 18th Century, was given away by her father Barry Lupino.

He was appearing that week at the Empire with his brother Mark, who was married to a Nottingham woman.

A PIRATE betting operation was rumbled by police during a four-day watch on a house in Taylor Street.

Officers saw the premises visited by 128 people, including 21 children who appeared to be younger than 14.

When the house was raided, they found 51 betting slips.

The occupier, a 40-year-old Great War veteran, said he was fed up with having no money and nothing to do. The venture had been a financial failure and he promised not to revive it.

A GOALKEEPER died in hospital after a collision during a match between New Hucknall Colliery and Heanor.

An inquest heard that he tried to smother the ball, but was accidentally caught by the boot of an oncoming forward. At first it was thought he was winded, but a ruptured intestine was later diagnosed.

A MOTHER admitted in court that she was unable to control her 12-year-old son. Instead of going to school he spent the day at race meetings. At the same Nottingham session, another mother admitted she could not get her 11-year-old daughter out of bed. In both cases, orders were issued requiring attendance at school.

LUCAS Broadhurst of Upton Hall, Notts, retired from riding to hounds after 80 years' membership of the Rufford Hunt.

WELCOME TO BOOTS: An open-top car bearing the Prince of Wales's feathers emblem arrives at the Island Street plant of Boots Pure Drug Co.

The prince, in a light grey suit and bowler hat, inspected the factories and chatted with staff.

He also laid the foundation stone of the Memorial Gateway at Trent Embankment. The monument was officially opened in 1927

Unions flex muscles as economy flops

NOTTINGHAM'S post-war housing programme was almost stopped because of a long-running national dispute between building firms and construction workers.

It was one of several industrial disputes in the spring of as Britain teetered on the brink of a depression.

Shipyard boilermakers, railwaymen, agricultural labourers and, in some areas, teachers, were locked in disputes with employers.

A prominent visitor to Nottingham was the general secretary of the Transport and General Workers' Union and future Labour minister Ernest Bevin.

He was known as 'the Docker's KC' [King's Counsel] because of his exertions on

'THE DOCKERS' KC':
Ernest Bevin in 1920

behalf of port workers in 1920.

Bevin told a union rally that chemical workers in the city had seen their working week reduced in stages from 84 to 40 hours — all because of union campaigning.

"I have not seen the employer who makes me nervous," he said. "The capitalist works as the wolf. The harder he works, the harder it is for you, the lambs."

In spite of the demand for slum clearance and the construction of new council houses, builders were struggling with costs in the supply industry — and wanted a 2d per hour cut in wages.

This led to the threat of a national strike that would have affected 7,000 Nottingham construction workers.

An 11th hour agreement saw the dispute go to independent arbitration.

Meanwhile Chancellor Stanley Baldwin tried to kick-start the economy with a generous budget in which several duties, plus parcel postage and telephone hire rates, were cut.

The *Evening Post* reported an immediate impact in Nottingham: Busier pubs as men took advantage of a 1d cut in the price of a pint.

Evidence of recovery came later in the spring when one of the Stanton Ironworks furnaces, unused since 1921, was recommissioned.

Furniture-sale Romeo fined

A NOTTINGHAM housewife alleged that her husband took another woman for spins on a motorcycle he had bought with the proceeds of the sale of the family furniture.

The husband, a 23-year-old tram conductor, had admitted as much to his wife, who then checked out his movements with one of his workmates.

The husband got to hear about it, a city court heard, and assaulted the woman several times.

He maintained he was acting in self-defence after his wife had threatened to "do" him with a knife.

The court fined him £2.

The Palais de Danse, city's nightlife landmark ➡ Page 62

The 'round Britain' bikers

HUGH Gibson, riding a Nottingham-built Raleigh 7hp motorcycle with side car, completed a 3,429-mile ride around British coastal roads in under 12 days.

Ten minutes after his return to his starting point in Liverpool, 23-year-old motorbike rider Marjorie Cottle completed the same route in the opposite direction.

She had ridden a 2.75hp Raleigh without side car.

Gibson and Cottle were carried shoulder-high by crowds of admirers to a Liverpool hotel.

She received a telegram of congratulations from Raleigh boss Sir Harold Bowden.

He called it "the greatest motor feat achieved by any woman."

Boots 5,000 at Wembley

MORE than 5,000 Boots employees were taken to Wembley to visit the British Empire Exhibition.

Workers were transported on eight special Wembley Express trains.

The earliest left at 5.47am and all arrived at the exhibition before noon.

An exclusive film of the occasion was made by Boots cameramen and shown later at the Elite cinema in Nottingham.

CITY PURCHASE: Wollaton Hall, sold by Lord Middleton

Wollaton sale for £200,000

LORD Middleton, the 10th baron, sold Wollaton Hall and park to Nottingham Corporation for £200,000.

The family had been seen less and less at Wollaton since the latter part of the 19th Century.

The first person to show an interest was Sir Jesse Boot who saw it as the location for University College. His offer to the 9th baron was refused.

It was the latter's death that forced the family hand as duties weighed heavily against them.

Long before their viability as tourist attractions, the maintenance of stately homes was becoming a problem for the landed gentry, with many mansions falling into decay.

Given Wollaton Park's history, the Middletons had no wish to see this happen, nor did they want to see it fall into private hands.

They were anxious that the people of Nottingham should benefit from the vision of Sir Francis Willoughby who built the hall in the 1580s. The new Lord Middleton agreed to the sale — but he died before the negotiations could be completed.

His heir finished the business at a sale price of £200,000 for the hall and park, and followed that by giving to the city the park deer and armoury weapons.

To recoup some of their investment the city fathers decided that 500 acres would remain untouched; 90 acres would be developed for smaller houses; land fronting Wollaton Road and a new road at the north west end would be sold for larger houses; there would be recreation grounds and playing fields, including an 18-hole golf course.

Buildings developed rapidly, with 500 houses let and favourable terms offered to those who wanted to buy at a freehold of £490.

The hall was converted for use as the natural history museum, which had been housed since 1874 at the natural sciences library in Shakespeare Street.

The natural history museum opened in 1926, and the 18th-Century stables were later turned into an industrial museum.

'Smokeless city' is forecast

THE introduction of a carbonisation process at Gedling Colliery was set to make Nottingham the first 'smokeless city'.

The process extracted motor spirit, fuel and lubricating oils from small coal, leaving a residue of smokeless fuel. The plant was capable producing 250,000 tons a year for Nottingham at the same price as domestic coal.

It was welcomed by Sir Albert Ball, *pictured right*, chairman of the city gas committee.

SNEINTON lad George Rideout became a hero for rescuing a girl from the River Trent.

He was cycling past Forest's ground when he heard children screaming and saw a girl struggling in the water.

George leapt over a fence and dived into the water, fully clothed, seizing the child just as she was about to go under.

Despite the current and his sodden clothes threatening to drag them under, he got the girl safely to the bank.

□ □ □

A CLIFTON Colliery loader strangled his wife and called for a neighbour to fetch the police. When asked why, he replied: "I have done her in."

When she was found, the mother of his five children was lying in bed, face covered, and with a prayer book on her breast.

□ □ □

PORTLAND House Home for Destitute Girls was opened by Lady Hickling, having been moved from Leen-side because there were "temptations for girls going to and from work".

□ □ □

GLASGOW MP T. Henderson, addressing a Co-operative Society meeting in Netherfield, commented on "the cunning method by which the city had hidden slums from the observer." He added: "They were as bad as those in any city in Great Britain."

□ □ □

THE Theatre Royal was taken over by the Moss organisation in 1924.

□ □ □

NOTTS County rose to the top of the First Division on November 1, but their championship hopes faded during a lean spell in January.

□ □ □

A.G. SMITH retired after 22 years as editor of the *Evening Post* and was succeeded by F.P. Pointon.

□ □ □

BOOK store and stationers Sisson and Parker, of 25 Wheeler Gate, extended the business to No 27.

Miners stick it out after General Strike folds ➡ Page 63

A YOUNG RAF pilot crash-landed his aircraft in Nottingham after the engine failed at 3,000ft.

Flight Officer A.R. Hamilton, based at No.2 Flying Training School at Digby, Lincolnshire, was in a Bristol fighter.

He landed in a field next to Basford gas works. The aircraft came to a standstill nose-down, but Hamilton escaped with only minor injuries.

NOTTINGHAM was blacked out for almost three days in June after fire spread through a cable subway at the power station in St Ann's Well Road.

Homes and factories were left without power or light, and trams stood stricken in the roads.

City Transport called up an assortment of buses and open-top charabancs to maintain local services.

THE Commercial Motor Users' Association organised a competition at Trent Embankment to encourage owners of lorries and vans to keep them smart and efficient.

The top prize went to three vehicles run by Boots Pure Drug Co.

THE Medical Officer of Health reported an increase in summer mosquito bites in 1925. The health committee authorised the spraying of stagnant ponds with paraffin solution.

FOREST finished bottom of the First Division in 1924-5. They won only six of their 42 matches.

A BROUGH motorcycle, made in Nottingham and steered by G. Patchett, was fastest in the trials on Skegness sands — at an average of 86mph.

NOTTINGHAM Ideal Home Exhibition was held at Derby Road Drill Hall. Attractions included a full-sized bungalow built especially for the show — and an appearance from fortune teller Madame Zada ("the mystery lady with the master mind").

PALAIS DE DANSE: The elegant interior of the dance club, with feature fountain, in 1925

Palais legend is launched

SID Reubens and his Savannah Band struck up the first notes to be heard at the new Palais de Danse.

The site had formerly been used by the old Nottingham House of Correction.

It was an impressive building, both inside and out.

The giant globe on the roof flashed red, white and blue ... until pilots objected.

Another impressive feature was a fountain in the middle of the dance floor, at that time one of the biggest in the country.

Sid Reubens was followed by the famous Billy Merrin, who was resident for many years, and others who graced the stage were Jack Hylton, Henry Hall, Billy Cotton and Harry Roy.

It was a fascinating building with its Cupid's Bar and La Paloma for the drinkers, and even a 'stag room' where men could shave and have their shoes polished and trousers pressed.

The only cost was a tip for the man in charge, Albert Mansfield.

Shy dancers could avail themselves of the services of professional partners, of both sexes, who could be booked on payment of a fee. They were known as Sixpenny Partners.

Clients paid their fee to a cashier and were then formally introduced to the partner of their choice. There was instant dismissal for a partner seen leaving the hall with a client.

One of those 1920s Sixpenny Partners was a teenager named Mae Walmsley who was spotted by famous dance band leader Victor Sylvester.

He got her jobs at the Carlton Hotel and Cafe de Paris in London, and she became world ballroom champion with her partner Sydney Stern.

'Mrs Warren' at the Royal

THE controversial play *Mrs Warren's Profession* by George Bernard Shaw, *above, in later life*, was given its first Nottingham performances at the Theatre Royal.

The play had been banned until 1924 because of its allegedly immoral content — the profession referred to in the title was that reputed to be the oldest in the world, prostitution.

Wilford power station opens

THE city council unveiled the £685,000 Wilford Power Station in 1925. The first phase provided generating plant for 30,000kw in three turbo-alternators. A £292,000 extension would increase generation power by 40%.

The corporation had been providing electricity since 1894, but it was clear during the war that more was needed. Wilford was selected because the Trent provided cooling water, railways were nearby and so was Clifton Colliery.

POWERFUL: The Wilford development

Trouble for Spencer as Labour exacts penalty  Page 64

Duke of York tours Raleigh

THE King's second son, the Duke of York, *pictured*, visited Nottingham in February.

The duke, later King George VI, attended a meeting of the Industrial Welfare Society, of which he was president.

He also toured the Raleigh cycle works in Lenton.

Poor 'Uncle Laurie'

NOTTINGHAM'S own wireless programme 5NG (on 323m) began broadcasting at 3.45pm with the Lyons Cafe Orchestra.

The mix of concerts, plays and discussions included a children's club. The *Evening Post*'s review bemoaned the illness of 'Uncle Laurie'. John Allwood of Loughborough became the 7,000th member of the 5NG Radio Circle.

The *Post* had its own children's column called The Wendy House which featured the Tinker Bell Club and items written by Billikins.

TO brighten up the pages of the *Evening Post*, a collection of schoolboy examination howlers were printed including:

● The plural of ox is oxo.

● The Menai Straits are spanned by a tubercular bridge

● Rhubarb is a kind of celery gone bloodshot

● Instruments used in an orchestra include viles, cellars, hornets, baboons, old boys and bubble bases

And finally...

● Christians are only allowed one wife. This is called monotony.

❑❑❑

MARL taken from sand and gravel pits at Cropwell Bishop, Cotgrave and Radcliffe was a key ingredient in the preparation of pitches at Trent Bridge.

Its fame spread in 1926, when orders were received from cricket clubs in Toronto and Philadelphia, and for tennis courts in Argentina.

❑❑❑

THE Nottingham Gleemen visited Bagthorpe Prison to perform a concert of hymns and popular songs.

In accordance with regulations, applause was not allowed but "it was obvious that the music was keenly appreciated by the prisoners".

❑❑❑

TRENT Bridge was reopened in April after being doubled in width to 80ft. The bridge had first been opened in 1871.

❑❑❑

INJURIES unsettled Notts County in 1925-6, and the club was relegated from the First Division.

❑❑❑

A FIVE-year-old boy met a tragic end when, as he was playing with other children, a dog dashed among them, knocking the lad under the wheels of a passing lorry.

❑❑❑

A HUGE housing shortage in West Bridgford saw 280 people apply for a single house to rent at 14s 6d [about 72p] per week.

Mayhem as workers back General Strike

THE General Strike began at midnight on May 3 following the breakdown of pay and conditions talks between the Government and miners' leaders.

The dispute had rumbled on since July 1925 when a stoppage was averted and a Royal Commission set up to investigate.

When it reported in 1926, talks were held between the colliery owners and the miners — but the two sides could not reach agreement.

That was on April 13. Three days later a ban on coal exports was approved by the International Miners' Conference and the growing threat of industrial action was discussed by the Cabinet.

But all talks failed and on May 1 the TUC called for a general strike.

It spread from the coal industry to include railways, road transport, iron and steel, and building and printing.

Nottingham bus services were suspended on May 4 as the strike began to bite. Employees were told to hand in their uniforms unless they reported for duty by May 10.

During the strike, six buses were operated by volunteers.

Nottingham newspaper

MAY MAYHEM: Crowds mill around an open-top motor bus which partially blocks Parliament Street outside the Theatre Royal

production was also hit from midnight on May 3. The *Guardian* was published daily, but no *Evening Post* appeared until May 10.

For the majority, the strike lasted only nine days, although the miners stayed out for six months.

Public disorder was widespread with windows smashed, vehicles overturned, hundreds arrested.

Queues formed outside pawnbrokers' shops, children

waited with jugs at the soup kitchens, and families scavenged for coal.

One Notts woman recalled: "One day I was so hungry I crept through a hedge and stole a stick of rhubarb and a potato which I ate raw because there was no means of cooking it.

"We had not one penny coming from anywhere."

Outside Shipstone's, a crowd confronted publicans who were collecting their beer because the draymen were on strike.

"One chap came out with two 56 gallon barrels on a little flat motor," a witness reported. "Shipstone's men did not interfere, but corporation men got on the back and rolled the barrels off on to the road."

On May 12, the day the General Strike ended, the corporation was able to put out 14 trams and 21 buses. Normal services were resumed on May 14.

Furniture fire tests city brigade

A MAJOR fire raged at the furniture store of Cullen Bros, 73-85 Carrington Street. Four fire crews were needed to bring it under control and save neighbouring buildings, including the Portland Hotel.

A report concluded that the fire brigade was not big enough. With only 31 firefighters plus 12 auxiliaries to call on, councillors feared the consequences if another blaze had broken out at the same time.

King and Queen open University College site ➡ Page 65

Row as square scheme cooks fair's goose

THE SQUARE, 1920s: The Exchange and market prior to redevelopment. The banner under the clock advertised an RAF band concert at the Castle

UNREWARDED:
Mr Lloyd George

THE Freedom of Nottingham was conferred on Liberal statesman and war premier David Lloyd George — but things did not go according to plan.

He accepted the honour, and a silver casket was made. However he was unable to attend a presentation, and suggested that the casket be forwarded to him.

The aldermen wrote back to the effect that, "If you don't fetch it, you don't get it."

The gift remains in the Council House.

❑ ❑ ❑

EVENING Post classified columns stretched to two full broadsheet pages by mid-1927.

Homes for sale included a five-bedroom house in Arboretum Street, at £550. In the motors section, a 1925 Morris Cowley four-seater was going for £100.

❑ ❑ ❑

HUCKNALL was the venue for the King's Cup air race, but the 'blue riband' of aero tournaments was overshadowed by tragedy. Two days before it, Captain Franklin L. Barnard, DSO, was killed while testing his Bristol Badminton aircraft near Bristol.

❑ ❑ ❑

THE extension of the Derby Road route to Wollaton Park was the final expansion of the electric tram system. By April 1927 there were almost 26 miles of route.

❑ ❑ ❑

NOTTINGHAM Writers' Club was founded at a meeting at the Black Boy Hotel in Long Row.

❑ ❑ ❑

THE Prince of Wales opened Gunthorpe Bridge in November. The £125,000 link replaced the toll bridge, unsuitable for modern traffic.

GOOSE Fair was held in the market place for the last time before the creation of a city square to match the new Council House, whose foundation stone was laid earlier in the year.

News that both the fair and the market were to be moved was broken in a rare local front page lead story in the *Evening Post* of July 5.

Traditionalists argued that the square had been a centre for trading for more than 1,000 years — but the majority on the council felt traders would be better off in the New Market planned for Parliament Street.

At a protest meeting, 12,000 people demanded that the fair be kept in the city centre. Speakers included Pat Collins, president of the Showmen's Guild.

But the corporation was unmoved. The planned split-level square with its fountains and flower beds was deemed to be unsuitable for England's biggest and oldest touring funfair

The final market place Goose Fair was held on October 6, 7 and 8.

Collins was back with his Scenic Whales and Over the Falls rides.

Other attractions included the Dolphins ride of Frederick Cox, two midgets and a lizard show.

Bostock's Menagerie commanded so much space that the rent was £80.

Labour kicks out MP after pit jobs rumpus

BROXTOWE MP George Spencer was expelled from the Parliamentary Labour Party in 1927 following his role in the previous year's national strike.

He had been secretary of the moderate Notts Miners' Association, many of whose members were reluctant to maintain the national pit stoppage following the collapse of the General Strike.

First he was suspended by the Miners' Federation for "negotiating agreements for the men to return to work". Spencer responded by saying he was merely enabling members to regain their jobs at pits where employers were already offering the terms demanded by the federation.

Labour loyalists were unimpressed. He not only lost his party whip in the Commons, following pressure from Broxtowe constituency party, but he was also expelled from Labour's NEC.

EXPELLED: George Spencer (pictured in the 1940s)

In a sequence of events repeated in Notts in the 1980s, Spencer led a non-political breakaway organisation. The Notts and District Miners' Industrial Union was immediately recognised by the colliery owners.

George Spencer was born at Sutton-in-Ashfield in 1872, the second of 18 children of a miner. He became an underground pit worker at 12.

From 1912 he held various posts in the NMA while serving as a member of Sutton-in-Ashfield UDC. In 1918 he became Broxtowe's first Labour MP.

The two Notts miners' organisations were eventually to amalgamate. Spencer became the first president of the unified Notts and District Federated Union, and represented it on the Miners' Federation.

Spencer was credited by his supporters for maintaining a spirit of co-operation with the pre-nationalisation colliery owners — a spirit which helped reduce disputes and improve output and wages.

But the term "Spencerism" was uttered by left-wingers with contempt.

Spencer was a Wesleyan preacher, a keen angler and chess player. He was president of Notts Cricket Club, 1949-50.

He lived in retirement in West Bridgford, and died aged 84 in 1957.

Market forces push chippies from old haunt

YOU'VE HAD YOUR CHIPS: October 1928 — and last night for the fish and chip stalls before builders moved into Nottingham market place. The redevelopment of the square also meant the displacement of the market traders' stalls. They were accommodated in the new Central Market, which opened in November on land between Parliament Street, King Edward Street and Huntingdon Street. It was the home of Nottingham's main retail market until 1972, when it moved to the Victoria Centre. Meanwhile, Goose Fair was held for the first time on The Forest recreation ground. There were more rides, and bigger rides — and city council income from rents increased by 18% to £3,556.

RALEIGH chairman Sir Harold Bowden fought off an American bid for the firm. "It will continue for the time being as a family concern," he said.

"I would rather see it, if the ownership does change, taken over by British interests."

◻ ◻ ◻

THE corporation built a new transport depot off Lower Parliament Street to accommodate buses, trolleybuses and 80 trams.

The Trent Bridge depot, built in the early years of the century, became the city transport department's main workshop.

◻ ◻ ◻

AUSTRALIAN import tariffs prompted British firms to build factories Down Under. Among them were Nottingham underwear specialists I & R Morley, who opened a plant in Ballarat.

KING George V and Queen Mary opened the new Nottingham University College buildings in July.

Sir Jesse Boot had provided the land at Highfields and the finances to enable college to move from the city centre. Because of his health, he did not witness the ceremony.

"The establishment of such a home of learning justifies all the jubilation which today will mark the occasion," reported the Nottingham *Journal*. "For Sir Jesse it represents the climax of a great and meritorious career."

Months later, he was raised to the peerage as Lord Trent.

The visit included the Royal Agricultural Show at Wollaton — which was also attended by the Prince of Wales.

A civic banquet was held at the new Palais de Danse — and late in the evening there was a surprise arrival. The prince turned up, asking if he could attend "as a citizen of this city" (in 1927 he had bought Grove Farm at Lenton).

The gathering gave an impromptu chorus of *For He's a Jolly Good Fellow*.

● Alderman Edmund Huntsman became the first Lord Mayor of Nottingham — the title was granted by the King in 1928.

◻ ◻ ◻

ROBERT Haimes of Nottingham invented the Quixen, a semi-automatic glass washer for use in pubs and hotels. The gadget consisted of a perforated horizontal plate that could be attached to taps. If the plate was pressed, water washed both the inside and the outside of the glass.

The royals arrive... and do it in style

ROYAL SHOW: The King and Queen at Wollaton

Safari hot-shot bags four lions

NOTTS big-game hunter Madia Foljambe, wife of Capt Edmond Foljambe of Osberton Hall, shot four lions with four bullets during a safari in Kenya and Tanganyika.

"I do not like parties, so I went on my own, engaging the services of a splendid white hunter, Mr Sydney Waller, and 30 natives," she told reporters.

"One day I almost stepped on a thick-maned lion. One shot killed him. The same afternoon I shot his mate, also with a single bullet.

"But the red-letter day was to be February 13. Suddenly my native gun-bearer pointed 100 yards ahead, where stood two lions. I shot them both with two shots, and at that moment six more lions rose all round.

"They offered easy targets, but I couldn't shoot any more, having already killed the licenced allowance. My companion shot three, one of which I finished off."

But fashion cred called in question

THE *Post*'s men's fashion correspondent questioned the assumption that the Prince of Wales was the leader of male sartorial style.

"Every gentleman who has the strength of mind to get his own ideas carried out by his tailor is unconsciously helping to mould tomorrow's fashions," he asserted.

"For instance I once learned a valuable tip, from a chance meeting with a sportsman while fishing in western Ireland, to improve the hang and comfort of the trousers.

"My tailor made good use of the hint when I passed it on."

The writer predicted success for a men's 'cricket-style suit' in which the hem of the shirt was attached by buttons to the trouser waistband.

Other essentials: Single-breasted jackets should have only three buttons; trousers must measure 22.5in in circumference at the knee.

Einstein lectures after breakfast at college  Page 67

A NEW casualty department opened at the General Hospital following concern about the rising number of road accidents. The cost: £6,500.

ASPHALT was laid on part of the Forest for the 1929 Goose Fair following complains the previous autumn about winds blowing dust and cinders into fair-goers' faces.

A MAN was fined £15 at Guildhall for conducting an illegal cash betting pool from his premises in Wheeler Gate. Police raided the building and found 800 coupons relating to forthcoming football fixtures.

THE Tramways Committee reported that 84 million fares had been collected on trams and buses, over an annual total of 7.6 million miles.

THOUSANDS of dead fish were seen in the Trent at the Embankment. Prof H.S. Holden of University College was called in to investigate.

BBC Radio announcer Eric Dunstan, from Nottingham, resigned after a rumoured disagreement with director-general Sir John Reith. The corporation declined to elaborate.

SAPPER'S stage version of *Bulldog Drummond* played at the Theatre Royal, with Hamilton Deane in the title role.

THE Sultan of Zanzibar visited Nottingham to inspect lace factories and the Raleigh Cycle Works. During his stay he was a guest at Welbeck of the Duke and Duchess of Portland.

THE *Evening Post* threw its weight behind a campaign to raise £115,000 to help Nottingham University College become a full university. In 1929, the college had 5,000 students.

SQUARE DEAL: The opening of the Council House

Prince does the honours

THE Council House, home of the City Council, was officially opened by the Prince of Wales in May 1929 — two years after the foundation stone was laid for T. Cecil Howitt's domed building.

The £500,000 civic headquarters was built on the site of the Exchange, which was adapted for corporation use in 1879.

Howitt used Portland stone from the same quarry used for St Paul's Cathedral.

The key stone for the entrance arch had been hewn for use in London after the Great Fire of 1666 — but had been left unused in Dorset for two centuries.

The scheme incorporated ground-level shops, producing rents of £25,000 a year. It also coincided with the redesign of the market place and the creation of the Processional Way.

The prince unlocked the main door with a gold key.

When Howitt died, his obituary in *The Times* described the Council House as "probably the finest municipal building outside London."

VIP: The Prince of Wales

£500 Derby ticket nets £62,500

WHEN the unfancied Trigo won the 1929 Derby, the winning ticket in the Stock Exchange sweep was held by financier Julien Cahn of Stanford Hall, near Loughborough.

Mr Cahn [later Sir Julien, who was to give Newstead Abbey to Nottingham Corporation] collected £62,500.

He had paid £500 for a half share of a ticket bought by his aunt. Members of his cricket team also bought £1 shares in his ticket, netting them about £1,000.

"What shall I do with the money? I haven't an idea," he told an *Evening Post* reporter. "I suppose I shall give it away, as I have with the rest of my money."

Five years earlier, when Sansovino won the Epsom classic, the winning Stock Exchange sweep ticket was held by another Nottingham investor.

S.P. Millard collected £32,000.

THE Lady Mayoress, Mrs A.R. Atkey, opened a craft fair in West Bridgford with a warning about not having a hobby.

"People who have no interest at home go abroad to the pictures a little too much," she said.

"I enjoy an occasional evening at the pictures myself, but some people go more often than they need."

That week's films included *The Divine Woman*, with Greta Garbo, and *The Last Command*, with Emil Jannings.

The 750-seat Majestic opened in Woodborough Road, Mapperley, in 1929. It was designed by A.J. Thraves of Nottingham.

Flying visit inspires stadium gift

HARVEY Hadden, who had made a fortune in Canada, returned to Nottingham for a single day and resolved to do something for the youth of his home city.

Hadden died in 1931. In his will he left £30,000 with instructions that it be used for a sports stadium. In 1959, the Harvey Hadden Stadium was completed. For 40 years it has been the home of athletics, cycling, football, rounders, American football and rugby league.

A nasty whiff of fraud at the gasworks

NOTTINGHAM police exposed a ten-year £67,000 fraud involving tradesman and employees of the city council's gas department.

The allegation was that invoices had been presented for goods which had not been delivered, and services which had not been performed.

The proceeds were shared between the tradesmen and some of the department's employees.

A joiner, a builder and a gas department employee were arrested in October. Several other people were later detained — and all were subsequently convicted at the Assizes of offences including larceny, false pretences and conspiracy to defraud.

Two of the accused were bound over to be of good behaviour. The rest were jailed for between six months and seven years.

An accountant's report showed a shortfall of £67,574. False claims could be traced back to 1920, but the feeling was that the corruption had been going on for longer than that.

In a further twist to the story, a council sub-committee investigated an allegation that a councillor had approached the corporation's gas engineer in an attempt to halt legal proceedings against one of the accused.

A fine way to give the kids a treat

TO fund a charity Christmas party for poor Nottingham children, members of Nottingham City Business Club agreed to be fined at their December lunch for breaches of modesty, etiquette and decorum.

Penalties were imposed on a member who used a menu card for lighting his pipe, and several others were fined for being bachelors and unwilling to get married in the following year.

Even journalists reporting the lunch were fined for failing adequately to report members' speeches during business meetings in 1930.

Members who escaped penalties were fined 4d for their excessive mirth at their colleagues' misfortunes ... and another 2d for being there.

GENIUS: Prof Einstein (centre) is welcomed at University College

Brightest, by a long chalk!

NOBEL prize-winning genius Albert Einstein visited University College on June 6 to lecture on his theories of relativity.

The blackboard showing his calculations was preserved for posterity, and the stick of chalk was jealously guarded by lecturers.

Einstein, born in 1879, graduated from Zurich Polytechnic in 1900 as a teacher of maths and physics.

He became a professor of physics in Zurich, then Berlin, and in 1916 published his Foundations of a Generalised Theory of Relativity. In 1921 he received the Nobel Prize for physics.

The visit to Nottingham was arranged by his friend Prof Henry Brose, and was such a red-letter day for Nottingham that it was filmed.

Before meeting staff and delivering his lecture, Prof Einstein had breakfast in the college dining room — coffee and eggs.

The guest delivered his lecture in German, with Prof Brose translating for the audience.

Einstein became resident in the US and was involved in the Manhattan Project, which was to develop the first atomic bomb. He later became a disarmament campaigner, and died in 1955.

LEGENDARY CUSTOMER: Aircraftman Shaw of the RAF collects his latest Brough Superior from the Brough motorcycle works in Nottingham. Proprietor George Brough is on sticks after a racing accident. Shaw was formerly Lt-Col T.E. Lawrence ('of Arabia'). He was to die in 1935 after an accident on his seventh Brough machine

Crackdown on joyriders

BRITAIN'S first traffic court was held in Nottingham on April 14, following the passage of the Road Traffic Act. The first applications were by the city transport department, who sought permission to continue existing services.

Later in the year, three men were jailed for a month each after magistrates applied the Act to joyriding.

A commercial traveller left his car in Beeston and returned to find it stolen. It was later found in a ditch near the Hemlock Stone.

Two men from Beeston and a third from Long Eaton admitted they had been drunk at the time. They also admitted stealing a suitcase.

"We feel there is far too much of this so-called joyriding," said the chairman of the bench. "It is a very great inconvenience to owners of cars, and we shall try to stop it."

❏❏❏

UNIVERSITY College student Sabir Ali Hashmy hosted a lunch at the Black Boy Hotel for the Nawab Sir Amin Jung, minister-in-waiting to the Nizam of Hyderabad. The student was a member of another family which had served the Nizam, and he hoped other delegates to the Indian Conference would be able to travel from London to attend. Also on the guest list were the Lord Mayor and Sheriff of Nottingham.

❏❏❏

DON Bradman played his first Test innings in England at Trent Bridge, and was on the losing side for the only time in a match in which he scored a century.

❏❏❏

THE Eastwood-born writer D.H. Lawrence died in the French Riviera town of Vence on March 2.

❏❏❏

THE Nottingham Corporation Act 1930 empowered the city to convert tramways into a trolley-bus network.

Demolition teams move in to Narrow Marsh ▶ Page 69

New HQ as Raleigh launches 'Karyall'

BIKE BASE: Raleigh's new office block opened in Lenton Boulevard. Left: An artist's impression of the plan by T.C. Howitt, who designed the Council House.

In 1931 the firm returned to the three-wheel market for the first time since the demise of the pre-war Raleighette cycle-car.

The product was the 500cc Karyall, with a roof and windscreen for the rider and a covered cargo compartment positioned over the two rear wheels.

Figs and goat's milk for smiling Gandhi

HEAVILY-guarded Indian pacifist leader Gandhi visited Beeston in October to call on his nephew, University College student J.V. Joshi.

"He wore his customary loincloth, but he was so far respectful to the cold nip in the air as to swathe himself in a flowing shawl," wrote the Evening Post reporter.

"The only visible part was his wizened, smiling face, with his grey head uncovered — and his feet, which were bare, with only sandals to protect him from the pavements.

"On stepping from the train at the Midland Station he hurried off to Beeston as fast as a car could carry him with his faithful disciple Miss Slade and two Scotland Yard detectives as well as a couple of Secret Service men."

Gandhi visited Ericcsons (later Plessey), where Mr Joshi studied accountancy when not at college lectures.

The firm's managing director recalled: "I spoke to him for a few minutes only. He struck me as being very kind, if fragile."

Wherever he went, he was followed by curious crowds. The Post reported: "Mr Gandhi appeared to be detached from the crowds but his smile was ever-present and he chatted in perfect English with anyone who gained an introduction."

Gandhi and his entourage visited 13 Linden Grove, Beeston, home of Mr and Mrs Davies, with whom Mr Joshi was staying.

In keeping with their guest's frugal needs, Mrs Davies prepared a light lunch of bananas, figs, orange juice and goat's milk.

'FLOWING SHAWL': Gandhi at Ericcsons

City takes over Newstead Abbey

GREEK premier M. Veniselos presided on July 31 when Byron's home Newstead Abbey was presented to the city. It was the gift of the philanthropist Sir Julien Cahn.

M. Veniselos, who had come to England especially for the ceremony, presented the deeds to the Lord Mayor.

He spoke of the veneration in which Byron was held in his homeland, whose freedom the poet had championed. He later went to Hucknall to lay a wreath on the poet's tomb.

Modern masterpiece takes shape at Boots site ➡ Page 70

City first to start calling all cars

THE city police force became the first in the country to equip two-way radio communication in patrol vehicles.

Chief constable Captain Athelstan Popkess had already proved himself an innovator, introducing the mechanised wing in 1931.

It was standard practice for officers in vehicles to keep in touch with HQ by using police or public phone kiosks.

Popkess ignored the sceptics and proposed an experiment with two-way wireless communication, perfected by H.B. Old.

On January 10, 1932, the first message was transmitted.

There was more to the project than prestige. The innovation enabled the city police force to reorganise patrols ... allowing officers to cut crime by 13.5% in 1932.

More innovations were introduced the following year, when Popkess unveiled his forensic science laboratory. It was later designated a national crime-fighting resource.

Plus-fours? No, shorts are best

RAMBLERS were given wet-weather tips by an *Evening Post* correspondent following Easter cloudbursts which ruined several organised walks.

"Plus-fours are abominable in wet weather and ordinary trousers little better," readers were told. "The former collect water where there is most cloth, and the latter hang like lead.

"Shorts are best. They may cause cold and wet knees, but knees can easily be dried and are soon warm again."

Walkers without waterproofs were advised to pack paper in their rucksacks. When clouds rolled over, the paper could be packed under outer garments.

"A newspaper will do, but stout brown paper is better. Roll two or three thicknesses around arms and legs, with a similar amount on the back and chest.

"It may feel uncomfortable, but will keep out the rain for several hours."

GOOD RIDDANCE: The creation of new housing in the Narrow Marsh district, with the Lace Market and St Mary's in the distance

Filthy slums gone at last

THE skyline was changing for ever — and for the better — with the clearance of the Narrow Marsh slums.

They were widely accepted as being among the worst in England, with overcrowding and filth dictating a life of squalor and disease. Until the 1870s, half of all Narrow Marsh youngsters were dead by the age of five.

Open sewers, cess pits and communal toilets all contributed to the high risk of disease, with typhoid among the most prevalent killers.

Nottingham did not get a sanitary department until 1867 when the ash pit privies were replaced ... by old paraffin barrels cut in half and fitted with lids and handles. They were emptied each day and the contents sold to farmers.

But it was the work of borough engineer Marriott Ogle Tarbotton which finally put Nottingham on the road to a cleaner future. He introduced a programme of slum clearance which would continue long after his death and into the 1930s.

It is recorded that in 1932 two houses in Sussex Street were demolished — but only after workmen had walked off the site until they had been fumigated, so alive with vermin were they.

GRACIOUS LIVING: Rufford Abbey, with the Savile family Rolls-Royce in the foreground. In 1932 the widowed Lady Savile announced her Notts home would be partially closed because of heavy taxation

GOOD news in April for thirsty residents of Aspley Estate. It had grown into a community four times the size of Southwell, yet had no licensed premises.

But there was still a fight before licensing justices allowed Bertie Miles to transfer his beer-off business from Radford Road to Melbourne Road, Aspley.

A Wesleyan Methodist Circuit spokesman told the court that there were already eight pubs within walking distance of the estate — and area in which poverty was rampant and hundreds were on the dole.

A Methodist minister argued that the shop was opposite a site intended for a public meeting hall and a school: "If the licence is granted, we shall suffer considerably."

◻ ◻ ◻

AN elderly man died in Sneinton after running into a brick wall. It happened at the junction of Sneinton Hollows and Dale Street, when a witness saw the 74-year-old gathering speed as he walked downhill with a small dog. By the time he reached the junction, he ran straight into the wall and collapsed with head injuries. He died in hospital 12 days later.

◻ ◻ ◻

A TOASTMASTER in Hucknall betrayed his feelings about women's hair fashions. Officiating at the silver wedding anniversary party of Mr and Mrs H. Critchley, he asked for glasses to be raised to those ladies present who had not had their hair bobbed and did not intend to do so.

◻ ◻ ◻

NOTTINGHAM boundaries were expanded for the first time since 1877, with the inclusion of Bilborough, Wollaton, parts of Bestwood Park and Colwick, and neighbourhoods of Beeston and Arnold.

◻ ◻ ◻

AN increase in cigarette smoking boosted employment in Nottingham, home of the John Player brand. Total UK employment in the tobacco industry had risen by 4,500 in six years to 43,000.

◻ ◻ ◻

TORIES forced the corporation to cut the city rate by 2d to 14s [70p] in the £ by creaming off £14,000 profits from Nottingham City Transport.

Water supplies: Alderman blasts wasteful men ➡ Page 71

NOTTINGHAM owner Colonel G.F. Storey had a three-year-old filly good enough to run in the 1,000 Guineas at Newmarket. However Lady's Lace was well beaten by the favourite, Brown Betty.

❏ ❏ ❏

EVIDENCE of economic recovery came with unemployment figures for Nottingham — 17,000 men and women were out of work in 1933, but the total had fallen by 29% since 1931.

❏ ❏ ❏

THE film star Anna May Wong visited Nottingham in August and took tea at the Council House with the Lord Mayor.

❏ ❏ ❏

AN anonymous benefactor gave £25,000 for a new block at the General Hospital, with the condition that it was for patients who could pay according to their income.

❏ ❏ ❏

THE sacking of a builder led to a lightning strike by 200 men working on the construction of the Ritz Theatre in Angel Row. They returned to work after management and their union agreed to refer the case to arbitration.

❏ ❏ ❏

THE Lenton farm owned by the Prince of Wales was sold to G.R. Shelton of Ruddington. The farm's prizewinning herd of shorthorn cattle was bought by his brother, W.B. Shelton of Holme Pierrepont.

❏ ❏ ❏

SIR Thomas Beecham conducted the London Philharmonic Orchestra in Nottingham in November, with Eva Turner the soprano soloist. The season also included performances by the Italian lyric soprano Amelita Galli-Curci and the violinist-composer Fritz Kreisler.

❏ ❏ ❏

AFTER a warm spring, a dry summer prompted fears of a drought. No water cuts were necessary, but the weather was so good that in West Bridgford a family were able to eat their garden-grown corn cobs.

'A MILESTONE': Boots 'Wets' factory, the D10 building, shortly after its completion in 1933

Boots opens D10 factory

ONE of the world's most famous industrial buildings opened in 1933 — D10, or the 'Wets' section of the Boots Company's new development at Beeston.

The Boots expansion in Beeston was presided over by the founder's son John Boot, who later succeeded his father Jesse as the second Lord Trent.

The manufacturing operation had been built up in the Island Street area. But by the 1920s there was no more room for expansion, and land was bought opposite Highfields Estate.

A works committee was formed in 1927, with the aim of creating a new soapworks, wet and dry goods factories, plus distribution centres.

D10's architect was Sir Owen Williams, who had designed the British Empire Exhibition at Wembley.

His achievement was celebrated in Nikolaus Pevsner's *Buildings of Nottinghamshire* (1951). D10, according to Pevsner, was "a milestone in architecture, especially modern concrete architecture in Britain."

The galleried interior behind the 550ft frontage reminded him of "a large department store."

It was the year Boots returned to British control.

Louis Liggett's United Drug Company, which had taken over Boots in 1920, was struggling in the Depression-hit American market, and agreed to John Boot's proposal for a sale.

The year also saw the opening of the chain's 1,000th retail branch, in Galashiels, Scotland.

Death of Fred Terry

NEWS of the death of the actor Fred Terry was broken to his daughter, who was performing at the Theatre Royal in April.

Phyllis Neilson-Terry had been playing in *Evensong*, and she was told of the death immediately after the curtain call. She left for London to be with the family, but returned for the rest of the run.

Fred Terry was the brother of Ellen Terry. He and his wife Julia Nielson had been regular visitors to the Royal, where he created the title role in *The Scarlet Pimpernel*.

Their last joint appearance at the theatre had been in 1925, in the drama *Henry of Navarre*.

80 spaces in first car park

ONE of the first municipal car parks outside London was opened in 1933 — a space for 80 vehicles on land next to Central Bus Station, Huntingdon Street.

Drivers were charged 1s [5p] a day, during which they could leave and return as often as they liked.

One of the aims was to provide work for disabled war veterans. Two ex-soldiers were employed, and kitted out in chauffeur-style uniforms of tunic, breeches and cap.

Larwood the hero of Ashes triumph

HAROLD Larwood, *pictured*, returned a national hero after his Ashes-winning fast bowling in the 'Bodyline' tour Down Under. He took 33 wickets, and fellow Notts seamer Bill Voce 15 — but their feat was overshadowed by the row which threatened relations with Australia. They were required by captain Douglas Jardine to bowl on the line of the batsman's body, with a leg-side field waiting for catches. Australians Woodfull and Oldfield were struck.

Dorothea Waddingham, city's 'nurse from hell' ➡ Page 72

Busmen parade their allegiance

LABOUR'S May Day parade from Old Market Square to the Forest included 50 decorated vehicles and seven bands.

One of them was the Nottingham Corporation Passenger Transport Band, whose attendance prompted questions at the next council meeting. Some councillors felt employees of the corporation should not be involved in a political event. Their defenders said they were members of a union and perfectly entitled to attend May Day rallies.

The Lord Mayor, Ald J. Farr, ended the debate, saying permission was not required because the men were parading in their own time.

Regional union official Arthur Hayday was one of the main speakers at the rally. That week he completed 25 years' service in the TGWU and was presented with a gold watch. "He is a man without trimmings and humbug," said a guest at the party. "He is straight and true and a damned good Englishman."

Post on the knock

KNOCKER Post became a Nottingham legend in the 1930s in a scheme to promote sales of the *Evening Post*. He and his team were employed to knock at doors in Nottingham and reward householders who could produce that night's *Post* with a ten shilling note [50p].

Waste not, want not is the cry on water

AS water consumption in Nottingham rose to 11 million gallons a day, women of the city were urged to persuade their husbands and sons to look after it.

Ald A.R. Atkey, chairman of the water committee, was giving a lecture at the Mikado Cafe to members of the National Council of Women.

The alderman, chairman of the water committee, said 25% of supplies were wasted through carelessness and the lack of thought.

"Those characteristics are more developed in the male than the female," he said, urging wives to keep an eye on wasteful use by their menfolk.

The supply of water was a matter of civic pride.

"It recently gave out in some rural districts, where villagers were seen buying water from handcarts," said Ald Atkey.

"But in Nottingham there is no fear of drought. We are fortunate to have an abundant supply of probably the finest water that can be obtained anywhere."

Its quality was improved by local geology, he told his listeners. Nottingham's rock formation formed a natural filter, and all the city needed to do was sink wells.

Arnold-born engineer Thomas Hawkesley had been

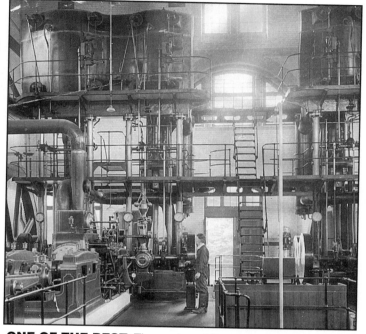

ONE OF THE BEST: The engine at Boughton Pumping Station was built in 1905, and much of the equipment remained in this 1971 photograph

the "father" of the system, and the waterworks in Haydn Road was working as efficiently in 1934 as when the equipment was new, in 1857. The Boughton pumping station was one of the best in the world.

HUNDREDS of men were laid off at Babbington and Newstead pits following a seasonal slump and the arrival of what unions described as "robots". They were referring to conveyor belts.

☐ ☐ ☐

UNIVERSITY College Rag Week raised £1,800 for the General Hospital. Prizes at the concluding ball at the Palais were presented by BBC entertainer Anona Winn.

☐ ☐ ☐

LONDON Suite, a work by Hucknall-born Eric Coates, was the finale at the 1934 Royal Command Performance. "Very thrilling," King George V told the show director.

☐ ☐ ☐

ARSENAL captain Charles Jones was appointed manager of Notts County, after an initial wrangle with the Gunners, who expected him to play in the 1934-5 season.

OVERHEADS: A change of policy by Nottingham transport department heralded the end of the trolley-bus era, although the vehicles still had years of service ahead of them. The city had Britain's largest fleet of trolley-buses — 106 — but experiments with motor buses running not on petrol, but diesel, showed savings could be made. The conversion of electric trams routes was continuing in Nottingham, but from 1934 they were replaced by motorbuses rather than trolley-buses. Thirty-seven new double-decker buses were ordered that year. Our picture shows a trolley-bus in Chapel Bar, 1934

Nottingham welcomes the Jarrow Marchers ➡ Page 73

Vicar raps 'armchair Christians'

THE Vicar of Bulwell warned that listening to religious services on the wireless was no substitute for worship in church.

Speaking from the pulpit of St John's, the Rev C.W. Whitacre said: "Listening by the fireside is an incalculable blessing to the aged and infirm.

"But for the young and active, to imagine that armchair Christianity is any sort of substitute for public worship is an insult to religion and to God.

"These people have grown soft. They are parasites living upon a Christian atmosphere to which they contribute nothing."

❑❑❑

THE 6.30pm Marylebone-to-Nottingham train on December 16 was involved in an accident in Northants. A slip coach detached at Woodford actually caught up with the train and collided with the rear carriage.

The ten injured passengers included Ivy Phillips of Forest Fields.

After treatment for a black eye, she recalled that her mother had been worried about the journey. "She said, 'Somehow I wish you weren't going. I shall be glad to see you back'."

❑❑❑

CITY licensing justices were impressed when told only four cases of public drunkenness had been recorded the previous Christmas. They granted Nottingham pubs 11pm extensions for Christmas Eve and Boxing Day.

❑❑❑

THE city council agreed to build 1,196 houses and 56 flats at land purchased in 1930 at Broxtowe Lane. The budget, including streets and sewers, was £394,042.

❑❑❑

NOTTINGHAM-based Boots introduced one of their most enduringly popular lines — the Boots No.7 range of cosmetics.

PIKES ON PARADE: A company of pikemen at a Wollaton Park tattoo, 1935. The event followed the Notts Historical Pageant, which saw the first official visit to Nottingham by a Lord Mayor of London. Twenty-four other civic heads were present

Letter snared killer nurse

NURSE DOROTHEA Waddingham might have got away with murder but for one mistake.

In 1935 the Sherwood woman took two patients into her care: Ada Baguley, 50, and her mother Loisa Baguley, 87.

Ada would stand to inherit a tidy sum when her mother died and when she was persuaded to change her will in favour of Waddingham and her lover Ronald Sullivan, it only needed the demise of the two ailing women to secure their future.

Within four months, both women were dead.

The deaths hardly raised an eyebrow until an extraordinary letter, purportedly signed by Ada two weeks earlier, was received by her doctor.

It read: "I desire to be cremated at my death ... and it is my wish to remain with Nurse and my last wish that my relatives shall not know of my death."

Exhumations were ordered and traces of morphine were discovered in the remains.

The trial became the sensation of the time. The case against Sullivan was dropped for lack of evidence. The jury rejected Waddingham's story and she was sentenced to be hanged.

Execution was carried out on April 23, 1936, with 12,000 people outside the prison gates.

THREE-WHEELER: Raleigh introduced a saloon version of the open-top Safety Seven (pictured), which had been launched the previous year. The company soon returned to a bikes-only policy. Manager T.L.Williams bought the equipment and set up in Tamworth, where three-wheel Reliants are still made

Nazi salute from boxers

THE Nazi salute was seen in Nottingham when a team of Stuttgart policemen arrived in December for a boxing tournament against the City Constabulary's finest.

The party was led by Herr Walther, superintendent of police and president of Stuttgart Sports Club.

When he laid a wreath at the war memorial, the Germans' right arms shot out.

"We think of those who gave their lives for their country," said Herr Walther at a reception that day.

"We think especially of the Lord Mayor's son, Captain Albert Ball VC. We hope there will never be another war between Germany and Great Britain."

He presented Nottingham police chiefs with a silver hock flask and a Christmas tree.

Chief constable Capt Athelstan Popkess responded by saying: "Wherever there is sport, there can never be bad feeling."

The boxing tournament ended in victory for Nottingham by seven bouts to two.

But the *Evening Post* reported that the visitors fought hard. Several bouts were toe-to-toe affairs, decided on narrow points margins.

'Carthorse' Blower smashes Channel record ➡ Page 74

Electric trams bow out after 35 years

THE last electric tram service completed its journey from Arnold to Lower Parliament Street on September 6, 1936.

Car No 190 was driven by transport committee chairman Ald J. Farr. The conductor was a City Transport inspector, Mr J. Vale, who had been conductor on Nottingham's first electric tram 35 years earlier. Special tickets for the journey bore the letters R.I.P.

The tram era continued in other cities. Nottingham sold 18 of its most recent vehicles to operators in Aberdeen.

DOOMED: One of the last electric trams, Colwick Terminus

Warm welcome for Jarrow marchers

THE footsore Jarrow Marchers spent an October night in Nottingham before continuing their southward journey.

The protest march began in the North-East, where the Depression and shipbuilding slump had caused 80% unemployment and poverty.

Two hundred men carried a 12,000-signature petition to the Government in London.

The march took them through Darlington, Leeds and Sheffield to Mansfield where, according to the *Shields Gazette*, the men received "a queer reception".

The reporter added: "It seemed as if the town was half afraid, and some of the authorities looked upon the men as if they were strange specimens of a barbaric race."

There was no such suspicion when the Geordies arrived in Nottingham.

The men were served supper by the Co-operative Society, and then put up for the night at a Sneinton hostel as the guests of the city council.

After 30 new cases of blisters were treated, artists from the Empire gave a variety concert.

Next morning, breakfast was provided by Nottingham Conservative Party. "You could hardly call it breakfast, it was more of a banquet," said marcher D. Riley. "We have had no better treatment anywhere."

The march continued to Loughborough and ended in London, after 26 days, on October 31.

GRIFFIN & SPALDING: The Long Row store took out one of the first full-page advertisements in the *Evening Post*. It promoted ladies' fashion labels including Braemar, Dorville, Linlaw and Rodex. A Rodex camel topcoat with horn buttons was available at six guineas [£6.30].

Barton pioneers coach packages

BARTON Transport ran what is believed to be the first Continental tour organised by a British coach company.

Coach No.270 went via the Dover ferry to Brussels, Cologne and the ancient German cities of Heidelberg and Rothenburg. The return leg was via Lake Constance, Strasbourg and Rheims. Customers, who paid 23 guineas [£24.15] for the tour, returned with pictures showing German streets festooned with swastika flags.

The following year, Barton repeated the offer, and added a tour to the French Riviera via Dijon, returning via Lyons, for 29 guineas [£30.45].

TWO drinking clubs were closed down after late-night raids by police. Both had been serving alcohol after hours.

Magistrates heard that 11 people were caught with drink when the Spiders Web Club in Derby Road was raided at 11.40pm. According to an officer, others in the club included "women of a certain type."

The secretary was fined £10, the others £1 each.

A few weeks later, officers arrived at 11pm at the Melbourne Social Club, Tokenhouse Yard, off Bridlesmith Gate. The secretary was fined £5, and five drinkers £1 each.

□ □ □

SHOPPERS and office workers were puzzled on March 3 by an hour of freak weather which plunged the city into near darkness in mid-morning.

It was so gloomy that pictures taken at 10.30am showed vehicles in Theatre Square with headlamps on.

Asked for his opinion, University College meteorologist G.O. Smith said it was "an extreme example of anti-cyclonic gloom which is associated with high-pressure systems and calm air in winter."

□ □ □

PART of the Raleigh factory was set aside for shell production amid fears of a war. A German contractor asked for asylum while equipment was being fitted. The Foreign Office said no.

□ □ □

NOTTS County signed Hughie Gallagher, one of the Scottish 'Wembley Wizards' who had beaten England 5-1 in 1928. His home debut in September 1936 added 10,000 fans to the Meadow Lane gate.

□ □ □

ST James's Church, a landmark on Standard Hill since 1808, was demolished. A nurses' home was built on the site.

□ □ □

THE site of County Hall, West Bridgford, was bought by Notts County Council for £15,600. Work began in 1938, but construction was suspended during the war.

Pay deal hailed by lowest-paid mineworkers ➡ Page 75

A PAIR of down-and-outs fought over newspaper bedding, and one was jailed for three months. Both were accustomed to sleeping in a brick kiln off Carlton Road, They argued about who slept where, and which of them was entitled to the newspapers. The younger man, 24, struck the other, whose cry of "Ho, murder!" woke other tramps.

□□□

TOM Breaks, whose father was Nottingham fire chief for 21 years, was appointed by the Home Office to help restructure Britain's fire brigades. He was chief of Sheffield's fire service before his 1937 appointment. Even as chief officer, he would lead his men from the front. He was praised for a gallant attempt, from the top of a ladder, to rescue four children caught in a Sheffield house fire.

□□□

THE city council agreed to publicise cremation as an economical and more hygienic alternative to burial. They were encouraged by the rising number of cremations in Nottingham — up from 70 in 1931 to 184 in 1936.

□□□

THE coldest Nottingham spring for 18 years brought snowstorms on February 28 and March 11 — the latter being the heaviest local snowfall since 1918.

□□□

NOTTINGHAM businessman W.F.M. Weston-Webb died aged 86. When a young man, he took on a black prize-fighter from Chicago after the local champion failed to turn up to the venue — a Nottingham pub.

□□□

FIFTY thousand fans at Donington saw Bernd Rosemeyer win the Grand Prix in his Auto Union car.

□□□

EVERTON goalscoring legend Dixie Dean, 31, signed for Notts County after the departure of Hughie Gallacher to Grimsby.

BILL-TOPPERS: Dame Sybil Thorndike and her husband Lewis Casson (pictured in the 1950s) appeared at the Theatre Royal in *Six Men of Dorset*, a play about the Tolpuddle Martyrs co-written by character actor Miles Malleson.

Other theatre news: Sir Julien Cahn built a private theatre at his home, Stanford Hall, near Loughborough. The philanthropist was a keen amateur conjuror and wanted a stage on which to perform tricks for his friends.

His 352-seat theatre included dressing rooms, cinema projection room and a pit containing the organ he bought from the Madeleine Theatre in Paris.

'Carthorse' surfaces as record seahorse

LONG-distance swimming hero Tom Blower, 23, smashed the cross-Channel record in 1937.

It was one of several feats that were to make Nottingham-born 'Torpedo Tom' a household name in the Thirties and Forties.

Blower was born in Dakin Street, Hyson Green, in 1914 and was educated at Berridge Road School — where he was nicknamed 'Carthorse' because he was so slow in swimming sprints.

In 1935 he became the first non-Lancastrian to win the ten-mile race across Morecambe Bay. In appalling conditions, he was the only swimmer to finish.

It was in August 1937 that Blower, a blubbery 6ft 5in and caked in a stone of wool fat, set out from Cap Gris Nez. He arrived in England after 13 hours and 29 minutes, breaking the record by 23 minutes.

After wartime service in the Royal Navy, during which he won a Royal Humane Society medal for rescuing a drowning swimmer, in 1947 Blower became the first man to swim the treacherous northern Irish Sea.

He swam from Donaghdee in County Down to Portpatrick in south-west Scotland in 15 hours and 26 minutes.

Other feats included a 30-hour

MARITIME MARATHON: Tom Blower pictured in 1937, while in training for his record-breaking Channel swim

non-stop marathon at Victoria Baths, Sneinton — 2,664 lengths and 39,000 strokes, during which he lost a stone.

Explaining his blubbery appearance, Blower once wrote: "Not only does the fat keep me from being chilled to the marrow, but it also 'feeds' me during the swim."

Other sustenance during his sea swims came from his devoted wife Clarice, who accompanied him in the escort launch. Jam sandwiches were a favourite.

In 1948, Blower joined the select band who had swum the Channel twice, once in each direction.

However an attempt, three years later, to swim the Channel both ways, non-stop, was abandoned because of fog and strong currents.

'Torpedo Tom' worked as a sales representative for Players, but died of a heart attack in 1955.

PC Rowe ... a match for a drunken braggart of a boxer

A DRUNKEN braggart met his match in burly city policeman PC Rowe.

The man was behaving in a disorderly manner. When he was approached by the officer, a court heard, he said: "You keep off, old chap. I am the boxing champion of the Indian Army." He did not know that PC Rowe was a boxer, Olympic wrestler and weightlifter.

The defendant alleged that he was placed in police custody, swung round "and given one on the chin." He added: "The fact that I didn't sleep a wink after being taken into custody proves that I was sober."

He was discharged for lack of evidence.

DISNEY DELIGHT: The Walt Disney animated film *Snow White and the Seven Dwarfs* was previewed at an invitation-only event at the Nottingham Ritz. "It is the first attempt to tell a full-length story through the medium of the cartoon, and there is no doubt whatever as to the success of the experiment," the *Evening Post* wrote. "Disney's extraordinary flair for the delineation of birds and animals was delightfully revealed. The forest creatures and their winning ways are a perfect joy, as are the dwarfs, each in his way a distinct character." The same month, Decca released the *Snow White* soundtrack on gramophone records. The tunes "were very likely to be whistled and hummed everywhere." Particularly delightful, readers were advised, were the numbers *Some Day My Prince Will Come*, and the dwarfs' marching song *Heigh-Ho!*

A warm-up for Rachmaninov

THE composer-pianist Sergei Rachmaninov made a return visit to the Albert Hall on March 21.

He agreed to be photographed during the interval, warming his hands in an electrically heated muff.

Pay victory for pitmen

A NEW wages deal for Notts miners was hailed as a triumph — especially for the coalfield's lowest-paid pit workers.

The mine owners also agreed to a savings scheme to fund pitmen's holidays, and confirmed their willingness to negotiate a new pension scheme.

"It is one of the best wage agreements in the British coalfields," wrote the *Evening Post*.

"It provides yet again an instance of the co-operation between owners and the men."

The deal was signed by both sides at a meeting of the Nottingham & District Miners Wages Board, under the chairmanship of Mr H.E. Mitton.

Under the terms of the agreement, all mineworkers were to share across-the-board pay rises.

Under the old system, those on lower-paid duties did not qualify for the general rise.

"It is one of the greatest things we have done," said miners' leader George Spencer.

"Formerly, when the highest paid were enjoying seven shillings [35p per shift], the lower-paid were receiving just coppers."

The concessions followed further signs that Notts was becoming the most profitable coalfield in the country.

Output per man shift in February 1938 rose to 77.91cwt — almost one third higher than the national average, and several pits broke their productivity records.

SECOND Division strugglers Forest escaped demotion by a whisker after surviving the last-match relegation decider at Barnsley.

Bottom-placed Stockport County were already down. Forest and Barnsley met on May 7 to decide who would join the Cheshire club in the Third Division.

Forest and Barnsley each had 35 points. Both clubs needed a win, but with a fractionally superior goal difference, Forest would survive with a draw.

It didn't look good for the Nottingham club as Barnsley came from behind to lead 2-1. And it got worse when Davies was injured and Forest were left with ten men.

But five minutes from the end, the home keeper Binns fielded the ball and was charged by Forest's Martin. Binns was knocked around, and the ball spilled from his hands into the goal.

Barnsley players protested, but after consulting the linesman, the referee confirmed that Forest had equalised. The 2-2 draw kept Forest in the Second Division.

❑❑❑

A BASFORD man was fined £2 for assaulting a boy of 11 — a friend of his son's. The boy had opened the door of the defendant's fowl coop and let out the hens. "Oh yes, I spanked him," the man conceded. It was also reported that he threatened "to break every bone in his body if he did it again."

❑❑❑

WITH fears of war mounting, Tollerton Aerodrome was used as an RAF Volunteer Reserve training school, with student pilots flying Miles Magisters, Avro Ansons and Hawker Harts.

❑❑❑

LAND in Shakespeare Street was bought for a new, bigger YMCA. The cost of the project was £49,000 — and an appeal fund was launched for the £28,000 still needed for the development.

❑❑❑

THERE was a rare white Christmas in Nottingham. Snow fell on December 24, 1938.

❑❑❑

NOTTS County centre forward 'Dixie' Dean went into hospital for surgery after chipping a bone in his ankle.

Thousands respond to appeal for Dad's Army ➡ Page 77

THERE was trouble on a Trent bus from Nottingham to Mansfield when a 72-year-old man began insulting fellow passengers and using foul language. A court heard he struck the conductor with a stick, and told a woman passenger: "You have a face like a monkey!"

Mr R.A. Young, prosecuting, said: "No Nottingham lady is going to stand for that." Magistrates heard that the man had 30 previous convictions, 13 for assaulting police. He was fined £2 for assault and £5 for obscene language.

AFTER the previous season's last-match escape from relegation, Forest again did it the hard way. The 1938-9 season ended with an away match against Norwich to decide which of the two clubs would join Tranmere Rovers in the Third Division. Norwich were relegated in spite of winning 1-0. They had needed a four-goal margin to survive.

THE Electrical Association for Women formed a Nottingham branch in the hope of interesting more housewives in labour-saving devices. The chairman, a Miss Haslett, said they wanted every woman "to know of electricity, what it can do for her personality and how she might get best results from its use."

A SEASIDE building known to hundreds of Nottingham holidaymakers went up in flames in February. Firemen fought in vain for two hours to put out the blaze in the south hall of the Butlin holiday camp at Skegness. Thousands of townsfolk turned out to watch as the fire destroyed bedding stored in the hall during the close season.

THE new John Player bonded warehouse in Wollaton Road was hailed as the last word in industrial building design.

Bombers: RAF chief defiant

AIR Vice-Marshal T.L. Leigh-Mallory told a Nottingham audience that bombers heading for the city could expect a "warm welcome" from his fighter squadrons.

Speaking at an Albert Hall dinner of the RAF Comrades organisation, shortly before the war, he said the air force had been strengthened in the previous two years.

The speaker, in charge of the air defence of eastern England, added: "We have made great strides. I don't want a war, but we will give a good account of ourselves. I have never seen better pilots in my life."

Leigh-Mallory was to play an important role in the Battle of Britain.

Later in the war, as Air Chief Marshal Sir Trafford Leigh-Mallory, he was appointed allied air commander-in-chief under General Eisenhower, supreme commander.

The toast to the veterans was given by Air Vice-Marshal Pattinson — who in 1916 flew in the same RFC unit as Captain Albert Ball, VC.

'NEVER SEEN BETTER': Pilots training. Inset: Leigh-Mallory

City's lead on civil defence

THE Chief Constable of Nottingham, Captain Athelstan Popkess, was credited with organising one of the best civil defence operations in Britain.

As chief constable, he became Chief Air Raid Precaution (ARP) Officer for the city, responsible for recruiting ARP wardens.

When fears of war rose in the spring, 150 to 200 people were stepping forward every week. When the number dwindled to 80-90, Capt Popkess made a public appeal for more volunteers.

A dozen First Aid Posts were created around the city, and the civil defence operation embraced 400 emergency vehicles — including regular fire engines and the 106 trailer pumps of the Auxiliary Fire Service, plus 70 ambulances.

From 1938 to 1944, ARP expenditure in Nottingham totalled £3.27 million — most of it paid by the Government, but £467,000 charged to local ratepayers.

By 1941, 288 public air raid shelters had been created.

The Home Office allowed £4 per man, woman and child for the creation of public shelters — but thanks partly to Nottingham's sandstone caves, the cost was kept down to £2 per head.

Throughout the city, free corrugated steel Anderson shelters went up in back gardens.

From October, 1939, the Government began charging households with an income of more than £5 — the cost per shelter was £10 18s [£10.90].

MOVING ON: Former Everton legend 'Dixie' Dean left Notts County after just nine matches over two seasons, and joined Sligo Rovers. Notts officials persuaded the Goodison club to waive £500 of the £1,000 still owing on the centre-forward

Cutbacks on the buses

The declaration of war soon had an effect on Nottingham public transport, which was required to cut back on non-essential fuel consumption.

Buses to the football grounds were withdrawn, as were scheduled services including 26 to Cavendish Road, 27 to Colwick, 30 to Strelley and 33 to City Hospital.

A week after war was declared, bus services after 9pm were cut by 50% — and by the end of September, services after 9pm were withdrawn altogether, although operators were later allowed to run buses until 10pm.

To comply with blackout regulations, City Transport experimented with blinds and blue and orange lacquers for bus windows.

The word 'Nottingham' was removed from bus liveries in the hope that German paratroopers would be confused. Trolley-bus booms were fitted with sliding covers so that overhead flashing would not attract enemy pilots.

ANTICIPATING blackouts, city police experimented in January with phosphorescent coats, helmets and gloves for constables on traffic duty.

GOOSE Fair was cancelled because of the outbreak of war. The event was lost to until 1945 — but in the last three years of the war, a Whitsuntide fair was held, with proceeds going to the Services Comforts Fund.

VC for soldier 'killed in action'

NOTTINGHAM-born Grenadier Guardsman Harry Nicholls won the second Victoria Cross of the war — and was then posted 'killed in action'.

But reports of the 26-year-old's death were later proved to be wrong.

Lance-Corporal Nicholls was badly wounded as he knocked out three German machine gun posts during fighting near the River Scheldt.

His citation, published in the *London Gazette* on July 30, read: "He was wounded at least four times in all, but absolutely refused to give in.

"There is no doubt that his gallant action was instrumental in enabling his company to reach its objective and in causing the enemy to fall back across the River Scheldt."

Although he was seen to fall, Nicholls was still alive. He was captured by the Germans and they tended his wounds.

Believing her husband to be dead, Constance Nicholls travelled to Buckingham Palace on August 6 to collect his VC from King George VI.

Then news filtered through that Harry was alive and recovering in a prisoner-of-war camp

'MISSING' HERO: Harry Nicholls

where he had become something of a personality because of the VC. The Germans even offered to give him extra rations, but Harry refused to have any more than his comrades. Constance returned his medal so that Harry could one day receive it in person.

Dad's Army: 3,900 answer Eden's call

MORE than 100 men enrolled at Guildhall within 12 hours of the Government's radio appeal for a new domestic security force.

Sir Anthony Eden, Secretary of State for War, had broadcast on May 14, calling for men to join the Local Defence Volunteers.

The first platoons went on duty in Nottingham on the night of May 23. By May 27, 3,900 city men had joined, with another 9,000 in units around the county.

On July 23, the LDV ('Look, Duck and Vanish', according to cynics) was renamed the Home Guard.

There was to be a waterborne equivalent of the LDV — Trent River Patrol. One of its main responsibilities was to guard Gunthorpe Bridge.

Vessels included a cabin cruiser, flying the Blue Ensign and crewed by volunteers with rifles and a machine gun. They patrolled 100 miles from Sawley to the Humber.

As with all home defence units, there were to be tragedies. Two members of the river patrol were killed during Lewis gun practice.

DEFENDERS: Home Guard on exercise 'somewhere in Notts'

DINGHY PATROL: A machine-gun section on the Trent

Ex-Notts squadron in action

PILOTS of 505 Squadron, based at Hendon, claimed 21 enemy aircraft shot down during the early days of the Battle of Britain.

The squadron had been formed at Hucknall in 1928, and before the war was a Special Reserve unit.

It became a fighter squadron in 1938 and in March 1939 it took delivery of new, eight-gun Hawker Hurricane Mk I aircraft.

In May 1940, the squadron was posted to France, briefed to reinforce BEF air cover in Belgium, and it later took up station in Wick as fighter cover for the Royal Navy's wartime base at Scapa Flow.

After the fall of France, Hucknall became temporary headquarters of No.1 Group, Bomber Command.

BUS companies began to rely heavily on women to keep services going. By July, City Transport was training 30 female clippies a week.

In January, Hilda Baldock became the first new conductress to be recruited by Barton's since 1919 — Nellie Goodson, the last one, was still with the company.

IN spite of wartime manpower demands, Notts CCC played six matches in 1940, three against RAF teams.

Observers were impressed with the strokeplay of young R.T. Simpson — later to open the England batting.

IN February, the city council agreed to the opening of cinemas on Sundays to cater for growing numbers of armed forces personnel based in Nottingham.

Managers, though, were required to give 50% of their Sunday profits to the Comforts for Troops Fund or other war charities.

Victoria Cross for Notts destroyer captain ➡ Page 79

Heroes of raid on Rommel HQ

NOTTS soldiers Col Robert Laycock and Sgt Jack Terry survived a daring raid on the North African headquarters of General Erwin Rommel.

Six officers and 53 other ranks from No.11 Commando were transferred from submarines to rubber boats, but only about 30 of them reached the shore on November 13.

Eighteen of them set out to attack Rommel's HQ at Beda Littoria, 18 miles away, and Terry was one of the three who would enter the building to capture or kill the general.

In the event, Rommel had left. Lt-Col Geoffrey Keyes

DESERT RAIDER:
Robert Laycock

was killed in the fighting, and the other soldier, a captain, was shot in the leg. Terry led the remaining raiders back to base, where Laycock was in command.

They split up, and Laycock and Terry spent weeks evading capture before rejoining British forces on Christmas Day.

Terry, awarded the DCM, later joined Notts police. 'Lucky' Laycock rose to major-general and succeeded Lord Louis Mountbatten as Chief of Combined Operations.

BOMBED BUT UNBOWED: Short Hill (left) and Shakespeare Street after the Luftwaffe raid

159 killed in bomber blitz

GERMAN bombers blitzed Nottingham on the night of May 8-9. By dawn, 159 people were dead and hundreds more were injured.

It was the worst of the 11 Luftwaffe attacks on the city.

Ninety-five aircraft were involved in the raid, dropping 424 bombs, and the damage would have been worse had not some German navigators been distracted by an illuminated 'Starfish' decoy site near Cropwell Butler.

Mapperley Park, St Ann's, Carlton Hill and the Lace Market were all hit.

Bombs also fell in Shakespeare Street, destroying part of University College, and The Esplanade, a small hotel.

Other buildings hit: Armitage's store at the corner of Victoria Street and High Street; Moot Hall and shops in Friar Lane; and a new office block in Castle Gate.

But it was the Sneinton, Meadows and Colwick area which bore the brunt.

The worst casualties were at the Co-op Bakery in Meadow Lane, where 48 employees and a member of the Home Guard were killed.

St Christopher's Church in Sneinton and St John the Baptist Church at Leenside were destroyed. Shakespeare Street Methodist Church and St Matthias's Church, on Carlton Road, were damaged.

West Bridgford was hit by 62 bombs, and the Beeston and Stapleford area by 28.

It was the biggest challenge yet for Nottingham's civil defence system. There were 12 serious fires, and another 100 smaller ones.

Two hundred houses were destroyed, 450 were severely damaged and 4,000 slightly damaged. In all, 1,286 people were bombed out of their homes.

WELLINGTON bombers based at RAF Newton raided Brest, in western France, in April.

Four bombs struck the German battle-cruiser *Gneisenau*, but she was not seriously damaged.

She and her sister ship *Scharnhorst* were later able to escape eastwards up the English Channel to German waters.

In July, RAF Newton was transferred from No.1 Group, Bomber Command, to Flying Training Command.

The commanding officer, transferring from Hucknall, was Group Captain Kepinski.

Polish pilots had been arriving at Hucknall Airfield from January with the creation of No.1 (Polish) Flying Training School. The students were taught in Tiger Moths, Battles and Oxfords.

☐ ☐ ☐

WARTIME newsprint restrictions led to smaller newspapers. From March 17, both the Nottingham *Guardian* and the *Evening Post* were reduced in size on two days a week.

☐ ☐ ☐

BY 1941 the conversion of some Barton buses to gas fuel had saved 75,000 gallons of precious liquid fuel. City Transport also experimented with 'gasbag' buses, but the idea was abandoned in November.

Teenagers perish as Bismarck sinks 'mighty Hood'

EIGHTEEN Notts seamen were among 1,418 who died when the battle-cruiser HMS *Hood* was sunk off Greenland.

"The mighty *Hood*" was revered among the Royal Navy's capital ships, but was outgunned by the German battleship *Bismarck* and heavy cruiser *Prinz Eugen*.

One Nottingham veteran later recalled his good fortune. Former rating Howard

Spence served in *Hood* until hours before she left Scapa Flow. He and 12 others — including future *Dr Who* actor Jon Pertwee — were sent on shore leave.

The Notts sailors who lost their lives included at least seven teenagers. The youngest was Boy 1st Class Billy Callon, from Gotham, who was just 16 (the Navy maintained the tradition of boy seamen).

King and Queen boost morale in city factories ➡ Page 80

Destroyer captain wins VC

NOTTS sailor Captain Robert St. Vincent Sherbrooke was awarded the Victoria Cross for his leadership of destroyers in the Battle of the Barents Sea.

As captain of HMS *Onslow*, he was in command of a convoy escort engaged by a superior German force.

Capt Sherbrooke lost an eye in the battle, during which the German destroyer *Friedrich Eckholdt* was sunk and the cruiser *Hipper* was severely damaged.

Sherbrooke, from Oxton, after recovering from his 1942 wounds, was to command the cruiser HMS *Aurora* and later the aircraft carrier HMS *Indefatigable*.

Promoted rear-admiral in 1951 he was High Sheriff of Nottinghamshire in 1958 and was appointed Lord Lieutenant in 1968.

He died in 1972.

In the case of emergency...

THE city council published the Nottingham Citizens' Handbook — a compilation of civil defence regulations and information on key organisations like the Home Guard, WRS and the National Fire Service.

The publication was supported by scores of city advertisers, including tobacconists Tyler & Co of Castle Gate, florist C.A. Wicks Ltd of St Peter's Gate, and scrap dealers E. Pownall & Co of Manvers Street.

In his foreword, town clerk J.E. Richards warned: "Modern warfare, waged according to Nazi technique, respects no rights whatsoever.

"It brings us all within the orbit of its destruction ... the hale and the infirm, the rich as well as the poor, are all within the range of Nazi hate and Teutonic barbarism, hence the need for trained and efficient civil defence services.

"This handbook tells Nottingham what they should do in certain emergencies, and how they can do their bit in defeating Hitlerism."

Advice to householders included:

● If you are evacuated from your home because of a time bomb, don't try to sneak back for your Sunday joint. A woman who did that was blown to pieces, and so was the police officer whom duty compelled to go after her.

● Make no unnecessary journeys; write no unnecessary letters. Be willing to accept no news as good news.

● Use the telephone sparingly, and be brief in your remarks. After an "incident", don't telephone all your friends to see if they are all right.

● Provide yourself with a good torch and use it as though every flash cost you sixpence. Torch lenses must be covered with at least one thickness of newspaper.

SWEENEY TODD: Tod Slaughter in the film

THE actor Tod Slaughter and his Lyric Players brought live drama to the Repertory Theatre, the old picture house in Goldsmith Street.

The curtain rose on *If Four Walls Told* on January 22, when Nottingham was gripped by freezing weather ... and the theatre heating system had broken.

Slaughter's leading lady was Patricia Hastings, and the company also performed plays by J.B. Priestley.

When the actor-manager arranged a tour for *Sweeney Todd* in the autumn, theatre owner Tom Wright set up a new company.

Slaughter was best known for his revivals of lurid Victoria melodramas. He died in Derby in 1956.

● John Gielgud appeared as Macbeth at the Theatre Royal. Lady Macbeth was played by Gwen Ffrangcon Davies.

CLIFTON Green saw its first May Day revels since 1939 — although labour shortages meant the traditional maypole was not erected. Jean Swain was crowned 1942 May Queen. Two others were crowned for the previous two years: Josie Moss (1940) and Olive Elliott (1941).

THE unsafe 177ft spire was removed from Holy Trinity Church in Trinity Square.

A MAN found lying face-down on the pavement in Forest Road at 3pm told police he had suffered from an epileptic fit. A police superintendent told magistrates that was the usual excuse on his several previous appearances for being drunk and disorderly.

Respected for 100 years

ROMAN Catholics celebrated the centenary of the building of their Nottingham parish church — later St Barnabas Cathedral.

The band of builders had been led in 1842 by Fr (later Bishop) Wilson. He was so respected in the town that people from other denominations offered help.

To mark the centenary, Archbishop Hinsley of Westminster made his first visit to the cathedral as Cardinal and presided at a pontifical high mass on May 10.

The Lord Mayor hosted a civic reception at which Cardinal Hinsley praised Nottingham for its public housing projects and its provision for young people.

"The passing generation may not be leaving youth an ideal world," he said. "But everything should be done to make conditions as good as possible for those who will carry on in the future."

CENTENARY: St Barnabas Cathedral, pictured in 1939

Wollaton GIs under fire in Normandy assault ➡ Page 81

POLICE charged a man with bribing a kennel boy to drug dogs at Long Eaton greyhound stadium.

It wasn't an attempt to 'nobble' favourites, but to make selected dogs run faster.

A detective inspector saw the defendant place a £10 bet on Bright Sam at 3-1. In spite of the drug, the dog was beaten.

Home Office analysis showed some confiscated tablets to contain Easton's Syrup, a tonic. Pieces of meat had been coated in a hypnotic barbiturate.

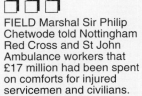

FIELD Marshal Sir Philip Chetwode told Nottingham Red Cross and St John Ambulance workers that £17 million had been spent on comforts for injured servicemen and civilians.

In 1943, some 2,000 Notts servicemen were being held in prisoner-of-war camps overseas. Sir Philip said the £43,640 raised by the Red Cross in the county would help them in their hours of need.

LT-COL John Dane Player, grandson of the founder of the tobacco empire, died of his wounds, aged 39.

LEADING Seaman Reg Bell, 23, from Kildare Road, was mentioned in dispatches for shooting down a Ju 88 aircraft from his stricken destroyer HMS *Gossamer*.

CITY Transport drivers and conductors staged a one-day strike on May 13 to protest at the way a pay claim was handled at arbitration.

Later in the day the TGWU executive ordered 1,000 men and women back to work.

T.H. Barton, chairman and managing director of Barton Transport, received the OBE for services to transport.

THE Home Guard celebrated its third anniversary with mock battles at the Embankment and the 'storming' of Mundella School.

CIVIC WELCOME: The Lord Mayor welcomes the King and Queen outside the Council House

Royal visitors boost morale

THE visit of King George VI and Queen Elizabeth to Nottingham on March 5 was supposed to be a secret.

At the height of the war, with cities across the country reeling from the effects of the blitz, the Royal couple were making a series of morale-boosting visits.

The citizens of Nottingham were told nothing about the visit, but somehow word got out and by the time the Royal couple arrived, 3,000 onlookers were in Market Square.

Their visits during the day included the Royal Army Ordnance factories at Chilwell and in the city, Wilford power station and Boots.

But those names never appeared in the local newspapers.

There were worries that the location of important installations could be revealed to Nazi spies.

At Boots the King and Queen mingled with workers and saw a squad of girls working out in the company gymnasium under the watchful eye of gym mistress Miss Turner.

At Chilwell, they met workers drafted in from as far away as Aberdeen and Glasgow.

From nearer home was Edith Cooper who travelled from Mansfield Woodhouse to help build the weapons needed to defeat Hitler.

She told Queen Elizabeth that her husband was fighting overseas. "I hope your husband will soon return safely to you," said the Queen.

The King, in the uniform of Field Marshal, inspected the Home Guard while the Queen visited one of the largest ATS camps in the country — location withheld.

And on a tour of the NAAFI cookhouse, 500 girls caught a glimpse of the couple.

As a morale-boosting effort, it must have worked wonders for the population and it gave Nottingham the only chance they would ever get to see the Royal couple visiting together.

'Knightsbridge' hero returns

GUNNER Tom Lynch, 23, of Hogarth Street, was repatriated in April from an Italian camp and returned with the story of the South Notts Hussars' heroic stand at the Battle of 'Knightsbridge' in North Africa.

One of a crew manning a 25-pounder gun, during the action he lost his right eye.

Gunner Lynch said he had been treated well by his German captors. After a spell in a field hospital he was driven back to Axis lines, and caught a glimpse of Rommel in his Mercedes before being handed over to the Italians.

The Italians had been fair, but there was never enough to eat and prisoners relied on Red Cross parcels.

£3.9m war-chest: City wins 'wings'

PLAQUE: Lord Sherwood

NOTTINGHAM was awarded its 'wings' by the Air Ministry for raising £3.9 million during Wings for Victory Week.

A plaque was presented by the Parliamentary Secretary to the ministry, Lord Sherwood.

As Sir Hugh Seely he was High Sheriff of Notts and later MP for Berwick. In the early years of the war he led No.504 (County of Nottingham) Fighter Squadron.

Lord Sherwood died in 1970, aged 71. In his will he left £10,000 to his butler.

33rd 'kill' for RAF ace

FORMER Nottingham University College student 'Johnnie' Johnson became the most successful RAF fighter pilot of the Second World War when he shot down his 33rd enemy aircraft.

Wing-Cdr Johnson's Spitfires joined a dog-fight over Normandy in July, during which he shot down a Me 109 with a three-second burst of machine-gun fire.

James Edgar Johnson, a policeman's son from Barrow-upon-Soar became articled to a surveyor following his studies in Nottingham. He was turned down by the Auxiliary Air Force, and only accepted by the RAF Volunteer Reserve when the service was expanded amid fears of a European war.

In May 1941, he recorded the first of his 38 wartime kills. He was awarded three DSOs, two DFCs, the American DFC and the *Croix de Guerre*.

After the war, Group Capt Johnson commanded three Sabre jet squadrons at RAF Wildenrath, and was commanding officer at RAF Cottesmore, the base of Britain's first operational Vulcan squadron.

Air Vice-Marshal Johnson retired from the RAF in 1965, pursued various business interests and set up a housing trust to provide homes for elderly and disabled ex-servicemen.

SPITFIRE LEADER: 'Johnnie' Johnson

Bloody campaign of Wollaton's '508th'

TWO thousand young Americans set out from Nottingham for the Normandy invasion — and only 800 of them returned.

The 508th Parachute Infantry Regiment was based at Wollaton Park, arriving in March from the isolated Port Stewart Camp in Northern Ireland.

Ray Pateracki was one of the advance party which prepared for the arrival of the 508th.

"We busted our butts during the daylight hours," recalled the former staff sergeant at a Nottingham reunion in 1990. "But once the sun set, we hustled those same butts into town."

It was dark when the main body of troops arrived in Nottingham. When they woke next morning and saw Wollaton Hall, some of them believed it was Nottingham Castle.

According to one report, soldiers shot at the park deer, thinking they were wild game.

Nottingham was a brief bright spot for the Americans, who were far from home and mindful of the fighting to come. The city's pubs also welcomed soldiers from another parachute regiment, based at Tollerton Airfield.

With pay four times higher than that of British servicemen, they were popular with Nottingham girls. There were some weddings — and when a New Yorker married a Radford girl, he called her "my greatest war souvenir."

There should have been more. Even in the 1990s, a few middle-aged Nottingham men and women were still trying to trace their fathers.

In the biggest invasion in history the regiment suffered dreadful casualties as they fought their way out of the drop zones. Only 800 fit men returned in July, and they were given a tremendous welcome by Nottingham.

BEFORE THE STORM: A chat with the locals for GI Tom Purcella at Wollaton Park

Soldier plays dead and survives

TROOPER G. Eason of Radford Road survived a mortar blast which blew his scout car off the road near the Meuse-Escaut canal.

Through the visor of the shattered vehicle he saw three German soldiers approaching. He shut his eyes, played dead and hoped for the best.

"The Huns inspected the car, peered inside and held a discussion," the *Evening Post* reported. "They evidently considered that Eason was as dead as mutton, and took cover in the lee of the car.

"Eason picked up a grenade and tossed it nonchalantly through the driver's hatch in the direction of their muttering.

"He clambered out of the car and almost fell over the three dead Germans."

TYCOON, philanthropist and sportsman Sir Julien Cahn died at his home, Stanford Hall, aged 62.

He had inherited both his baronetcy and a fortune from his father, and his gifts to the community included the transfer of Newstead Abbey to Nottingham Corporation.

He was at various times masters of three hunts. As a cricketer he captained his own XI, and led teams to all corners of the British Empire. He had been president of Notts CCC.

RAF radio operator Ronald Jephson, 26, from Nottingham, was honoured by the Russians for his work with Balkan partisans.

The Hucknall-trained airman was one of two who parachuted into Yugoslavia to work with Marshal Tito's forces fighting the Germans.

He was awarded the blue and grey ribbon of the Soviet Order of Valour and was offered a pension of ten shillings a month for life, to be drawn at any Soviet embassy.

CANON C. Dudley Hart was installed as Grand Superintendent of the Royal Arch Masonry in the Notts Province.

NOTTINGHAM and other Midland towns experienced an earthquake on December 30. Damage was slight and nobody was hurt.

'BEVIN BOY' Jackie Sewell joined Notts County from Whitehaven, and made his debut as a 17-year-old.

DEFERRED by the war, plans for a Sandiacre by-pass on the Nottingham-Derby road were revived when Derbyshire County Council agreed to a southern rather than a northern route.

VALERIE Clark became the smallest baby ever born at the City Hospital. She arrived on July 25 and weighed just 1lb 14oz.

CITY magistrates criticised the Board of Trade's use of *agents provocateurs* to obtain convictions for breaches of rationing regulations.

A Goosegate business was accused of selling a raincoat to a ministry inspector, posing as an ordinary shopper, without taking the appropriate clothing coupons.

The court heard that the inspector told the shop manager she "could not spare the coupons".

The business owner was fined £5, but the chairman told the Board: "I do not like this method."

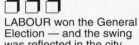

LABOUR won the General Election — and the swing was reflected in the city polls, too.

The party took control of the council for the first time, gaining ten seats while winning 19 of the 25 at stake in 16 wards.

The election left Labour with 36 seats and the Conservatives with 25. There were two independent councillors and one Liberal.

WHEN the war ended, Nottingham faced a new housing crisis.

The city's reconstruction committee reported that 18,000 homes were needed but there was land only for 5,000.

The council issued a purchase order on 936 acres in the parish of Clifton-with-Glapton. In the 1950s it would become Clifton Estate — the largest public housing project in Europe.

A HUGE crowd gathered at the Embankment on November 11 for the first Armistice Day of the peace. *Last Post* was sounded by a bugler of the 9th Bn, Rifle Brigade.

THE Nottingham registrar reported a big demand for yuletide marriages. There were 40 in the three days before Christmas.

NOTTS branch of the British Limbless Ex-Servicemen's Association was formed after an inaugural meeting at the Strathdon Hotel, Derby Road.

IT'S OVER: Crowds in Old Market Square celebrate VJ Day

Dancing in the Square

THOUSANDS of citizens danced the night away in Old Market Square after Winston Churchill's announcement the war against Nazi Germany was over.

The date was Tuesday May 8, a few hours after General Jodl signed his country's unconditional surrender.

Loudspeakers were set up in the city centre and crowds flocked down Long Row to hear the long awaited news.

Flags and bunting appeared overnight and outside Henry Barker's furniture shop — now the Central Library — in Angel Row, the flags of all the allies were proudly displayed.

Around the suburbs, victory parties were hastily convened in the streets.

On August 15, they all turned out again, swamping the Old Market Square in their thousands to celebrate victory against Japan.

General Dwight D. Eisenhower, victorious Allied commander in Europe, visited Nottingham on October 26.

Schoolchildren were given a holiday, shops and offices closed and 20,000 people packed into the city centre.

At the Council House, Eisenhower was guest of honour at a civic luncheon — during

TRIBUTE: Supreme commander Gen Eisenhower at the Council House

which crowds in the square shouted "We want Ike". The meal was interrupted so that he could appear on the balcony.

The purpose of his visit was to launch the Roosevelt Scholarship, which continues to give young Notts people the chance to travel in the USA.

Eisenhower spoke of the "genius and intelligence" of local people who had contributed so much to the war effort.

VC back from the dead

LANCE Corporal Harry Nicholls travelled to Buckingham Palace on June 22 to receive his Victoria Cross from King George VI.

Grenadier Guardsman Harry, from Sneinton, had won the medal five years earlier but it had been presented to his wife Constance because he had been reported killed in action.

In fact, he had been taken prisoner by the Germans and when Constance heard the news, she returned his medal.

That led to the moment when, for the first time in the history of the VC, the same medal was presented twice.

Pilot wins and loses speed record

GROUP Capt H.J. Wilson smashed the world air speed record in a Gloucester Meteor jet — and lost it an hour later to another pilot, Notts rugby footballer Eric Greenwood.

Wilson completed the four test runs over the Thames estuary at an average 602mph. The previous official record was the 469.2mph recorded by a Messerschmidt 109 in 1939.

Greenwood's four runs averaged 606mph. But when cine-film times were checked, Wilson was recognised at the record holder, with 606mph — Greenwood's average was recorded as 603mph.

Action plea on Broxtowe 'death traps'

RESIDENTS of the Bilborough and Broxtowe estates demanded a council clean-up of the suburban environment after a spate of accidents involving children.

Parents complained that the area had become "a veritable death trap", with ...

● Unsecured reservoirs.
● Unattended building sites.
● Burning slag heaps.
● Dangerous pit shafts.

There had been three fatal accidents within 12 months, the latest involving a six-year-old boy who drowned in a colliery reservoir.

In June, there was nearly a fourth and fifth death when a mother and child fell into smouldering slag.

A petition organised by the Communist Party and the residents' association had been signed by 800 adults from the Broxtowe and Bilborough neighbourhoods.

But when residents tried to present it at a city council meeting, they were told it was not customary to accept petitions at public meetings.

"We think lives are more important than customs," countered residents' leader Arthur West.

Labour leader Alderman Bowles agreed to refer the matter to councillors.

Damages for dancer in crash

A DANCER was awarded £2,500 damages for injuries to her legs when she was hit by a runaway car in Chapel Bar.

The accident happened in September 1944 when Marjorie Rowland, then 36, was peering into a shop window.

An unattended car careered down the hill, mounted the pavement and pushed her through the plate glass window, trapping her legs on the sill.

Miss Rowland, who had danced as a Tiller Girl in the West End and had appeared at the Folies Bergeres in Paris, said she believed she had three of four years left as a stage dancer.

But her legs needed make-up to hide her scars, and since the accident she had received psychiatric counselling for nerves, nightmares and her fear of traffic.

FARE DEAL: Passengers at Midland Station await a holiday special

TWENTY thousand Midlands railwaymen backed Government plans to nationalise the railways — and demanded a voice for workers.

Their delegates met at the Albert Hall and approved the nationalisation plan. They suggested it be extended to embrace all forms of public transport.

The NUR resolution demanded area boards of management with representatives not only from the Government, but also from the railway unions: "An efficient transport system is an imperative necessity for the restoration of Britain's economic life, and the workers' participation in its management is an indispensable condition of this."

● Rail fares were increased in July, hitting holiday budgets. A return to Skegness rose from 15s 4d to 17s 7d [about 87p].

Bread ration angers mums

NOTTINGHAM Advice Bureau was founded to provide housing information for demobbed servicemen and women returning to their home city.

The driving force was Alan Quin, a Canadian who was the city council's emergency planning officer.

Situated at the Nottingham Hippodrome, the bureau was run by the city's information officer, Louis Pollock.

Housing was not the only problem. Bread rationing was introduced in July, prompting a protest from 150 Nottingham members of the National Housewives' Revolt Campaign.

Nottingham fruit traders complained when the Government ordered that jam-makers get first call on the strawberry crop.

There was also a tobacco shortage. Courts did a brisk business in people charged with stealing or handling tobacco. In the worst theft, 86,300 cigarettes were taken from a lorry at Cinderhill.

HONOURS were even when Wolverhampton did battle with Nottingham to see which town had the prettier girls.

Nottingham won the first of two beauty parades.

For the re-match at the Palais de Dance, the city chose ten girls from the 16 who had paraded for selectors at Jessops. Seven were brunettes.

But the Wolverhampton team had been strengthened. Their ten included six new faces, four of them blondes.

The contest was adjudicated by entertainer Billy Reid and his stage partner Dorothy Squires — and they made Wolverhampton the winners by 369 points to 314. The event made £100 for the Women's Hospital and RAF Benevolent Fund.

□□□

CONCERT pianist Benno Moiseiwitsch lost an appeal against £52 breach-of-contract damages for his non-appearance at the Theatre Royal in 1942.

The pianist had withdrawn with fibrositis in his arms, and was sued by impresario Harold Fielding, who said he had incurred additional expenses in booking a stand-in performer.

COUPON COUNTER: A Food Office in Nottingham immediately after the war

Charter gives city the first post-war university ➡ Page 85

AN ex-soldier wrote to the *Evening Post*: "I was discharged from the Army, and my job in London, where I lived for 24 years, was no longer open. Nottingham has given me a wife, a home, a job and the finest bunch of people as friends."

☐ ☐ ☐

THE pre-war Sheffield-to-Marylebone express was restored to the winter timetable at Victoria Station — the A3-hauled Master Cutler, departing at 7.40am. The return service left London at 6.15pm.

☐ ☐ ☐

A GARDENER reported the theft of chrysanthemums from his Nottingham garden. A policeman followed a trail of petals to another house, where the occupant produced 60 blooms and admitted he had sold another 16 for four shillings [20p].

☐ ☐ ☐

SIX Nottingham butchers were fined for selling beef sausages with a meat content less than 50%. The court accepted that they were marginal offences by reputable butchers, but said an example had to be made.

☐ ☐ ☐

THE 1st Test against South Africa at Trent Bridge was drawn after England, following on, scored a huge second-innings 551. Following their half-centuries in the first innings, Denis Compton and Bill Edrich followed up with 163 and 50 respectively.

DELUGE: Drivers splash their way through the Nottingham floods

The big freeze ...then floods

THE worst winter weather since 1895 saw sub-zero temperatures for six weeks, snow lying 21in deep in parts of Nottingham, and outlying villages isolated by 6ft drifts.

Weddings were spoiled when the temperatures froze camera shutters.

Blizzards were still being recorded on March 15. But then temperatures fell.

Swollen by a torrent of thawing Peak District snow, the Trent began rising by an inch an hour on March 17. By March 29 it was two inches an hour. Emergency workers were put on floods stand-by, low-lying homes were sandbagged.

North of the river, the flood waters submerged 2,425 acres of the city — including 298 miles of streets and 4,704 homes, offices, factories and shops.

A three-week-old child and a woman of 84 were among 35 people evacuated from Lenton homes to a relief centre in Church Street.

Loughborough Road, Melton Road and Wilford Lane were all impassable.

Homes in The Meadows were particularly badly affected, and nearby railway lines were also flooded. At its height, flood water rose to within an inch of platform surfaces at Nottingham Midland Station.

The flood began to recede on March 20, and the Lord Mayor, Alderman Robert Shaw, opened an appeal fund for victims.

Notts miners gave £1,000, and collections in the city and in churches topped the fund up to £4,500.

Public health was a constant concern as householders cleared their homes. West Bridgford Council distributed two tons of soap and 3,000 bottles of disinfectant.

Power cuts anger Notts industry

A COLD snap in December forced up electricity consumption, and led to twice-daily power cuts. Industrialists blamed over-consumption by householders.

City electricity engineer M. Wadeson said: "There are two ways of overcoming power shortages. One is to appeal to people to be as economical as possible. The other is by cuts. "The appeals have failed, so we have had to enforce cuts."

Business leaders called for householders to cut back on the use of electric heaters — and to take advantage of plentiful stocks of coal.

It had been a productive year in the Notts coalfield, with output records set at Gedling, Hucknall and Clifton collieries. Regional output, approaching 800,000 tons per month, was at its highest level for years.

☐ ☐ ☐

COLWICK Park racecourse announced its first-ever three-day National Hunt meeting to cope with a phenomenal weight of entries for the two-day meeting planned for February 1948. The 232 first-stage entries for the Annesley Novices Hurdle was a record for any jumps race in England.

☐ ☐ ☐

SNEINTON Windmill was damaged by fire on July 10. The building remained unused until the 1970s.

Record transfer: Tommy Lawton quits Chelsea for Magpies

NOTTS County smashed the transfer record in the autumn to sign the England centre-forward, 28-year-old Tommy Lawton from Chelsea.

The move shocked many in football. Lawton was at the peak of his powers and was leaving a top club for the Third Division (South).

But Notts were determined to buy back the glory days. "We are prepared to spend to put the old club back where it belongs," said director H.J. Walmsley.

The £20,000 deal was agreed at the Great Western Hotel, Paddington. Notts would pay £17,500, and allow £2,500-rated Bill Dickson to move south to Stamford Bridge.

Lawton fever swept across Nottingham.

On Boxing Day, a record 45,116 fans were locked into the match against Swansea; 10,000 could not get into the ground.

In 1949-50, when Lawton's goals helped Notts to the Third Division (South) title, the club had an average home gate of almost 35,000.

HERO'S GUARD: Tommy Lawton protected from fans

Quincentenary festival lifts post-war blues  Page 86

RAF appeals to city

THE biggest post-war recruitment drive by the RAF came to Nottingham, with exhibitions and displays on the Forest and in Old Market Square.

The event was opened by the Under-Secretary for Air, Central Nottingham MP Mr G. de Freitas.

Displays featured the Spitfire and Hurricane fighters, and the RAF's latest jet aircraft, including the Vixen. Recruitment officers received inquiries from 150 young men.

Still no bananas

THE *Post* reported that tomatoes were available in Nottingham shops. Savoy cabbages and spring greens were value at 5d [2p] a pound. There were hopes for oranges, but still no sign of bananas.

The Ministry of Food urged *Post* readers to make the most of their meat ration, by pot-roasting joints instead of cooking them in the oven.

PRISON CAMP: Wollaton Park PoW compound

GERMAN prisoners-of-war made several appearances in Notts courts.

Hermann Joeddicke, 21, from Aslockton Camp, admitted breaking into a shop in West Bridgford and stealing property worth £17.

Notts Quarter Sessions heard that he told a

Prisoners-of-war in court

policeman, in English, "Come and get me." He was overpowered.

Ernst Wagner, 22, was accused of breaking into a NAAFI canteen in Ollerton and stealing 227 bars of soap.

Heinrich Otten, 22, was charged with stealing a package containing 186 pairs of stockings. He told the court he had been sleeping under haystacks since absconding from Langar Camp.

CHALLENGE:
Lord and Lady Trent

At last, a new university

A ROYAL charter conferred university status on Nottingham's 67-year-old University College.

The seat of learning, based at the Highfields estate given in the 1920s by Sir Jesse Boot, was Britain's first post-war university. The first vice-chancellor was Bertrand Hallward, former headmaster of Clifton College, Bristol. He has been appointed University College's last principal in 1947.

Under Hallward's leadership, the Highfield campus was transformed, with the addition of the Portland Building, ten halls of residence, library, sports centre and departmental blocks.

The first post-war university was soon popular with Britain's school-leavers, offering a variety of quality degree courses in a leafy campus on the edge of an exciting city.

The first honorary degree ceremony was held in 1949. Among the recipients was the university's first Chancellor, Sir Jesse's son, the 2nd Lord Trent.

Mechanics' strike hits City Transport

CITY Transport and other operators with coach workshops were hit by a spring strike by the National Union of Vehicle Workers. About 150 Nottingham-based members backed a national claim for an extra 3d [about 1p] on their basic hourly pay.

The Ministry of Labour, fearing the effect on the post-war export drive, referred the dispute to arbitration.

BOYS with catapults were blamed for holding up house-building on Broxtowe Estate.

A contractor at Helstone Drive complained: "It's vandalism. As soon as houses are ready to be handed over, window breakages begin — and evidence in each case points to catapults."

Because supplies were short, sub-contractors had to wait weeks for replacement glass.

Thirty windows had been shattered, and another four were broken on April 11.

WEST End star Selma Vaz Dias joined the new Nottingham Playhouse company. Other autumn recruits were Michael Aldridge, cast in the title role of *Othello*, and Maxine Audley.

Seat prices were fixed at 2s 6d to 5s [about 12 to 25p], with performances at 7.15pm (5 and 8pm on Wednesdays and Saturdays).

The box office opened on October 25, and the first night — Shaw's *Man and Superman* — was set for November 8.

BRITISH Railways introduced the *South Yorkshireman* service on the Bradford to London route, leaving Nottingham at 10am. The return service left London at 4.50pm.

CYCLIST Reg Harris, riding a Raleigh bike, won two silver medals at the 1948 Olympics in London — just months after his back was injured in a car crash.

RUMOURS of a nudist camp followed the discovery of unauthorised huts in the heart of Newstead Abbey Park.

NEWARK-born Shakespearean actor Donald Wolfit married his leading lady Rosalind Iden. Later in 1948 they appeared at the Theatre Royal in Ibsen's *The Master Builder*.

Clifton, Europe's biggest public housing project ➡ Page 87

500 years up – and we step out proudly

WATER officials appealed to householders to cut consumption after weeks without rainfall.

"If you have the petrol to take you to the Derwent Valley reservoirs, you will see that levels have dropped badly," a city water engineer said.

An alderman pointed out that 500,000 local customers were each using, on average, 22 gallons of water a day.

"If an accident occurred and outside supply was cut off, it would be a disaster," he said. "I ask those people who have a bath every morning to cut it to three times a week. I have already done so."

❏ ❏ ❏

BARBERS were desperate to employ male apprentices ... but drew the line at allowing women to cut men's hair.

"There has been a falling off in recruits since the war and lads are still going away for military training," said C. Atkinson of the Nottingham branch, Incorporated Guild of Hairdressers, Wigmakers and Perfumers.

"There has been some talk of women taking over men's hairdressing in some parts of the country. The chances of this happening in Nottingham are hardly worth thinking about."

❏ ❏ ❏

RALEIGH cyclist Reg Harris became the first Briton to win the world professional sprint title. Racing in Copenhagen, he beat former champion Van Vliet in a best-of-three semi-final, and won the championship in two heats against Jan Derksen.

❏ ❏ ❏

THE Royal Ordnance Factory made 180 redundant after reduced demand for lace machines. Although still a gun plant, it had taken on civilian manufacture as an "insurance policy" against arms cuts.

❏ ❏ ❏

THREE hundred infants were entered for the baby show at Bulwell Lido. First prize of a canteen of cutlery, went to the parents of six-month-old Lynn Dianne France.

SQUARE DANCE: The quincentenary dancing display in Old Market Square. Right: Princess Elizabeth admires lace at the trade exhibition

POST-WAR gloom was brightened by Nottingham's quincentenary celebrations — the 500th anniversary of the charter of 1449.

The highlight was the visit on June 28 of Princess Elizabeth and the Duke of Edinburgh.

The couple toured exhibitions at the Broad Marsh and Guildhall, and watched the primary schools' sports day at the Forest.

After watching a display of country dancing in Old Market Square, and lunch at the Council House, the princess was presented with a china and silver coffee set as a gift from the city.

The celebrations also included a historical pageant, a medieval fair and a shop window display for traders. Classes were won by the Co-op branches in Broxtowe Lane and Plains Road, Mapperley; Hopewell & Sons and Smith Englefield, both of Parliament Street; Kaye's Fashions, King's Walk.

A cycling tournament on the Embankment included a race for vintage bikes, in which 72-year-old R. Watson rode a Referee Safety model of 1877.

The festival was spoiled by a fire which destroyed the former Canaan Street Chapel, where a local government exhibition included several valuable items.

After the event the council praised citizens for their enthusiasm.

Council rejects rag week appeal

STUDENTS asked permission to hold a rag week, but the council said no. During a rag week in Loughborough, students "captured" an aeroplane propellor, and councillors wanted no such incidents in Nottingham.

Coun W.G. Dyer fought in vain for the youngsters. He said the students of the old university college had raised £18,000 for the General Hospital in the 15 years before the war — largely through rag week street collections.

A survey in Nottingham showed that only 48 out of 6,414 interviewees were against a student rag week.

Festival of Britain honour for village of Trowell ➡ Page 88

Banks have too much money!

IN October, Nottingham banks complained they had too *much* money. To be more exact, they complained they had too many coppers.

The Thurland Street branch of the Westminster Bank found itself with £23,000 worth of penny pieces — 5,520,000 coins.

Branch head cashier Mr G.D. Bretland explained: "Most of the city's pennies come from transport, electricity and gas, and other banks assist the Westminster in coping with the rush of pennies that come in.

"Now the dark nights are coming, there will be a bigger demand for pennies. But after Christmas the surplus will be as big as ever."

The problem had become so acute, across the UK, that he couldn't see other banks coming to his aid.

"When we ring up other branches in different parts of the country and ask them if they want any coppers," he said, "they just laugh.

"They would like to pass a few million to us."

'Human' pony at 655th Goose Fair

AMONG the attractions at the 655th Goose Fair was Blitz, 'the Shetland Pony with the human brain', and her new-born foal Lucky, who measured just 18in high.

Nearly 800 applications had been made to the Nottingham Fairs and Markets Committee for just 400 sites.

The 1950 fair opened amid an unusual heatwave, the temperature in Nottingham that opening Thursday reading 73F.

CLIFTON ESTATE: Rows of new houses in Sturgeon Avenue

Estate with a big future

THE main construction work began on what was to become the biggest public housing project in Europe.

Nottingham Corporation began work on the design of Clifton Estate in the late 1940s, directed by planning officer Bill Dennis.

His aim was to recreate the neighbourhood spirit that characterised urban streets of back-to-back housing — but in an open, green environment.

Mr Dennis had grown up in Finkhill Street, a high density slum area which was later levelled for the creation of Maid Marian Way.

He divided the Clifton site into distinct neighbourhoods, each with 600 to 1,500 homes, shops, open spaces and primary schools.

Construction of sewers and 25 miles of roads and sewer construction began in September 1950. In that year, the average wait for a council house was five years, so speed was a priority.

So as well as traditionally-constructed houses, the estate included Wimpey No-Fines concrete homes where a mixture of aggregate, cement and water was poured into timber moulds. The method enabled the corporation to create 30 homes a week.

What the planners could not envisage, however, was the boom in car ownership in the second half of the century.

In 1950, most families living on council estates would not have owned a car.

"We didn't build many domestic garages," Mr Dennis said years later. "You couldn't foretell the future.

"In the same way, no one would have thought that in years to come, people would drive off to huge supermarkets on the outskirts of the city and forget about the neighbourhood shops we created."

The first residents collected the keys to their homes in September 1951. When Clifton Estate was completed, it was home for 30,000 people.

ABOUT 1,000 Nottingham schoolboys were sent to help farmers pick potatoes on the first day of the new season. They were packed off to farms in Lowdham, Sutton Bonington and the area around the new Clifton estate.

The scheme, carried out for the Nottingham Education Authority, was organised by Mr W.P. Hadrill, head of the Ellis School. Boys had to be 14 and girls weren't allowed. The previous year there had been no such restrictions and 3,500 children were involved.

□□□

BEESTON held a photo exhibition to mark the centenary of the Public Libraries Act. The local library was itself celebrating a record, having stamped out 480,000 books in the year.

□□□

SYLVIA Glenn, 12, from Ford Street, New Basford, received an unexpected letter from a 13-year-old boy in Denmark. She had been on holiday in Ingoldmells where she put a message in a bottle and tossed it into the sea. It arrived on the coast of Jutland where the lad found it.

□□□

A SOLICITOR put up an unusual defence for a Glasshouse Street baker accused of selling a cake containing a dead beetle. The lawyer asked the Guildhall court: "Does there being a beetle in it make a cake unfit for human consumption?" Magistrates thought it did, and fined the baker £40.

□□□

OWNERS of radios were warned by the Post Office in the autumn that detector vans would be patrolling Nottingham and listening for anyone who was tuning into the airwaves without a wireless licence.

□□□

THE West Indies won the 3rd Test at Trent Bridge by ten wickets after scoring an unassailable first-innings 558. Frank Worrell hit 261 and Everton Weekes 129.

GOING FAR: Barton Transport, based in Chilwell, celebrated its 42nd anniversary. The firm had started out with a 28-seat charabanc shuttling between Long Eaton Market and Stanford Street. Founder Thomas Barton hired the vehicle from a firm in Sheffield. Within three days, he had taken £100 and was on the road to success. In the picture is a 1950s replica of the Daimler charabanc used for the first Barton services in 1908.

The Mousetrap: 'Nice little run' starts in city  Page 89

1951

CLARENDON College announced a cookery course for 'bachelors and married businessmen' so they would no longer be so heavily dependent on their mothers and wives. The idea had stemmed from a course the previous year aimed at 'brides and business girls'. Principal Miss K. Waters said men would be taught "the basic rules regarding nutritional values" and would be shown it was "possible to prepare a meal on a gas ring."

☐ ☐ ☐

THE city transport department experimented with one-man bus operation. The single-decker Service 32 between Old Market Square and City Hospital operated without a conductor — even though it was a rear-entrance vehicle. The driver was required to collect fares before returning to his cab to continue the journey.

☐ ☐ ☐

ONE of the exhibits at the Nottingham and District Aquarists Society's show was Bertie, a 10ft boa constrictor. Before leaving home for the event, at the Regent Hall, Bertie was given a meal of two rabbits. Afterwards he slept through the show.

☐ ☐ ☐

THE *Post* recorded the death of a singular Carlton man, with an unlikely but lifelong hatred. Thomas James Brooks, 91, put his longevity down to the fact that he had given up tea 72 years earlier.

☐ ☐ ☐

NOTTINGHAM was facing a milk shortage. To ensure the position did not deteriorate, the Nottingham Co-op imposed a 10% cut in all domestic supplies. The shortage was explained away as 'seasonal'.

☐ ☐ ☐

A SHORT story called *Mountain Jungle* won a prize at Nottingham Writers' Club. The author: 21-year-old Alan Sillitoe.

☐ ☐ ☐

NOTTS County record goalscorer Jackie Sewell signed for Sheffield Wednesday for £34,500.

Festive spirit comes to city

THE travelling Festival of Britain Exhibition spent three weeks in Nottingham, attracting thousands of visitors to displays covering 35,000 square feet in Lister Gate.

Visitors paid a shilling [5p] to pass through a foyer and enter five different exhibition areas.

● Discovery and Design demonstrated the influence of science and featured relatively new materials like plastics and polystyrene.

● People at Home showed the latest in home furnishing, including "a bedsitting-room for a businesswoman".

● People and Travel displayed oddities like the non-rusting suitcase.

● People at Play included an array of toys and hobbies.

● People at Work featured the manufacture of jet engines, at which Britain was a pioneer.

Other Festival of Britain events in Nottingham included a historical pageant, a gymnastics display on The Forest, illuminations at Wollaton Park and a trades exhibition at Queen's Drive recreation ground.

Trowell was chosen as the 'Festival Village of Britain' — symbolic of the rural way of life (this was a decade before the M1 was built through the parish).

The choice was criticised by those who felt a prettier village should have been selected.

Answering in the Commons, Broxtowe MP Seymour Oaks said: "Trowell combined the strength of modern industry with the peaceful beauty of the countryside."

Celebrations lasted from May to September and included a parade by the Ruddington Silver Prize Band, the planting of commemorative trees and a village concert party.

While London's Festival of Britain celebrations had a budget of £70 million, events in Trowell were subsidised by a door-to-door collection of £29.

The village had no restaurant or pub at the time. A pub was built in 1956. To mark Trowell's unique role in the events of 1951, it was called the Festival Inn.

CALL SIGN: City police were pioneers of walkie-talkie radios

A tall order for bobbies

CITY police launched a major recruitment drive. The key thrust of the campaign was a comparison with pay and conditions in 1903.

Then they earned 26 shillings [£1.30] for a 48-hour week, and didn't get a day off.

The *Post* pointed out: "Today's policeman draws a pay packet that compares favourably with most wage earners. Even discounting the way pounds, shillings and pence have devalued since 1903, the present day policeman is much better off then he was 50 years ago.

"And the policeman of today is treated with respect. He is no longer a figure of fun."

The average bobby was earning about £400 a year. A constable with 25 years' experience was on £505. A new superintendent earned just under £1,000. The campaign was aimed at making up a ten per cent deficit in manpower and stressed the fringe benefits, such as a canteen and sports facilities.

Would-be recruits had to be aged between 19 and 30 and a minimum 6ft tall. The reason, said the *Post*, that Nottingham police had to be taller than the 5ft 9in national requirement, was so that they would stand out in a crowd, and be able to command authority.

The tallest Nottingham policeman at the time was PC Peter Gilbert at 6ft 5in.

FESTIVAL PAGEANT: The story of Edward III and Queen Philippa is told in the city's historical pageant

Scottish play hits director's debut

THE *Macbeth* jinx struck the first Nottingham Playhouse production by newly-appointed artistic director John Harrison.

Actors are so wary of the bad luck attached to Shakespeare's tragedy that they won't even utter its title. True to form, disaster struck at the dress rehearsal in January. The actor playing Macbeth, John Lindsay, fell from the stage and broke his ankle.

Bernard Kay was promoted from the role of Banquo, and an actor was summoned from London to learn Kay's old lines.

Lindsay later returned to the production, his ankle encased in plaster.

Gremlins strike as TV exhibition is opened  Page 90

Quick thinker averts a major disaster

FIREMEN praised corporation engineer Stanley Shipman for his quick thinking in tackling a fire that could have blown a huge hole in the city centre.

The blaze was at a garage opposite Central Fire Station, in Shakespeare Street.

Mr Shipman had been working with oxyacetylene when he saw flames on the top of a tank containing 2,000 gallons of petrol.

"There was a sudden flash in the garage," he said.

Somehow, the fire hadn't spread into the tank. If it had, experts told the *Post*, "it would have caused a devastating explosion."

Mr Shipman, having initially tackled the fire, rushed out of the building and raised the alarm by shouting across the street to the firemen, who were outside doing a drill exercise.

"Was I scared? Yes, but something had to be done," he said.

Walking tall at state funeral

KING George VI, who had died in his sleep at Sandringham on February 6, was laid to rest in St George's Chapel, Windsor.

As the funeral cortege moved slowly from Westminster Hall to Paddington Station, the eyes of thousands were fixed on the gun carriage bearing the coffin, draped in the Royal Standard.

It was flanked by the party of pall-bearers — huge soldiers of the King's Company, 1st Battalion, Grenadier Guards.

Among them were two men who were to become familiar faces in Nottingham.

Guardsmen Dennis 'Tug' Wilson and Geoff Baker later joined the city police force, whose chief constable, Captain Athelstan Popkess, required his bobbies to be at least six feet tall so that they could be easily spotted in crowds.

Wilson and Baker had height to spare, even by Popkess's standards.

The former was 7ft to the tip of his policeman's helmet, and the latter 6ft 8in.

Mousetrap's first night

THE WORLD'S longest running theatrical production opened at Nottingham's Theatre Royal on October 6.

Agatha Christie's *The Mousetrap* was presented by the impresario Sir Peter Saunders.

"Christie kept the audience guessing right up to the unexpected if unlikely end," wrote *Evening Post* critic Eileen Ritchie.

Her colleague on the Journal, Bernard Stevenson, wrote that the thriller showed "every evidence of being likely to enjoy a satisfactory run."

The author was just as confident. Her first Det Sgt Trotter, the young Richard Attenborough, later recalled chatting with the cast after the opening performance.

"We sat talking about the play for some time, and then Agatha Christie decided that she would go to bed.

"As she went upstairs, she put her head over the banisters and said, 'You know, darlings, there is no need to worry. I am sure we will get a nice little run out of it'."

The Mousetrap went on a provincial tour before opening at the Ambassador's Theatre in

POLICE ROLE:
Richard Attenborough

London in November. The "nice little run" has lasted 47 years and shows no signs of ending.

The Theatre Royal had been chosen for the premiere because Saunders and Christie regarded Nottingham as a "lucky" city for their shows.

The Hollow, Witness for the Prosecution and *Spiders' Web* were all introduced at the Nottingham theatre and went on to money-spinning West End and touring runs.

As it happened, Christie never made a penny out of *The Mousetrap*. She gave the rights to her eight-year-old grandson.

Opera star's 'kidnap' exaggerated

A NEWS agency reported the "kidnap" in Berlin of Nottingham-born international opera star Constance Shacklock.

The contralto had an engagement at the East Berlin State Opera, in the Soviet-controlled sector of the divided city.

She arrived at Tempelhof Airport, in the American sector. It turned out that she had been driven from the airport in an official East Berlin car — which agencies later confirmed was normal procedure.

Constance Shacklock sang her first solos, aged 13, in a church choir at Bulwell. She launched her professional career after the war, singing contralto and mezzo-soprano roles at Covent Garden and the world's other major opera houses.

She was celebrated especially for her dramatic

CONTRALTO:
Constance Shacklock

Verdi and Wagner roles, but had a popular touch. For several Prom seasons she sang the last-night *Rule, Britannia*; she appeared as the Mother Abbess in the West End production of *The Sound of Music*.

Miss Shacklock was awarded the OBE in 1971. She died in 1999.

AN Anglican minister was appointed to the new Clifton Estate —- former wartime spy the Rev Stephen Verney.

Capt Verney wore grimy clothes and lived with peasants during the German occupation of Crete. He passed on vital intelligence and carried out behind-the-scenes work to aid Allies in the Mediterranean theatre.

Because St Francis' Church was not fully finished, early services were carried out in the living room of the council house he and his wife had taken so he could live, as he put it, side by side with his congregation.

In an effort to find out more about his parishioners Mr Verney worked alongside them at Raleigh Industries.

Verney later became Bishop of Repton.

❑❑❑

NOTTINGHAM took measures to preserve its reputation for the prettiest girls in Britain. Mr E. Howard, the city's lighting engineer, gave a radio talk where he suggested that sodium lighting was unflattering to a woman's complexion. As a result, he said, city policy was to install tungsten filament lighting — much kinder to appearances — within a mile-a-half's radius of Old Market Square.

❑❑❑

A YOUNG actor from West Bridgford landed a leading role in a new late-night revue at London's Irving Theatre. Nineteen-year-old Leslie Crowther was the son of Mariede Lisle, who had been Britain's first female stage manager. His father, also called Leslie, had been a character actor on the London stage.

❑❑❑

THE Parliamentary Secretary at the War Department received several letters of complaint from staff at the Central Ordnance Depot, Chilwell. They were angry that they were being forced to retire at 65.

❑❑❑

MEADOW Lane hero Tommy Lawton was transferred from Notts County to Brentford, where he was appointed player-manager.

Parents lectured as head finds horror comic  Page 91

SCORES of Nottingham families began counting the cost after the East Coast floods smashed holiday homes and caravans in Skegness and other Lincolnshire resorts.

More than 300 people died and 32,000 properties were damaged or destroyed as sea defences burst down the whole length of the North Sea coast.

Nottingham became a regional WVS clothing collection centre, and parcels arrived from all over the country.

□ □ □

A BUMPER sugar beet harvest was predicted after a sun-and-rain summer free of crop diseases. Notts was expected to produce 18,000 tons of sugar, processed at Colwick, and Kelham.

□ □ □

NOTTINGHAM completed the building of 23 new schools since the war when seven were opened by the chairman of the National Coal Board, Sir Hubert Houldsworth.

□ □ □

A NEW bus depot at Bilborough was opened by the Sheriff in January, following delays caused by mining subsidence.

□ □ □

A THOUSAND Nottingham women signed a petition calling for the reinstatement of food subsidies. A Bestwood mother of six said it was impossible to buy eight meat, butter and bacon rations on her husband's pay — £6 3s [£6.15] a week.

□ □ □

NOTTS County Council approved a £185,000 contract for the completion of County Hall. Work on the Trent Bridge site had been suspended during the war.

□ □ □

MR and Mrs George Hickling of Waldeck Road, Carrington, celebrated their 74th anniversary. Mr Hickling worked in the lace trade from eight to 66. The couple, both in their early nineties, had recently become great great-grandparents.

Korea PoWs return

THE Victoria Station loudspeaker announced: "The next train on Platform 4 will be the troop train from Southampton."

Families were waiting for the return of the latest batch of prisoners-of-war to be released following the Korean conflict. Fifteen local soldiers arrived on September 16, either on the troop train or scheduled services.

Cpl Joseph Kenworthy was anxious to return to the Far East as a colonial policeman. "Civvy life is too slow," he said. In Hucknall, flags were raised for the return of Lance-Cpl David Kaye.

No high heels, girls!

GIRLS at Hucknall Secondary School were told not to wear high heels and jewellery.

It wasn't just a question of what was appropriate for the occasion, argued headmistress Mrs N.P. Wilson.

"Recently a girl lost a watch," she said. "It turned up in a rice pudding.

"We had a fire practice and a girl wearing high heels sprained her ankle while running to her station.

"The rules all come from bitter experience."

Gremlins spoil TV technology show

A GLIMPSE of a TV revolution was offered to the people of Nottingham — when independent television companies showed off their ideas at a major trade exhibition.

The radio and television trade fair was the second-biggest event of its kind after Olympia's version, and thousands flocked to the Albert Hall to see celebrities perform pilot shows which were relayed to the public on closed-circuit screens.

Opened by radio television announcer McDonald Hobley, the exhibition also included displays of the latest TV sets.

The independent companies were keen to show they could do as well as the BBC, and pilot shows included celebrity interviews with Joan Gilbert, plus kitchen tips for housewives.

Another idea was a game show to identify the most happily married married couple in Nottingham.

The winners, who received a hair dryer, were Mr and Mrs Bert Simpson of Port Arthur Road — married 26 years "and we've never had a serious argument."

Mr Simpson told the audience: "She doesn't know how much I earn, but I give her housekeeping money every week. Up to now, she's always made a good job of it."

Unfortunately, to the embarrassment of organisers, there were gremlins in the exhibition technology, and no closed-circuit pictures were

TV FACES: Eamonn Andrews, who endorsed the GEC TV sets, and McDonald Hobley (inset), who opened the exhibition

available for the first few days of the show.

The trade fair prompted advertising interest in the Evening Post.

A smiling Eamonn Andrews extolled the virtues of the GEC

TV set, encased in walnut veneered cabinet.

A Ferguson 998 model cost 55 guineas, and Wigfalls of Clumber Street offered rental deals from five shillings [25p] a week.

Blind woman, 50, sees at last

A 50-year-old woman who had been blind since birth had ten per cent of her sight restored after an operation at Nottingham Eye Infirmary.

Selina Lilliman never knew her father, and lost her mother when 13. She went to live in an institute, where she was trained as a machine knitter.

"When they took off the bandages I saw bright light," she said. "I had to learn colours by name, because I had not imagined they would appear as they are. The size of things was

surprising. Everything seems larger than I had imagined."

The story was reported prominently in Nottingham newspapers, which were making headlines of their own in 1953.

T. Bailey Forman, proprietors of the *Nottingham Guardian* and the *Evening Post*, bought the rival morning and evening newspapers from Westminster Press. In September, the morning papers amalgamated and appeared as the *Guardian Journal*.

Tragedy of RAF pilot who tried to save trainee ▷ Page 92

END OF AN ERA: Skinner & Rook, the wine and provisions merchants, pictured in the early 1950s. The site at the corner of Long Row and Clumber Street was to be sold for redevelopment in 1955

Chief raps horror comic

NOTTS director of education J. Edward Mason wrote an angry open letter to parents after a head sent him a horror comic that had been confiscated at an infants' school.

"It was evil in concept, illustration and design," wrote Mr Mason.

"This revolting publication contained stories of girls torn to pieces by wild animals, parents murdered by their children, daughters whipped to death by their fathers and other atrocities too terrible to mention.

"I have never read anything that has revolted me or distressed me more.

"How any parent can place such a document in the hands of a child I do not know. Yet this parent received the comic from a neighbour and presented it to her six-year-old son, who took it to school.

"When school libraries have rich and almost unlimited facilities available, it is sacrilege to let filthy trash of this kind fall into the hands of unsuspecting, innocent children."

'Drinkers won't stand for it'

CITY members of the Licensed Victuallers' Association pleaded for a cut in beer duty.

"If a man spends 10s on beer," said president John Farr, "he gives 6s 8d to the Chancellor. How much longer will the British public fork out at that rate?"

Panthers bag second title

NOTTINGHAM Panthers won the English National League title for the second and final time.

The league made way for a British championship the following year and Panthers would win that competition, along with the Autumn Cup in 1956.

The Panthers had been formed in 1946 when coach Sandy Archer, star of the pre-war Wembley Lions, brought a dozen players over from Canada, including legendary winger Les Strongman and defender Kenny Westman.

But it was the arrival of another city sporting legend Chick Zamick that really set the Panthers alight.

He scored 100 goals in his first season and by the time he left the Panthers in 1958 his total had reached a staggering 750.

He was twice voted Nottingham's Sportsman of the Year, finishing ahead of such luminaries as Tommy Lawton and cricketer Reg Simpson.

The high cost of imported Canadian players was a constant problem for ice hockey's administrators and rink owners and the writing was on the wall when Panthers asked their coach Archie Stinchcombe to resign "because of high running costs".

The sport struggled on until the 1959-60 season when the Panthers' name was laid to rest for more than 20 years.

Bike-builder Brough rides again

GEORGE Brough, *left*, and Harold 'Oily' Karslake took part in the golden jubilee run of the London-to-Edinburgh motorcycle rally.

Brough, who lived at Daybrook, had first taken part in the event in 1908, when he was just 13.

The 1954 rally was the last major competitive outing for the bike builder whose Brough Superior models were a legend.

The Superior, created in a little works in Basford, was described as 'the Rolls-Royce of motorcycles'. Customers included Lawrence of Arabia, who had seven of them.

As a competitive rider, Brough set a world speed record in 1928 of 130.5mph. A streamlined Brough later clocked 180mph.

Brough died in 1970, aged 79.

TENS of thousands turned out at Mapperley Plains on January 23 for a football clash between pitmen and Oxbridge undergraduates.

It was a second-round tie in the FA Amateur Cup. Gedling Colliery were playing the most successful amateur team of the day — Pegasus, who brought with them 25 coachloads of supporters.

Pegasus were leading 2-0 at half-time, then Gedling Colliery centre-forward Joy Kay scored.

The pitmen's hopes of getting back into the game were dashed by a third Pegasus goal, scored by Kent county cricketer Tony Pawson. The visitors scored three more times.

WEST Bridgford clerk Raymond Hodson was briefed to get textile exhibits to Iraq for a British trade exhibition in Baghdad. He drove there, towing a caravan.

When the car broke down in Yugoslavia, locals fixed it for nothing. "You are British, so you are a friend," they told him.

Driving through Syria, Mr Hodson picked up a traveller on the outskirts of Damascus. He said he was hitch-hiking to New Zealand.

CITY Transport drivers hit back when accused by other unions of trying to impose a colour bar on the recruitment of black staff — the local depots were short of 280 bus staff at the time.

They explained that the reaction would have been the same had jobs been offered to Scots or Welshmen: A driver's wage of £7 a week was below the industrial average, and the shortage of staff enabled them to claim more overtime.

A POCKET transmitter developed by Nottingham engineers, led by Frederick Hopwood, was tested by entertainer Tommy Trinder.

He wore it in rehearsals for a London show, *Cinderella on Ice*, to see if his voice could be heard from all parts of the stage rink.

Inter-city helicopter taxi service fails to pay  Page 93

1955

Royal Show comes to Wollaton Park

ABOVE: Workmen put up a marquee at the Royal Show. **RIGHT:** The Queen, who attended with the Duke of Edinburgh, escorted by the Lord Mayor

THE Wembley dreams of both Forest and County ended in controversy.

Forest and Newcastle took their fifth round tie to a second replay before the Reds lost 2-1, manager Billy Walker claiming the ref was the only man who did not see Newcastle's Jimmy Scoular handle in his own penalty area.

Notts went a stage further and were drawn at home against York. But a crowd of 47,301 saw them lose 1-0, the winner allowed only after the ref had consulted his linesman.

▢ ▢ ▢

A CASKET containing a scroll, coins and a newspaper was placed in the foundations of the new Clifton Bridge.

The bridge was part of a strategy to reduce traffic jams in the city centre. The development of Clifton Estate had made the scheme even more urgent. It opened in 1958.

▢ ▢ ▢

HEAVY snow arrived in February, causing numerous accidents. In Bramcote, 16 people needed hospital treatment after a British Celanese works bus skidded and crashed on its side.

The double-decker crushed a new car, whose driver was among the casualties.

▢ ▢ ▢

THREE crews, including two school boats, sank in rough water during the Head of the Trent races.

Five pupils had to swim 200 yards to reach safety.

Grieving mother honours pilot hero

AN RAF pilot from Chilwell sacrificed his life in a vain attempt to save the pupil he was training.

The death of Flight Sgt Delwyn Brown, 33, whose mother Mary lived at Chilwell, led to the withdrawal from service of the Harvard training plane.

He had taken off from RAF Feltwell in Norfolk, with a trainee alongside him, when he radioed: "Mayday. Propeller and engine adrift. Am baling out."

Again and again over the intercom, he told the young pupil to bale out, but without success.

So he remained in his cockpit in a courageous attempt to crash land. Both men died instantly.

Brown's mother provided a memorial trophy for RAF Feltwell, a silver replica Harvard to be given to the outstanding trainee pilot.

The *Post* reported: "A lonely figure in black will stand on the dais as the last pilots trained on Harvards march past. With pride and sorrow Mrs Brown will hand over the replica."

OLD TESTAMENT 'MYTH': The Bishop of Southwell, Dr Russell Barry (pictured at a diocesan conference in 1957) stirred up a controversy by declaring in a newsletter that the story of Adam and Eve was nothing more than a myth

Notts star fined: Manager blamed for wedding delays

NOTTS County manager George Poyser had a problem. He was blamed for stopping winger Albert Broadbent's wedding.

Bride-to-be Margaret Proctor, 19, told the *Post* she had called at Woolwich Register Office to postpone the wedding for the third time because her fiance was serving a disciplinary ban imposed by his club.

Broadbent had allegedly defied team orders by going out for a drink on the eve of the York cup tie, was seen and reported to the club. He was dropped for the next match and also pulled out of an FA tour to the West Indies.

His fiancee told the *Post*: "There has not been any trouble between Albert and me. It's a matter of finance."

But Mr Poyser denied any ban had been imposed and described Miss Broadbent's statement as "only hearsay".

22 points: Gran scoops football pools fortune ⮕ Page 94

All-rounder Iremonger dies at 80

JAMES Iremonger, one of Nottingham's greatest all-round sportsmen, died aged 80.

As a cricketer he played for Notts from 1897 until 1914, scoring 16,328 runs and taking 616 wickets. He toured Australia with Pelham Warner's MCC team in 1911-12.

He was also a noted mentor of young talent, and as coach at Trent Bridge from 1921 to 1938 he helped develop the skills of Ashes-winning England bowlers Harold Larwood and Bill Voce.

He was a talented footballer, serving Nottingham Forest for 15 years at left-back and winning three England caps. He was also player-coach at Notts County.

Iremonger's Notts and England contemporary John (Jack) Gunn celebrated his 80th birthday in 1956 by declaring that the current Australian tourists were the worst he had ever seen.

The Aussies included Richie Benaud, Ray Lindwall, Neil Harvey, Slasher McKay and Keith Miller.

During his career Gunn scored 30,000 runs and took more than 1,000 wickets.

City soldier dies in Cyprus blast

A NOTTINGHAM soldier became a terrorist casualty in Cyprus when he was killed by a bomb in Famagusta.

He was a private serving with the 1st Bn Royal Leicestershire Regiment, stationed on the island where EOKA terrorists were fighting to expel British troops and unite Cyprus under the Greek flag.

He had been planning to leave the Army and return to Nottingham.

A few days later, another Nottingham soldier died in Cyprus. The 24-year-old, serving with the Warwickshire Regiment, accidentally shot himself with his own gun.

EARLY WHIRLYBIRD: The first helicopter to land at the Lenton Heliport (in 1955) was this Westland.

BEA 'copter scheme flops

TRANSPORT Minister John Profumo was among the passengers on the inaugural flight of Nottingham's commuter helicopter service.

The plan was to provide fast travel from Lenton Heliport to Leicester and Birmingham.

The first BEA passenger service, using a seven-seater Sikorsky, took off on July 2. As well as Mr Profumo (later the War Minister who resigned, infamously, in 1963), passengers included the Lord Mayor.

A single to Birmingham cost £1 9s [£1.45] and to Leicester just 11 shillings [55p].

BEA chairman Lord Douglas believed all Britain's major cities would be linked by helicopter by the mid-Sixties. He forecast that the Nottingham-Leicester-Birmingham flights would eventually need 20-seaters.

However operating costs proved to be prohibitive, made worse because of fuel shortages and rising prices during the Suez

INAUGURAL FLIGHT: Transport Minister Profumo

Crisis. In November that year, the service was suspended — and it was never resumed.

The heliport served as an off-road driving instruction area then as a go-kart venue.

Princess at Clifton's new church

CHURCH PARADE: Princess Margaret attended a service at the part-built St Francis's Church, on the new Clifton Estate

'Gormless' star in the making

THE farce *Something About A Sailor* played at the Theatre Royal. According to the *Post*'s reviewer, "a most promising 23-year-old repertory actor, Richard Briers, waffles around ... there are times when he overdoes his gormlessness but there is no doubt that he will make a nice light comedian."

Round the corner in Goldsmith Street, the Playhouse announced the appointment of a new director, Val May.

PROMISING: Richard Briers

Tom breaks the hoodoo

THE agency caption with this 1957 photograph of Tom Graveney, *right*, said the England batsmen would be travelling to Trent Bridge for the 3rd Test "trying to break the hoodoo that has dogged him in recent tests".

He did break the hoodoo, hitting 258 in England's massive first innings 619.

But the West Indies fought back for a draw, with a century in the first innings by Frank Worrell and another in the second from O.G. Smith.

DOUBLE TON: Tom Graveney

THE city came to a momentary standstill when the Civilian Defence siren whined through the air, sparking fears of an emergency.

It was later revealed that a GPO technician, putting back the fuses for a test planned for a week later, had accidentally touched off the alarm.

Over at C&A, managers had to deny it was a publicity stunt to mark the opening of the new menswear department. C&A should have opened its first store in the city in 1939, but the war intervened.

A CHEESE weighing half a ton passed through Nottingham on its way to the London Dairy Show. It was four feet in diameter and three feet deep.

To mark the occasion, the Lord Mayor was given a 40lb cheese which he passed to Portland Training College for the Disabled.

AN application for a juke box at the Bulwell Cafe, Cinderhill Road, was rejected by Nottingham Transfer Sessions on the grounds that it would attract undesirables.

However, Nottingham's oldest established milk bar, the Farmer Giles in Chapel Bar, was granted a licence for a record player and a light orchestra.

FOREST returned to the First Division after finishing runners-up in the Second. Promotion was secured with a 4-0 victory at Sheffield United.

Gran scoops pools fortune

FIFTY-two-year-old grandmother Mrs Ivy Howkins of Nuthall scooped the staggering sum — for 1957 — of £51,000 on the pools.

The shopkeeper and her husband had 22 points, but it was revealed that Mrs Howkins, a mother of two married sons, nearly did not bother to send the coupon in.

Mr Howkins said: "My wife had been ill on Thursday when she usually makes out the coupon. We nearly were not going to bother with it but on Friday I was going down to the local, so we posted it off then."

Mrs Howkins added: "Saturday would not be the same without the results. I seem to be lucky with them, I won £68 a short time ago."

The news of their win was broken to the couple at their Glasshouse Street shop.

Mrs Howkins said: "We think we will put the money into the business and take a holiday."

A pools spokesman said that if the win was invested, it would pay interest of £30 per week.

Monty does the honours

FIELD Marshal Viscount Montgomery is pictured during a visit in September to open Raleigh's No.3 cycle factory in Triumph Road. Three thousand dealers were invited to the ceremony at the £5 million plant.

Who saw Smoky wed?

BILLY Smart's circus was in town — and construction manager Walford Lotus had a special mission.

Eleven years earlier, Smoky, as he was known in the circus world, was married at Nottingham Register Office to bride Nancy after a three-week whirlwind romance.

They asked two strangers to act as witnesses and ever since, Smoky and Nancy had wanted to meet them again.

He hoped an appeal in the *Post* would enable him to contact Joseph McIlwaine and Charles Wright for a reunion drink.

GIRL and boy students clad in jeans and sports shirts jived to Humphrey Lyttleton at Victoria Ballroom.

JAYNE Torvill was born in Nottingham on October 7. Her future skating partner Christopher Dean was born in the city on July 27, 1958.

NEWARK-born actor Sir Donald Wolfit took part in a city debate on the state of theatre in Britain.

Murder law: Professor fears death penalty anomalies

A NOTTINGHAM law professor criticised the new two-degree murder law.

J. C. Smith of Nottingham University said that under the new law, if Ruth Ellis had used a hatchet instead of a gun she would have escaped the death penalty.

He said there were infinite varieties of murder "from the most atrocious to the most excusable. Formerly murder was unique in that only one punishment was prescribed — death.

"If a mother killed her imbecile and suffering child from compassion she was a murderer. Under the 1957 Act — supposed to differentiate between degrees of murder — she may kill her child by shooting and still be sentenced to death."

A Royal Commission had suggested it should be left to juries to decide the punishment but the Government pressed ahead with the legislation, ruling that the death penalty be retained for the worst cases.

Forest fever as Reds beat Luton for FA Cup  Page 96

FINAL CURTAIN: The variety theatre in 1968, the year before it was demolished

Farewell to city's grand old Empire

UNTICKLED:
Empire regular Ken Dodd

OPEN AND SHUT:
The neglected stage door

THE Empire Theatre, Nottingham, closed on June 21 — and variety fans were suspicious of assurances that it would re-open. It didn't.

Campaigners included broadcaster Dennis McCarthy, and an *Evening Post* correspondent wrote: "Surely the craze for demolition in the city does not extend to the destruction of a theatre."

But there were dissenting voices. A *Post* correspondent signed Lady Godiva bemoaned falling standards and wrote: "I cannot agree that it is a cultural loss to the city.

"The spectacle of brassy-faced wenches getting undressed is neither elevating nor entertaining. Good variety exists no more."

Another wrote: "Week after week at the top of the bill is usually a young man who can't sing ... and teenagers in the front row yell or scream at him.

Is there any wonder music halls are closing all over the country?"

Increasing ownership of television sets was one of the reasons for declining business.

In its heyday, the 2,200-seat theatre had welcomed artists as diverse as Charlie Chaplin, Houdini, the Beverley Sisters, Ken Dodd, Morecambe and Wise and Bruce Forsyth.

The Empire was eventually demolished in 1969, but the location was not lost to entertainment. It became the site of the Royal Concert Hall.

Meanwhile the Odeon was pinching the best musical acts.

A little-known comic called Des O'Connor introduced Buddy Holly and the Crickets on March 8, 1958.

The *Evening News* described "a deafening steam-hammer beat... a noise to drown even the din of all the city's many demolition projects."

Singing star appeals for racial calm

SUPERSTAR Paul Robeson sought to quell tension following the 1958 race riots in St Ann's. The black American actor-singer booked into the Black Boy Hotel on October 26 prior to his concert at the Nottingham Odeon.

"Nottingham gave me one of the warmest welcomes I have ever had," he told reporters. He said he was concerned about the rioting, but optimistic about the future of coloured people in Britain, "a place of great tolerance."

Reds face Munich survivors

FOREST played in one of the most emotionally charged fixtures in the history of football — the first match at Old Trafford after the Munich air disaster in which eight Manchester United players were killed or fatally injured.

The stars were among 22 who died following United's 3-3 draw with Red Star Belgrade in the quarter-final of the European Cup.

On February 22, 66,000 spectators crammed into Old Trafford to watch a makeshift team including crash survivors Harry Gregg and Bill Foulkes, and reinforced by Taylor of Blackpool and Crowther of Aston Villa.

A memorial service was held before a match which proved to be a hard, physical contest full of aggressive tackling by a home team determined to win for their departed team-mates.

Stewart Imlach fired Forest into the lead in the 32nd minute. But United earned a draw with a 74th-minute goal.

Not even Forest fans wanted United to lose, according to one of the Nottingham players.

Goalkeeper Chick Thompson said later: "We said the crowd at one end was blowing it in, and at the other end they were sucking it in. It just got there — and it was probably the right result."

After the match, referee Les Howarth said Forest had not only earned a point, but also United's gratitude for "keeping their heads" in a difficult game.

☐ ☐ ☐

NOTTS County were relegated to the new 'combined' Third Division, composed of the top teams from the old Third Divisions North and South.

☐ ☐ ☐

PRINCESS Alexandra toured the Boots site at Beeston on June 5, where she was greeted at the D6 building. She also opened Nottingham and District Technical College.

City setting for Lawrence and Sillitoe movies  Page 97

A MAN proposed to the woman he loved — from the dock at Nottingham Guildhall.

The defendant had admitted stealing clothes from lodgers at a house in Sherwin Street.

Although he had a long prison record, he asked the court for another chance, saying: "If you give me the chance, I will get married."

At that moment, a woman hurried out of the court, apparently to meet prisoner as he was released on probation.

DURING August, in response to a rumour sweeping through the city, Forest chairman H. W. Alcock issued the following statement about the club's colours.

"It is too ridiculous to think about anyone wanting to see the Cup holders play in anything else but red shirts and white knickers."

THE *Evening Post* failed to appear from June 22 to August 5 because of a national dispute.

A news sheet was produced to keep readers informed of local events. It began as a four-page Roneo-printed publication, but production was later switched to a press.

By the end of the strike it was selling up to 109,000 copies a night.

A STOCK car driver died in a collision at the Long Eaton speedway stadium. At the inquest, it was said that the 21-year-old was testing his home-built go-cart.

A 54-year-old man who had spent 17 of the previous 26 years in prison was sent back to jail for stealing an alarm clock and some cloth, worth £3. He had recently completed a six year sentence in Dartmoor.

NOTTINGHAM-born author Alan Sillitoe's story *The Loneliness of the Long Distance Runner* was published to great acclaim. It was later adapted for the cinema, with an early starring role for Tom Courtenay.

FOREST FEVER: Fans in Nottingham await the return of the Forest team from Wembley. Right: Skipper Jack Burkitt with the Cup

Reds triumph in Cup Final

FOREST won the FA Cup with a 2-1 win over Luton Town at Wembley, thanks to goals from Roy Dwight and Tommy Wilson.

The campaign began unpromisingly on January 10 when the Reds travelled to London for their third round tie.

Non-league Tooting and Mitcham United held their illustrious visitors to a 2-2 draw — Forest's scores coming from a penalty and an own goal!

With home advantage, Forest won the replay 3-0, then knocked out Grimsby Town 4-1.

It took three matches to settle the 5th round tie with Birmingham City. After two 1-1 draws, the Reds thrashed the Blues 5-1 in the second replay, with a hat-trick from Dwight.

In the next round Bolton Wanderers were beaten 2-1 at the City Ground, and a John Quigley goal decided the semi-final against Aston Villa.

A full house of 100,000 saw the Final on May 2, when the only sad news concerned scorer Dwight.

Forest had opened in brilliant style, sweeping into a two goal lead after 17 minutes. Then Dwight went down with a broken leg.

With no substitutes in those days, Forest were left to battle on with only ten men. Luton pulled a goal back, but the gallant ten held on.

By the time the final whistle blew, Dwight was in hospital — so he was unable to watch skipper Jack Burkitt receive the Cup from the Queen.

Next day the traditional open top bus ride around the city saw tens of thousands of fans lining the streets and Old Market Square.

Caine at the Royal

WILLIS Hall's play about an army patrol in the Malayan jungle, *The Long And The Short And The Tall*, arrived at the Theatre Royal. The cast included an unknown Cockney actor with a future ... Michael Caine, *pictured left*.

Meanwhile at the Playhouse, near the bottom of the cast list was a certain Brian Blessed in *Two For The See Saw*.

PC rescues boat couple

NOTTINGHAM'S 'Canadian' bobby PC Richard Cooke was awarded the Mountbatten Medal for diving into the River Soar to rescue two non-swimmers.

The couple fell into the water when their motor cruiser began to negotiate the Ratcliffe lock.

PC Cooke was off duty and convalescing from a serious illness. He dived into the stream, fully clothed except for his jacket, and first secured the man with a rope thrown from another vessel.

Then he helped save the man's wife, and applied artificial respiration. It was 15 minutes before she recovered consciousness.

He received his medal from Lord Mountbatten, president of the Royal Life Saving Society.

PC Cooke was born in Canada and took part in the D-Day landings. He married a Nottingham girl and settled in Canada before returning and joining city police in 1952.

Post office raid: Sweeney on the robbers' trail ➡ Page 98

Mapperley Tunnel closed

IN April, British Rail closed "unsafe" Mapperley Tunnel — effectively shutting down the Nottingham suburban line.

Extra coaches were put on for the final service from Nottingham Victoria to Netherfield, Gedling, Daybrook and Basford North. One passenger, a first-class season ticket holder since 1932, told a reporter: "It's disgusting. These local trains are better than the bus any time." Chalked on the engine was the Latin phrase *Fidelis ad Mortem* (Faithful unto Death).

'Chucking' at Trent Bridge

TRENT Bridge was the scene of a 'throwing' controversy when Notts played the South Africans in late May.

The tourists' opening bowler Geoff Griffin was no-balled eight times for an incorrect bowling action. The match was drawn.

Griffin was not in the team which returned to Trent Bridge in July for the 3rd Test. England won by eight wickets, Fred Trueman taking nine wickets in the match.

Two premieres as film fever grips city

NOTTINGHAM saw two movie premieres in 1960. *Saturday Night and Sunday Morning* and the D.H. Lawrence classic *Sons and Lovers* were both partly shot in the area.

The adaptation of Alan Sillitoe's best-seller was directed by Karel Reisz.

It starred Albert Finney as Raleigh worker Arthur Seaton, Shirley Ann Field as his girlfriend and Rachel Roberts as his married lover.

"A brilliantly unpretentious slice of realism," said the *Evening Post* critic.

The director attended the provincial premiere at the ABC in November. So did Field, described by promoters as "the starlet whom casting directors wouldn't let through the cheesecake barrier."

Nottingham and the West End shared the UK premiere of Jack Cardiff's movie *Sons and Lovers*.

The film starred the American actor Dean Stockwell as Paul Morel and British performers Trevor Howard and Wendy Hiller as his parents.

Mary Ure and Heather Sears played the two women in Paul's life — but there was no appearance for Joan Collins, who was named in the cast in 1959.

Produced by Jerry Wald for 20th Century Fox, the project included location work in Eastwood. Some £2-a-day extras recalled Lawrence, who was born in the village in 1885.

● Penguin won the 'Lady Chatterley Trial' at the Old Bailey in 1960, allowing publication of the unexpurgated version of Lawrence's novel.

ABOVE:
Shirley Ann Field and Albert Finney in the film adaptation of Nottingham novelist Alan Sillitoe's *Saturday Night and Sunday Morning*

RIGHT:
Mary Ure in the screen version of D.H. Lawrence's novel *Sons and Lovers*

CAPTAIN Athelstan Popkess retired in 1960 after 30 years as chief constable of Nottingham.

In the 1930s he introduced two-way radio linking control centres and patrol cars (Nottingham police were the first in Britain to use the system successfully). His other innovations included a forensic laboratory.

In the 1940s he led Nottingham's efficient civil defence organisation.

Popkess was succeeded by Thomas Moore, former acting chief of the county constabulary.

In 1960, the city force took delivery of a consignment of motor scooters, for use by officers patrolling outlying housing estates.

▢ ▢ ▢

RALEIGH and their main competitors, the British Cycle Corporation, merged under the ownership of BCC's parent company Tube Investments.

Later in 1960, Sir Harold Bowden died. He was the son of Raleigh's founder Sir Frank Bowden and had been chairman until 1955.

▢ ▢ ▢

NOTTS County, second in the Fourth Division, were promoted back to the Third.

Robeson's plea for racial justice

FINAL SHOW:
Paul Robeson

PAUL Robeson returned to Nottingham on April 26 for a concert at the Albert Hall.

The American actor-singer said: "I am very conscious of my colour and will be until it is accepted in every part of the world that black people are as good as white. My art can help my people."

In 1960, black immigrants reported problems obtaining mortgages in Nottingham. Some complained that interest rates they were offered were higher than those offered to white English citizens.

The *Post* quoted building societies as being more interested in offering loans on newer properties than on "the type usually required by coloured people."

Robeson's concert was the last in a series in Nottingham that began in the 1930s. He died in 1976.

Threat to Bobby Kennedy: Woman committed ➡ Page 99

Cliff at the Odeon

CLIFF Richard, *pictured right*, and The Shadows headlined a show at the Odeon on April 13, 1961.

Three years earlier he had made his first live appearance under the name Cliff Richard at the Regal in Ripley.

Harry Greatorex, who ran the Regal, spotted Cliff's group at a Soho club and invited them to Ripley, but under a different name — saying Harry Webb and The Drifters "wasn't rock 'n' roll enough". They came up with Cliff Richards (the 's' was soon dropped).

At the Regal they played for 40 minutes, covering numerous hits of the time including *Hound Dog* and *Heartbreak Hotel*.

The four were paid £15 and slept on the seats in the ballroom afterwards before jumping back on a train to London.

● Cliff bought a 78cc Raleigh Roma in 1961, but the Nottingham bicycle firm's move into the scooter market was to fail.

CID officers from city and county police forces joined the joint Special Inquiry Squad — a forerunner of the regional crime squad. It became known as 'the Ghost Squad'.

THE council approved the winding down of Nottingham's trolley-bus system in 1961. The first service to be converted to motor bus operation, the following year, was the 45 route between Trent Bridge and Wollaton Park.

VALENCIA came to the City Ground and thrashed Forest in the Inter-City Fairs Cup. Billy Cobb scored for the Reds with a dipping free kick.

DEBENHAMS, owners of Griffin & Spalding in Long Row, acquired the neighbouring Mikado Cafe for £200,000. The building was soon demolished.

ODEON STAR: Cliff Richard, the former Harry Webb

'Sweeney' in chair puzzle

FLYING Squad detectives were involved in the hunt for a gang of thieves who threatened to kill a city postmistress before escaping with £1,000. The manhunt spread to London after the raid at Bobbers Mill.

Robbers entered the post office, locking the door and pulling down the blind. The postmistress was struck from behind and she and her husband were tied up.

When the woman screamed, a hand was clamped over her mouth and she was told to be quiet or she would be killed.

The third member of the gang grabbed about £1,000 before they were disturbed by a customer and escaped.

Two days later, a Nottingham landlord was beaten unconscious by two men who were later seen boarding a London-bound express.

From their lodgings, police took away a chair with three legs. In the garden outside the Bobbers Mill post office, police had found a chair leg which had been used as a cosh.

Police believed the landlord was beaten as a warning to keep quiet if he knew anything about the post office raid.

Snow misery for Easter trippers

IT was one of the most miserable Easters on record, ending with a heavy snowfall.

Rain and cold kept people at home, leaving bus companies with few people for their bank holiday day trips.

The director of parks in Nottingham said the fall of snow would be "disastrous" for spring flower displays.

For about 1,000 Easter holidaymakers, the weekend got off to a disappointing start — they were stranded in the Weekday Cross tunnel when a coupling on their Skegness-bound train broke.

The incident caused bedlam at Victoria Station as bored youngsters leapt from the stranded train and started running up and down the platform.

SOME of the world's leading golfers were in Nottingham contesting the £3,600 Cox Moore tournament played at Wollaton and Beeston Fields.

New Zealander Bob Charles, South Africans Bobby Locke and Harold Henning, and Ryder Cup star Peter Allis were among the field.

But £1,000 winner's prize went to little known Irishman Eddie Jones, playing in his first major PGA event. Allis was second, two shots behind.

ALBERT Finney, star of city author Alan Sillitoe's *Saturday Night and Sunday Morning*, returned to Nottingham to appear at the Theatre Royal in the new John Osborne play *Luther*.

Swift battles on

NOTTINGHAM boxer Wally Swift failed in his bid to regain the British welterweight title after a 15-round battle with Empire champ Brian Curvis.

Curvis had taken the title from 24-year-old Swift the previous November, at the Ice Stadium. On this occasion, at the same venue, he claimed a decisive points victory.

Swift, knocked down several times, ended with severe cuts to his face but received the acclaim of the crowd.

POINTS DECISION: Swift (left) throws a left at Curvis

Beatlemania: 'Fab Four' visit city three times ➡ Page 100

FAITH IN HIS FANS: Adam Faith signs autographs at the Theatre Royal stage door in 1962. The former £4 10s-a-week messenger boy was then earning £80,000 a year

Playwright Hall weds Jill Bennett

NOTTINGHAM playwright Willis Hall married actress Jill Bennett following his divorce from his first wife Kathleen.

Born in Leeds, the writer settled in Nottingham in 1953. A year later his first radio play, *The Nightingale*, was produced by the BBC.

He became a regular writer for TV and radio, going to endless lengths to ensure authenticity.

He once trained for three days with Forest to get the atmosphere right for a play about a disabled footballer, and spent three nights in Hyson Green police station before writing *The Claverdon Road Job*, a play about police and teddy boys.

But it was the production at the Playhouse in 1958 of what later became titled *The Long And The Short And The Tall* that made his name.

The play — about a patrol of British soldiers in the jungle — was an immense success, winning the London *Evening Standard* best drama award.

Willis Hall sold the film rights for £30,000 and it was made with Laurence Harvey taking the lead role.

In 1961 he collaborated with his old friend Keith Waterhouse to produce *Celebration*, which had its premiere at Nottingham Playhouse.

They also teamed up for the stage and film versions of Waterhouse's novel *Billy Liar* and the hit films *Whistle Down The Wind* and *A Kind Of Loving*.

THE curse of 'the Scottish play' struck a Nottingham Playhouse touring production when one of the actors suffered a sprained ankle.

Colin George, associate director, made a dash to Mansfield and arrived five minutes before curtain for the first of eight performances seen by 4,000 local schoolchildren.

THE Midlands most revolutionary school, featuring a honeycomb design, was earmarked for a site in Wilford.

Classrooms at Wilford Meadows School were designed with six corners to enable teaching in small groups to be conducted.

EX-England footballer Frank Forman, of West Bridgford, who had died aged 86 the previous December, left more than £35,000 in his will.

A member of Forest's FA Cup winning team of 1898, he left his medals and memorabilia to his son and grandson.

NOTTS County celebrated their centenary on May 2 with a match against an England XI including Alan Hodgkinson, Jimmy Bloomfield and Alan Peacock. The guests won 3-1, with Tony Hateley scoring the County goal.

RFK threats: Woman held

THE US government dropped charges against a former Nottingham woman accused of sending threatening letters to Attorney-General Robert F. Kennedy and Senator Edmund Muskie.

The 46-year-old had been committed to hospital, so the Baltimore district judge was ordered to drop the charges.

The woman had emigrated in 1949 with her husband. She was arrested by the FBI who alleged she had sent letters threatening to kill Kennedy and Muskie.

Her former neighbours in Forest Fields said they were amazed by the news.

"The last person you would have thought would have done anything wrong," said one.

Another described her as "charming, petite and dainty, ... she wouldn't say boo to a goose."

ARTHUR SPOONER:
The distinguished Nottingham artist died in 1962, aged 89

Our 'Enery too good for Erskine

HENRY Cooper battered old rival Joe Erskine to defeat in their British and Empire title fight at the Nottingham Ice Stadium.

Erskine had looked the winner until a cut eye forced the referee to step in.

It was the fifth time they had met, Cooper winning the last three bouts, but Erskine's manager Benny Jacobs said: "It was only bad luck that beat Joe this time. I am convinced he has the beating of Cooper."

Pearsons store founder dies at 91

TOM Pearson, founder of Pearson Bros of Long Row, died aged 91.

He had built a small ironmongery and silverware business into one of the city's biggest shops, and the last of the major family owned stores in the city centre.

Despite his years, he was still looking to the future, having made the first donation towards the cost of modernising the store.

The funeral service was held at the Albert Hall, which Mr Pearson had helped to buy for the Wesleyans in 1902.

Motorists beware ... traffic wardens on patrol ➡ Page 101

'Pretty Windows' mystery

POLICE were baffled by one of the most notorious of Nottingham's post-war crimes — the so-called 'Pretty Windows Murder'.

The victim was the licensee of the Fox and Grapes pub at Sneinton Wholesale Market. The hostelry had decorative window frames, hence the nickname.

After closing time on the night of September 7, the licensee took his dog for a walk.

In the early hours of the following morning, his body was found on the pavement outside the pub's side door.

He has been stabbed several times in what detectives described as a frenzied attack.

Rex Fletcher, head of Nottingham CID, personally took charge of the case, and Scotland Yard officers were also called in.

A huge operation was mounted, and later a knife was found which officers were able to link to the crime.

There were to be several confessions to the crime — but only from cranks and time-wasters.

REAR-engined buses were introduced to the Nottingham fleet.

The 18 Daimler Fleetlines were followed in 1964 by a batch of Leyland Atlanteans.

NOTTS County's powerful strike force of Tony Hateley and Jeff Astle jointly scored 30 goals in the last 25 games of the 1962-3 season.

But the Magpies could finish only seventh in the Third Division. In the close-season, Hateley was sold to Aston Villa.

THE Nottingham *Evening News* was merged with the *Evening Post*, whose publishers had acquired the newspaper ten years earlier.

FAB FOUR: Paul, Ringo, George and John

Beatlemania ... eventually

THE Beatles played their first show in Nottingham on March 7 — but even though they were at No.1 with *Please, Please Me*, there was no sign of Beatlemania.

The Fab Four unloaded their own equipment from the back of an old van in preparation for a gig in the Elizabeth Rooms, above the Co-op in Parliament Street.

In spite of the presence of Gerry and the Pacemakers, Billy J. Kramer and a young Cilla Black, it was only half full.

The Beatles returned to share top-billing with Roy Orbison at the Odeon. Again they topped the charts, this time with *From Me To You*.

But it was their third appearance, again at the Odeon, that is best remembered.

With the nation in the grip of Beatlemania, all local police leave was cancelled and special constables and a fleet of ambulances were drafted in for the show on December 12, 1963.

Old Market Square and Angel Row were packed with tearful, fans who hadn't got a ticket.

Meanwhile, John, Paul, George and Ringo were holed up in Central Police Station.

They made it to the Odeon thanks to a series of decoy vans — and brought the house down.

Their final visit to the Odeon was on November 5, 1964, after which they simply became too big for any Nottingham venue to hold.

The young Stones hit town, too

THE Rolling Stones first came to Nottingham to support the Everly Brothers at the Odeon on October 23, 1963.

Others on the bill included Bo Diddley, Mickie Most, Julie Grant and Little Richard.

The *Evening Post and News* passed over the Stones — complaining that they were "almost inaudible behind the barrage of electronic sound."

IN TOWN: Mick Jagger

Snowdon opens new Playhouse

THE new Nottingham Playhouse was opened by Lord Snowdon on December 11 and VIPs were treated to excerpts from *Coriolanus*, which opened the following night.

Architect Peter Moro's project at Wellington Circus had been beset with financial and political problems — but these were soon forgotten as the Playhouse became, during the mid-Sixties, the most admired provincial theatre in England.

Internationally-renowned director Sir Tyrone Guthrie staged *Coriolanus* in Victorian dress. The cast included the theatre's joint artistic director John Neville, in the title role, Dorothy Reynolds, Leo McKern and the young Ian McKellen.

DIRECTOR: John Neville

Reviews in the national press were mixed — but visiting critics praised the new theatre, which replaced the old Playhouse in Goldsmith Street.

There were headlines, too, about what happened after the gala show.

Civic dignitaries and guests went from the theatre to the Council House for a civic buffet.

When the actors and backstage team arrived, hungry and thirsty, food was in short supply.

There were arguments and even a scrap between a member of the company and a council official.

The opening season also included Oscar Wilde's *The Importance of Being Earnest* (with Neville, Michael Crawford and Angela Baddeley).

Pollock brothers crush England at Trent Bridge ➡ Page 102

Ella, Arthur ... and 'Sing Little Birdie'

ELLA Fitzgerald delighted audiences at the Odeon with some of her favourite songs, like *Goody Goody, Sunny Side Of The Street, Miss Otis Regrets* and *Lady Is A Tramp.*

Also in the city, at the Theatre Royal, was comedian Arthur Askey.

Other performers in 1964 included Eurovision runners-up Pearl Carr and Teddy Johnson. Their song *Sing Little Birdie* took second spot in 1959.

THE ENTERTAINERS: Fitzgerald and Askey

'Whitehall snoopers' take to the streets

ON January 20, rush hour drivers saw something new. At 8am, the city's first shift of traffic wardens marched from Central police station to their beats.

The Road Traffic and Road Improvement Act 1960 empowered towns to recruit wardens.

Former chief constable Captain Athelstan Popkess was an early believer in wardens, and his successor presided over the creation of a new department in the autumn of 1963.

In the new year, 42 men reported for a two-week training course. There should have been 43, but one recruit failed to show.

Nottingham newspapers reported an immediate effect on the city's streets. Kerbside congestion was reduced as drivers observed restrictions and headed for car parks.

However, there were early signs of the wardens' unpopularity. Newspaper letters pages referred to them as 'Whitehall Snoopers' and 'The Yellow Peril'.

Throughout the Sixties, more wardens were taken on. By the end of the decade there were 74, of whom eight were in supervisory roles.

'YELLOW PERIL': Traffic wardens on parade in Nottingham

Raleigh strike: 300 return to work

THE longest post-war strike in Nottingham ended when 300 toolmakers at Raleigh returned to work after a dispute over redundancies.

The strikers were hoping to save the jobs of 25 colleagues made redundant six months earlier.

They had demanded that Raleigh institute a job-share scheme to keep the men in work, but management declared the idea impractical. The final blow for the strikers came when AEU members in other parts of the country voted against calls to have Raleigh work 'blacked'.

More than 2,000 workers had been laid off because of the dispute.

When the strike ended, the union levied members to pay the redundant workers £5 per week until they found jobs.

NOTTINGHAM got its first taste of late night shopping and hundreds hunted for bargains.

Shoppers made trips from as far away as Derby to sample the experience and all the major store managers predicted a future for the innovation.

□ □ □

THE finishing touches were put on a new motel on the West Bridgford side of the Trent.

Built on the site of the old Plaza cinema, the building eventually became the Bridgford Hotel before being turned into Rushcliffe Civic Centre.

□ □ □

FOREST offered £27,500 for Mansfield's prolific goalscorer Ken Wagstaff.

It would have been a record for the Stags, but the club held out for another £10,000, and Wagstaff eventually signed for Hull City.

□ □ □

LABOUR relations in the coal industry continued to be tense as local NCB chief Wilfred Miron attacked miners for persistent absenteeism.

Notts NUM secretary Albert Martin blamed the absenteeism on the high rate of accidents and an increase in cases of pneumoconiosis.

□ □ □

HEADTEACHERS, police and politicians met to discuss the growing problem of under-14 crime in Nottingham. Plans were announced to establish an after-school playcentre in a bid to combat the rising tide of burglaries by children as young as 11.

□ □ □

NOTTINGHAM had never seen a wedding quite like it. St Barnabas Cathedral was the setting as ex-Miss Poland Alicia Barbara Soltysik married Russian aristocrat Marc Stanislaw de Costres, with Sultan Hamid Kaykavousi among the guests.

□ □ □

INVESTMENT in the *Evening Post* allowed a 24-page broadsheet paper to be produced in Nottingham for the first time. The first 24-page paper was sold on November 6.

Pilots and villagers survive mid-air collision  Page 103

THE introduction of a new one-way system in the centre of Nottingham even had the police heading in the wrong direction.

New, continental-type letterless one-way signs went up in George Street and, according to the *Evening Post*, motorists happily ignored them.

Even a police car was seen to drive in the wrong direction, followed by a lorry whose driver said: "What's good enough for the police is good enough for us."

The problem was the positioning of the signs which made them almost impossible to see. And some motorists, seeing a red disc with a broad horizontal stripe, did not know what it meant.

RALEIGH scored a huge success with its small-wheeled RSW 16.

Alex Moulton, pioneer of the small-wheeled bike, approached Raleigh in 1958. A design was prepared, but the plan was shelved and Moulton went ahead independently.

His bikes sold so well that Raleigh responded with chief designer Alan Oakley's RSW.

Motor Cycle and Cycle Trader wrote: "Not since the last century has cycle design been so expanded at one step."

TORIES failed in an attempt to force the Labour-controlled education committee to rethink its plans for comprehensive secondary education in Notts.

RACING at Colwick Park was reprieved when the city council offered to guarantee meetings for two years.

SCORES of weapons were handed in during a Notts police amnesty, including a machine gun.

VALENCIA were at City Ground for a friendly to mark Forest's centenary. Chris Crowe scored from the spot in the 1-1 draw.

JOHN Neville, director of Nottingham Playhouse, was in London to collect his OBE from the Queen.

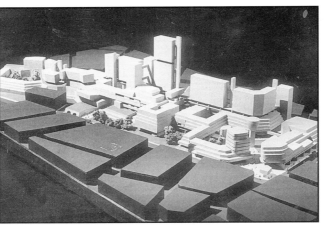

VIC VISION: An early model for the Victoria Centre

Shopping malls: Plans take shape

THE council was criticised for plans to redevelop doomed Victoria Station.

Architecture East Midlands wrote: "The 350ft high residential block will dominate the city.

"The balance of the central area will be changed. There is no way in which sufficient disgust can be expressed."

Meanwhile the council approved a £10m redevelopment of the Broad Marsh, creating 130 shops on land once occupied by the city's worst slums.

Also planned for the site were a new bus station, two car parks, offices and a restaurant, pubs and three tower blocks containing 360 flats.

Families flee as fire nears diesel tank

FAMILIES in nightclothes fled their homes when fire caused at least £50,000 worth of damage to a three-storey bleaching factory in Alfred Street South.

More than 50 firemen manning 11 pumps, backed up by auxiliary crews, fought a desperate battle at the premises of Wrights and Dobson to keep flames from a 1,200 gallon diesel tank.

"If the fire had got to the oil, the whole street would have gone up," said a housewife who was among families evacuated to a public house.

"The firemen deserve a medal. The heat was amazing."

One firemen was rescued when his breathing apparatus broke down in thick smoke.

Occupants of four houses, including an 18-month-old baby, were taken to the Alfred the Great pub for safety, while firemen used the inn for supplies of thirst-quenching lemonade.

Mr M. A. Phillips, managing director of Wrights and Dobson, said the damage could run as high as £100,000.

SOFT CENTRE: Ex-world heavyweight champion Rocky Marciano presented the Lord Mayor, Alderman Bill Derbyshire, with £50 worth of toys for needy children. Marciano also met Bingham boxer John Pritchett, just a few days before his British title fight with Nottingham's Wally Swift, which Pritchett won.

Pollock brothers crush England at Trent Bridge

THE 2nd Test at Trent Bridge was turned into a family showcase for the talents of Graeme and Peter Pollock. The brothers dominated throughout as South Africa beat England by 94 runs in four days.

Graeme, the 21-year-old left-hander, scored a first-innings 125 in just two hours and 20 minutes. He began steadily, then in a 70-minute period he flayed the England bowlers for 92 out of 102.

Seasoned commentators reckoned it was the finest Test innings seen at Trent Bridge since the war. In his second knock, Pollock scored another 59.

Elder brother Peter, opening the tourists' attack, took five wickets in each innings for an analysis of ten for 87 in 48 overs.

● Leicestershire's Clive Inman clubbed his way into the record books at Trent Bridge. His unbeaten 57 included 51 in eight minutes as Notts offered cheap runs in the hope of an early declaration.

Victoria Station axed in Beeching rail purge  Page 104

Village and airmen survive jets' collision

TWO RAF Provost jet trainers collided over Woodborough on May 26. Amazingly, none of the three airmen involved was injured. "There must be a lot of guardian angels in Woodborough," the vicar said.

The aircraft, from RAF Syerston, were being used for formation training.

A ten-year-old witness said: "One plane's wing seemed to touch the other plane and caught fire. It came spinning down with smoke coming from it."

Wreckage narrowly missed children who were on their way to school. Pieces from the planes were scattered in roads and gardens.

Meanwhile two instructors and a student pilot were parachuting to the ground — one of them landing in the village's main street. All three were taken to hospital, checked over and found to be unhurt.

NEAR MISS: Calverton villagers and the wreckage of a Provost trainer

CID men grab armed suspect

TWO young Nottingham CID officers struggled with a desperate man who was armed with an eight-inch knife.

Detective constables Melvin Musson and Trevor Rawding went to a house in The Meadows to trace a man suspected of armed robbery.

The powerfully built man resisted arrest and produced the knife. He lunged at DC Musson, who deflected the blow. Both officers were involved in the struggle until the knife fell to the ground and the suspect was overcome.

They received the Queen's Commendation for brave conduct, presented at a ceremony at the Council House by the Lord Lieutenant of Notts, Major-General Sir Robert Laycock.

● In 1961 Sir Robert opened the city's first boys' probation hostel, in Woodborough Road.

Trent House, fitted out for £42,000, was designed to accommodate 21 youths, aged 17 to 19.

4-2 to England, but touts also win

ON July 30, hundreds of Nottingham fans made the trip to Wembley to see Sir Alf Ramsey's England team defeat West Germany 4-2 in the World Cup Final.

Some returned admitting they had paid London touts £4 15s [£4.75] for tickets to the match. Their face value was 15 shillings [75p].

As the nation was gripped by World Cup fever, local shops and businesses reported a very quiet Saturday afternoon.

Trent body: Jumper clue

THE discovery of a dismembered body in the Trent at Burton Joyce sparked a nationwide manhunt.

Clothed only in a grey jumper, and minus the legs, the decomposed body had been in the water for weeks.

Police first had to establish the identity of the young woman and after the *Post* published a picture of her jumper, a caller recognised it as belonging to 19-year-old Glaswegian girl.

A phone call to the newspaper sent police to an address where identification was confirmed. She had come to Nottingham months earlier, sharing a flat with a friend.

A hundred officers from across the region joined the inquiry and quickly began to piece together vital clues.

At one point they enlisted the help of dustmen as they searched for other items of the girl's clothing.

A week later, Notts police predicted a successful conclusion to the murder hunt. Shortly afterwards a salesman was arrested in Anglesey and confessed to the crime.

Farewell to the trolley-buses

A LITTLE bit of old Nottingham disappeared as the last trolley-bus wound its way from Queen Street to Nottingham Road.

Watching it go was 63-year-old Bernard Parker who had put up the first trolley-bus wires 39 years earlier.

"As it pulled away, a little bit of me died," he said.

The driver for the last run was Albert Parish, the conductor Fred Cooper.

Sixty members of Nottingham Trolley-Bus Group marked the occasion by hiring number 510 to follow the last service.

LAST STOP: VIPs on the final service

By the time it reached Valley Road, 20 cars were following behind. At the Parliament Street depot, a chorus of *Auld Lang's Syne* was struck up.

ROD Stewart appeared at the the Boat Club in 1966 with blues-based band Shotgun Express, featuring Peter Green and Mick Fleetwood.

Stewart returned in 1968 with the Jeff Beck Group, before joining The Faces then launching his solo career.

□□□

THE village of Bunny had some apt but surprising visitors — Bunny Girls from the Playboy Club.

There at the invitation of a local car dealer, the scantily clad beauties shook hands with the vicar, the Rev H. Evans.

□□□

JUST down the road, soap queen Pat Phoenix — *Coronation Street*'s Elsie Tanner — arrived at Radcliffe-on-Trent in a chauffeur-driven Rolls-Royce. She opened the new cattery at the village's RSPCA animal shelter.

□□□

THE West Indies won the 3rd Test at Trent Bridge by 139 runs, thanks mainly to Basil Butcher's undefeated second-innings 209, supported by 94 from captain Gary Sobers.

□□□

CITY MPs Michael English and George Perry supported a Labour motion condemning US bombing of North Vietnam.

□□□

SAINSBURY'S were advertising for store assistants in Nottingham, with a starting wage of £10 17s [£10.85].

Crowds mob Burtons at Nottingham cinema ➡ Page 105

FOREST, managed by Johnny Carey, narrowly failed to win the two biggest prizes in English football.

They were runners-up to Manchester United in the First Division, and reached the semi-final of the FA Cup, losing 2-1 at Hillsborough to Spurs.

The 1967-8 season included an autumn outing in the Inter-City Fairs Cup. Joe Baker scored three of Forest's five aggregate goals in the defeat of Eintracht Frankfurt, but the Reds lost the tie against FC Zurich.

The first leg at the City Ground was marred by disgraceful scenes. Police moved into the Trent End after the visiting keeper was pelted with coins.

● Carey and Notts boss Billy Gray backed moves to abolish the offside law for free kicks. Gray went further by calling for no offsides between the 18-yard line and goal line.

NOTTS motorists got their first warnings about the dangers of drinking and driving as transport minister Barbara Castle introduced the breath test.

"You can call me a Hitler for restricting the freedom of the British drinking driver, and some enraged licensees have done just that, but the overwhelming weight of the evidence supports what we have done."

COIN boxes in phone kiosks across the city were raided in a two-day crime blitz. The Post Office said the villains were well organised and had "a lot of nerve".

THE *Evening Post* became the first newspaper in the United Kingdom to install a general purpose computer for setting editorial text and advertisements.

THE possibility of a new concert hall receded when city councillors were told there was no space within the Victoria Station redevelopment scheme.

Hollywood star's pay cut

HOLLYWOOD star Robert Ryan took on two huge parts at Nottingham Playhouse at the start of the 1967-8 season.

He played the title role in *Othello*, with the theatre's artistic director John Neville as Iago, then James Tyrone in Eugene O'Neill's *A Long Day's Journey into Night*.

Ryan commanded £70,000 fees for films like *King of Kings* and *The Battle of the Bulge*. At the Playhouse, he earned the going rate of about £50 a week.

As the Moor, Ryan failed to make an impression on the critics — but the reviewers were impressed with his performance as the formidable patriarch Tyrone.

Earlier in the year, the 6ft 3in Chicagoan saw the Playhouse production of Arthur Miller's *Death of a Salesman*, in which Neville gave one of his finest performances in the central role of Willy Loman (Michael Rudman's production also featured Ronald Magill, Gillian Martell and John Shrapnel).

Ryan was impressed with their American accents — with the exception of one word: "Americans never say 'been'," he commented. "They always say 'bin'."

£50 A WEEK: Robert Ryan arrives in Nottingham

Beeching axe falls on Victoria Station

THE last passenger train pulled out of Victoria Station on the evening of Saturday, September 2, driven by George Chambers of Bilborough.

The old Great Central main line from to Marylebone had failed to survive Dr Beeching's rationalisation.

There was no fanfare of trumpets, or crowds of wellwishers. Only the resident pigeons and a few members of the press and public saw the grand station's final departure.

It was a far cry from Victoria's glory days. When it opened in 1900, it was the finest railway building in the East Midlands and among the grandest outside London.

In its heyday, specials like the Master Cutler, East Midlander and the South Yorkshireman all passed through Victoria.

Seeing off that last service to Rugby was station master Bill Dobbs, who was also bringing the curtain down on his 50-year career.

The last permanent member of staff was Wilfred Cook, who was puzzled by the decision to leave the Midland as the city's only major station.

Freight services continued to pass through, but soon the demolition teams moved in. The site is now the Victoria Centre.

ALL ABOARD: The final passenger train leaves Victoria Station

Jimi Hendrix in 'thunderous' form

GUITAR legend Jimi Hendrix, *left*, visited three times in 1967.

On January 1 he played at The Beachcomber, and in August he was at a Sherwood Rooms blues gig with Long John Baldry.

On December 3 he appeared with The Move, Pink Floyd and The Nice.

A *Post* review read: "Only the entire resources of East Midlands Electricity can have averted a power-cut when the Jimi Hendrix Experience... shook the Royal with thunderous electronic reverberations."

The Black Boy, hotel to the stars, is doomed ➡ Page 106

Rampant Sobers

HEAVY HITTER:
Gary Sobers

NOTTS skipper Gary Sobers, the great West Indian all-rounder, made cricket history by becoming the first batsman to hit six sixes in a six-ball over.

It happened at Swansea, where the unlucky bowler was Glamorgan's Malcolm Nash.

Notts' first innings was already past 300, thanks mainly to 140 from opener Brian Bolus.

Sobers drove and hooked the maximum off Nash's over.

His final blow sent the ball into a nearby street, and it was not recovered until next day. Notts won by 166 runs.

Grateful Plant

HEAVY ROCKER:
Robert Plant

HEAVY rock pioneers Led Zeppelin had a special relationship with the Nottingham Boat Club.

It was as Robert Plant and the Band of Joy that the band first appeared at the Trentside venue, on February 9, 1968.

Soon they would blossom as the Led Zeppelin but Plant didn't forget 'The Boat'.

In a Radio 1 interview he thanked the venue for helping them along the road to cult-dom. Despite their stadium-filling appeal, Led Zeppelin would play a free concert there, with a law-busting 400 people squeezing in.

First woman Lord Mayor

ALDERMAN Mrs Joan Case became the first woman Lord Mayor of Nottingham.

For Lady Mayoress she chose her student daughter Pamela who, at the age of 21, was believed to be the youngest to hold that office.

Mrs Case later became the first woman to have held the offices of Lord Mayor and chairman of the county council.

❏❏❏

THE Queen spent more than an hour at Raleigh chatting with directors and staff to acknowledge the cycle maker's export success.

She was driven around the factory in an open Land Rover — while outside, where 15,000 children had gathered along the route to the Council House, the heavens opened.

❏❏❏

TEN performing polar bears, worth £15,000, arrived at their new home — in Hucknall. They were the first arrivals at the 17-acre Sherwood Zoo which cost £30,000 to set up.

Crowds mob the Burtons

SUPERSTARS: Taylor and Burton in their 1968 film *Boom!*

A CROWD of 1,000 mobbed Richard Burton and Elizabeth Taylor when they visited Nottingham for the East Midlands premiere of their film *Dr Faustus*.

The most glamorous couple in showbiz were welcomed to the Moulin Rouge by the cinema's owner, Bill Cook, and were introduced to the Lord Mayor and Lady Mayoress of Nottingham, Coun and Mrs Fred Roberts.

Burton was presented with a rugby ball and a bottle of ale by five-year-old Richard Oxley.

Taylor was given a bouquet by nine-year-old Elizabeth Jones.

After the screening, the Burtons made a brief appearance on the cinema stage. Then it took police several minutes to clear the crowds to allow the couple to leave in their Rolls-Royce.

● They were accompanied by John Neville — embroiled in a row over his departure from the Playhouse following a dispute over Arts Council funding.

At first the Playhouse board tried to persuade him to stay, but his resignation was accepted after four months. Neville then withdrew his resignation, but the board stuck to their decision.

Forest at Meadow Lane after blaze

FIRE tore through the main stand at City Ground during Forest's match against Leeds. The cause was a mystery, although an electrical fault was suspected.

Fans evacuated the stand while the first half was being played out. The match was abandoned at half-time, the score 1-1.

Autumn home matches were played at Meadow Lane, but play resumed at City Ground in November.

POP idol Adam Faith returned to Nottingham to team up with Dame Sybil Thorndike, in Emlyn Williams' thriller *Night Must Fall* at the Theatre Royal.

Post theatre critic Emrys Bryson described the chart-topper's performance as "very creditable" while commending 85-year-old Dame Sybil for not acting down to the newcomer.

❏❏❏

NOTTINGHAM Corporation took over West Bridgford UDC Transport, with its 73 employees and 28 AEC buses.

❏❏❏

EASTWOOD-born Jeff Astle, a former Notts County player, scored the winner in the FA Cup final as West Bromwich Albion defeated Everton 1-0 after extra time.

❏❏❏

A HOUSE in Mapperley Road, which had been designed by Nottingham's celebrated architect Watson Fothergill, was demolished. Fothergill built the turreted house in 1872 and died there in 1928. It had been turned into flats but the site was was scheduled for redevelopment.

❏❏❏

A SIX-sided church costing £38,000 was built on the Killisick estate in Arnold.

❏❏❏

A NOTTS mother, Emma Smith of Ravenshed, set a world record of 100 days for being buried alive in a coffin.

Paul Smith starts his business in 12ft room ➡ Page 107

THE balding headmaster of a city school paid for ten long-haired pupils to have their hair cut.

Ex-RAF officer J. I. Williams told parents of pupils at Bilborough Grammar that he had paid out of school funds. He would be grateful if they repaid, but added: "I will not press for the money."

Two boys agreed to have their hair cut after the head threatened expulsion. But what was short enough for them was not short enough for Mr Williams, who took them back to the barber with strict instructions on style and cut.

Mr Williams denied he was jealous of the boys' "lush heads of hair", saying the school had high standards. "The irony of it is that I am the only bald person in school."

Some pupils hit back, distributing a leaflet accusing Mr Williams of being an "extreme dictator". But the head was defended by his sixth formers.

❏ ❏ ❏

NOTTS miners travelled to the London headquarters of the NCB to join comrades from around the country in a demonstration calling for a shorter week for surface workers.

They arrived to find NCB chairman Lord Robens had left for a visit to Derbyshire, but an NUM spokesman said: "It is unfortunate ... but there will be plenty of officials who can tell him about it when he returns."

❏ ❏ ❏

A SMALL fortune in rare stamps went missing when a city dealer left his briefcase in a bank.

Roy Gilbert, who had only just taken over the Midland Stamp Centre in Mansfield Road, raced back to the bank, but the briefcase, containing £1,200 uninsured British commemorative stamps, was gone.

❏ ❏ ❏

NOTTS cricketer Deryck Murray, the popular West Indies wicketkeeper, announced his retirement from the first class game so he could take a three-year course in industrial economics at Nottingham University.

Long-shot Whetton wins European gold

NOTTS athlete John Whetton shocked the cream of European 1,500m runners by winning the European title in Athens.

The Sutton Harrier had only just scraped into the British team and was not given a chance. But he ran a brilliant tactical race, and his career-best time broke the championship record.

After twice reaching the Olympic finals, in Tokyo and Mexico, Whetton had suggested Athens would be his last championship, but on the strength of his success, he continued until after the following year's Commonwealth Games.

A college lecturer, he pioneered the Robin Hood marathon in 1981 and was director of the race for many years.

VICTOR: John Whetton, *left*, in a local event

Black Boy: Farewell to the stars' hotel

THE Black Boy Hotel in Long Row closed on March 8 prior to the most controversial demolition in post-war Nottingham.

King Charles II had stayed on the site when it was a coaching house.

The imposing modern structure was created by Watson Fothergill in the 19th Century, and refurbished in 1928. It had 78 bedrooms.

It was the first choice hotel for celebrities visiting Nottingham. Guests included film stars Margaret Lockwood, Laurence Olivier and Gregory Peck, and stage performers Gracie Fields and George Formby. Touring Australian cricketers also stayed at the Black Boy.

However it was open to non-residents, and its public bars were popular with Nottingham drinkers. One was for gentlemen only, and another was devoted to cocktails.

The site was acquired in 1963 by Littlewoods, who later secured permission to demolish and build a store.

A 1969 menu in the Grill Room offered a starter of whitebait, a main course of Tournedos Colbert at 18s 6d [about 92p] and a dessert of zabaglione.

The building was levelled in 1970.

LAMENTED: A fire alert at the Black Boy Hotel in 1969

Anti-apartheid protesters make their mark

THE visit to Nottingham of the South African ambassador caused controversy.

The envoy's scheduled appearance at the Monday Club meeting in the Albert Hotel had to be cancelled when a crowd of about 100 anti-apartheid demonstrators arrived chanting slogans and waving placards.

Some of them got into the building, and there were clashes with police. Three people denied assaulting police officers.

£20-a-night Paper Lace are discovered in pub  Page 108

Raleigh launches the Chopper

RIGHT: Raleigh's chief bicycle designer Alan Oakley with the Nottingham-built bike that was to dominate the youth market in the Seventies, the Chopper.

The launch came five years after the company's success with the RSW. The revolutionary Chopper had the looks of a dirt-track motorbike, with high-rise handlebars and an extended saddle with lumbar support.

Death of Dame Laura

DAME Laura Knight, the Long Eaton-born artist, died aged 93.

Laura Johnson had been born into poverty. The single-parent family moved to Hyson Green where her mother earned a meagre income with painting classes.

Orphaned at 15, Laura trained with Nottingham Art School. She was still in her teens when she met her future husband, fellow painter Harold Knight.

Together they opened a studio in Nottingham, and painted in Yorkshire and Cornwall before settling in London.

Laura Knight also travelled with circuses and

CITY STUDIO: Dame Laura Knight

ballet troupes. She painted the portraits of George Bernard Shaw, the actors Sir John Gielgud and Paul Scofield, and (in 1950) Princess Elizabeth.

She became the first woman elected to the Royal Academy since the 1700s, and was chosen as the official British artist at the Nuremburg Trial.

She was a Doctor of Literature at the University of Nottingham.

Paul Smith gets started

PAUL Smith, who started in fashion by making ties on his mum's sewing machine, opened a shop in October.

The 12ft square room in a Nottingham city centre side-street became the foundation of an international fashion empire with late-Nineties turnover of £142 million.

Beeston-born Smith developed an interest in clothing while working in the Lace Market. He helped out at a friend's boutique in Bridlesmith Gate.

With the help of his girlfriend Pauline Denyer, he sank £600 into his new business, which initially opened only on Fridays and Saturdays — the rest of the week he was busy buying, cutting and studying.

Within four years he had formed a company to market his early designs, and the shop in Byard Lane was extended.

By 1976, Smith's clothes were being shown in Paris and in 1979 he opened a London outlet.

In the 1980s he broke into the Japanese market and opened a

DESIGNS ON SUCCESS: Fashion maestro Paul Smith, pictured in 1973

shop in New York's Fifth Avenue.

In the 1990s there was a franchise in Hong Kong, a 60th store in Japan, a CBE and a Queen's Award for Exports. Customers included the England football team. Terry Venables' Euro 96 squad wore Paul Smith suits, as did Glenn Hoddle's 1998 World Cup team.

'Bishop and the showgirl' scandal

THE Bishop of Southwell, Dr Gordon Savage, resigned and became a Anglican chaplain in Tenerife, where he was joined by Amanda Lovejoy, described as his housekeeper.

As Joy Shaw, she had been a dancer at the Eve Club in Regent Street, London. It emerged that Dr Savage had been a frequent visitor to the club where, according to one columnist, "statuesque showgirls appeared topless in the exotic cabaret."

He resigned the chaplaincy and later settled in Hereford. He died, aged 75, in 1990.

TRENT Bridge staged the 2nd Test in an unique series, England v Rest of the World, arranged following the cancellation of South Africa's tour.

The Nottingham match provided England with their only win in five tests.

Gary Sobers captained the World XI, for whom Clive Lloyd (West Indies) and Eddie Barlow (South Africa) scored centuries in the first and second innings respectively.

For England, Ray Illingworth hit 97 in the first innings. Needing 284 to win, Brian Luckhurst (113 not out), Colin Cowdrey and Keith Fletcher saw England home.

❑ ❑ ❑

GUITAR legend Eric Clapton returned to Nottingham in July for a Boat Club gig with Skid Row, which also included Rory Gallagher and Peter Green.

Clapton had appeared in the city several times during the Sixties — on the first occasion, in 1966, with influential rock band Cream.

They played at the Sherwood Rooms (later MGM, now Oasis) as part of the graduation ball for University of Nottingham students.

❑ ❑ ❑

THIRTY-year-old Nottingham barrister Kenneth Clarke was elected Conservative MP for Rushcliffe.

An old boy of Nottingham High School and a past president of the Cambridge Union, he had twice unsuccessfully contested the safe Labour seat at Mansfield before his adoption in Rushcliffe.

❑ ❑ ❑

THREE Notts police officers received the Queen's Commendation for brave conduct following the arrest of violent men in St Ann's. They were Sgt James Montgomery, PC Graham Davies and PC David Parker.

❑ ❑ ❑

NOTTINGHAM acquired a new institution of higher education with the creation of Trent Polytechnic, formed from the Regional College of Technology and the College of Art and Design.

New look for market in Vic Centre setting ➡ Page 109

NOTTS drinkers pondered on a distressing piece of news — the price of a pint was about to hit 40p.

The general consensus of opinion among city drinkers was that pubs would soon be empty.

One said: "I have about six pints at lunchtime and ten pints at night. I will just have to go in for a drink later at night."

The price hike was being forecast to pay for a proposed move to continental opening hours to come in line with the Common Market.

NOTTINGHAM Corporation's multi-million eastern by-pass scheme — which had been dubbed the city's Berlin Wall — was rejected by the Department of the Environment.

The idea had been to build it through Sneinton and St Ann's and link with the Sheriff's Way, a major highway slicing through the city centre.

FRANK Yexley, who had been in the ring with Randolph Turpin, Henry Cooper and Cassius Clay, announced his retirement — without a mark on his face.

He was relinquishing his role as a master of ceremony because of ill health. He had come to Nottingham in 1940 to run boxing courses for the Army School of Physical Training.

NATURAL gas was coming to the region with East Midlands Gas Board planning to connect 278,500 homes and businesses over the following 12 months.

The board was planning to complete all connections by the mid 1970s — a total of 1,314,703 customers.

ST Ann's Church, a local landmark for more than 100 years, was demolished in 1971.

EIGHT years after the merger of the two papers, the words *'and News'* were dropped from the title of the Nottingham *Evening Post*.

Tony on target

NOTTS County, powered by 22 goals from Tony Hateley in his second spell with the club, were champions of the Fourth Division and promoted to the Third.

Over the Trent, Forest chairman Jack Levy was leading the clamour for Sunday football. It was to be discussed by the Football League, along with a proposed ban on re-runs of controversial incidents in televised matches.

On the playing front, Forest sacked their coach of five years, Tommy Cavanagh.

SCORER:
Tony Hateley

Drugs warning

THE number of drug addicts being treated at Mapperley Hospital was rising dramatically. From a figure of only eight in 1967, the hospital dealt with 78 in 1970.

Most were born in England, all were white, and 19 admitted taking drugs while still at school.

Nottingham's Medical Officer said: "Drug abuse is developing as a serious national problem and can only be curtailed by frank and complete co-operation by those concerned, whether they be police, social works, doctors or chemists."

Brothers celebrate as envoy is released

EIGHT months after his kidnap by guerrillas in Uruguay, British ambassador Geoffrey Jackson was released — much to the relief of his Hucknall brother Seymour.

The envoy had been snatched by Tupamaros guerrillas and held in 'the people's jail' before being released unharmed.

It was the news Rolls-Royce worker Seymour Jackson had been waiting to hear.

He and his twin Frank, who had travelled from Bolton to share the moment, toasted the release of their brother.

And it was revealed that the extraordinary affinity between the twins had led Seymour to be at the bus stop to meet his brother — without knowing what time he was arriving.

Seymour said: "We are both so happy about Geoffrey's release, and we plan to do some more celebrating."

Mr Jackson was held for a total of 246 days during which he gave up smoking.

He was reunited with his wife and son in Madrid and later knighted by the Queen.

His release by the Tupamaros was part of their campaign to discredit the conservative government of President Jorge Areco.

LEFT: 'Maid Marian' caused consternation as she set off for a promotional trip to the US. Airport security officers at Manchester confiscated her bow and arrow.

Anna Freyne was travelling with the Sheriff to promote Nottingham when she ran into the red tape.

"An official said he had better take the bow and arrows in case of hijacks. I thought he must be joking. I told him I couldn't hit anything if I tried.

"He didn't sound serious — but he still took them away from me."

In America Anna appeared on three TV shows and four radio programmes.

Manager discovers £20-a-night band Paper Lace

SHOWBIZ manager Brian Hart turned up at the Grey Goose in Gedling to hear an unknown band playing for £20.

"I was impressed," he said later. "They were a superb close harmony group. I asked them about becoming their manager."

Phil Wright (vocals), Chris Morris (keyboards), Michael Vaughan (guitar) and Cliff Fish (bass) liked what they heard. Paper Lace, the biggest band ever to come out of Nottingham, were on their way to chart success.

Hart was a former army major based in Burton Joyce. His clients then included unknown comics Little and Large, and singer Wayne Fontana.

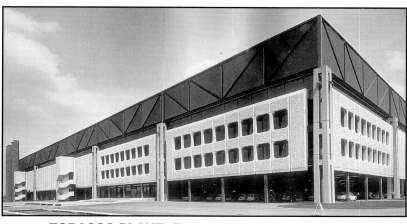

TOBACCO PLANT: The award-winning Horizon factory

'Horizon' costs £14m

THE Horizon tobacco factory was opened on a 45-acre site at Lenton, at a cost of £14 million.

It meant the closure of John Player factories in Radford. The highly automated plant, which won three architectural awards, was capable of producing 100 million cigarettes a day.

Wings debut at university

PAUL McCartney's new band Wings played their first ever gig at Nottingham University — purely on a whim.

McCartney was travelling with wife Linda and the rest of Wings on the M1 when he made the decision to return to the live circuit.

He made a call to Nottingham promoter Tony Sherwood and the following day — February 9, 1972 — Wings played in front of 1,000 people at the university's Portland Building.

It was the first time that McCartney had performed on stage in five years.

With Linda on keyboard and their children at the side of the stage, Wings ran through a mix of new and old numbers, from *Lucille, Wildlife* and *The Mess I'm In* to the controversial *Give Ireland Back To The Irish.*

McCartney told the *Post* after the show: "It was very pleasing. We wanted the chance to appear without much fuss at first and this was a really good response."

End of an era for tripe factory

TOM Sanderson and Sons Ltd, the tripe factory at Cloister Square, Lenton, went into voluntary liquidation.

It was founded at the turn of the century with a small shop in Arkwright Street. The business flourished, and another 11 shops were opened.

The founder's sons, Rupert and Thomas, kept the tradition going and opened the Lenton factory.

As the business expanded, their brothers Herbert and Eric also joined the company.

'Vic' market doors open

UNDER COVER:
Shoppers at the new market

A QUIET revolution in market trading began in Nottingham with the opening of the £700,000 Victoria Centre market.

There was no fuss. The traders simply moved on to their stalls and opened up business.

To make the occasion special however, several stores which have moved into the new Victoria Centre, chose the day to open their doors for the first time.

W.H. Smith, Wineways and shoe shop Peter Lord were among the newcomers.

The general consensus of opinion about the new market was favourable.

Deputy markets clerk Eric Rowe said: "I think Nottingham will have a market to be proud of."

And Clive Kay, the centre manager, added: "The stalls are very impressive indeed. The corporation has done a wonderful job."

The two floor market featured miscellaneous trades on the lower level with 138 stalls operating while on the upper tier were 136 stalls selling foodstuffs.

Traders did their bit by promising not to put up prices.

It was the third home for the city's main market, which had originally stood in the Old Market Square for around 800 years before moving to the Central Market in 1928.

MP Jack Dunnett was among the first VIPs to tour the new centre, giving his thumbs up approval, and plans for an official ceremony to be conducted by the Sheriff were revealed.

THEY could hear him crying, but little Daniel Hansworth's parents did not know where he was.

They searched their Dunkirk home from top to bottom until they finally located desperate Dan — in a hole under the floorboards.

It took the fire brigade, armed with a hacksaw and crowbar, to prise the two-year-old free.

□ □ □

A CALL to pedestrianise the centre of Nottingham, linking the new Victoria and Broad Marsh shopping centres, was made the Civic Society.

Their view was that such a move would solve the problem of traffic congestion.

□ □ □

A SATURDAY park-and-ride bus service was introduced at the Forest recreation ground in November. It dropped passengers near the Theatre Royal.

The second park-and-ride service took passengers from a car park at County Hall to Maid Marian Way.

□ □ □

EMMANUEL Church in Woodborough Road, known as 'the Church on the Hill', was demolished in 1972.

□ □ □

OBJECTIONS were being lodged against plans to demolish the Elite Cinema in Upper Parliament Street. A development company was proposing a department store and restaurant.

□ □ □

FOREST were relegated from the First Division in a miserable season in which they were knocked out of the FA Cup in the third round, by Millwall. Manager Matt Gillies resigned early in the 1972-3 season.

□ □ □

FRANK Carson, Duggie Brown and Colin Crompton were among the comedians performing at the Theatre Royal. The New Seekers followed up their second place in the Eurovision Song Contest with a sell-out concert at Nottingham's Albert Hall.

Pitch invasion denies Forest in FA Cup tie ➤ Page 111

Premier opening

BOAT-owning Prime Minister Edward Heath officially opened the £1½m National Watersports Centre at Holme Pierrepont.

He declared the centre, built with the help of a £400,00 grant from the government, a valuable asset for the nation as well as the sport.

And Ald Mrs Anne Yates, chairman of the county council, said the opening was the most important red letter day of her career.

Also present was Dr Roger Bannister, first man to break the four minute mile, who attended as chairman of the Sports Council.

ABOVE: Ted Heath

RIGHT: The new water centre

A FORMER city fireman returned from the tiny Canadian village where he had lived for ten years to find that Nottingham "has no breathable atmosphere now...we can smell it."

Ralph Whittlesey, was visiting his mother-in-law Mrs Danby on the Bulwell Hall Estate.

□ □ □

ENGLAND won the 1st Test and Trent Bridge by 38 runs, overcoming a heroic fightback by New Zealand. The tourists hit 440 in the final innings of the match, with 176 from captain Bev Congdon and 116 from Vic Pollard.

□ □ □

THE AA in Nottingham was investigating an incident in which a family turned up for a cricket match — with three children in the boot of their car.

□ □ □

THE Notts County revival continued. In 1971-2 the newly-promoted Magpies had finished fourth in the Third Division. At the end of 1972-3 they were promoted to the Second.

□ □ □

HAROLD Larwood completed his family XI. The 68-year-old former Notts and England bowler was celebrating the arrival of his 11th grandchild.

□ □ □

THE *Evening Post* teamed up with police across Notts to wage war on 'vicious and mindless' vandals.

Saved only by her fingertips

NOTTS police inspector Richard Cooke — who 14 years earlier had saved two non-swimmers from the River Soar [see 1959] — was the hero of another rescue drama.

Called to an address in Tennyson Street, Nottingham, he found a woman who had crawled on to a third-storey roof with the intention of committing suicide.

Insp Cooke talked to her at length, trying to entice her from the ridge of the roof.

Suddenly she fell backwards, but held on by her fingertips. The officer crawled along the ridge and secured her. Even though she struggled violently, he was able to hold on to her wrists until the fire brigade arrived.

Insp Cooke was recommended for the Queen's Commendation, which was awarded in 1974.

Two Notts CID officers also received commendations for their roles in a city centre disturbance in 1972.

Detective Constables Bill Wright and Dave Greasley were caught between two rival gangs of youths in Clumber Street following a fight in the Lion Hotel.

One faction made off towards Parliament Street, pursued by a group of 30 youths, some armed with bricks and scaffolding poles,

The detectives shouted that they were police officers and tried to restrain one of the gangs — but they were caught up in a "furious melee" and both were injured.

At the trial of seven of the people involved in the fight, the Crown Court judge praised DC Wright and DC Greasley for their courage.

Time for Emmett

MAGICAL MOMENTS: The Emmett Clock

ROLAND Emmett, the eccentric inventor and cartoonist , unveiled his latest masterpiece — the 23ft water fountain and clock in the Victoria Centre.

More than 1,000 people watched Emmett set the £20,000 creation in motion.

A whirling confusion of colourful birds and butterflies, it chimed on the hour and half-hour, followed by harpsichord music by Purcell.

Since its opening it has fascinated millions of visitors.

● Shoppers had to walk the plank after floods cut off part of the subway at the Broad Marsh Centre. It was caused by waste paper, thrown by shoppers, clogging up the gullies.

Final Guardian Journal edition

AFTER more than 100 years, the *Guardian Journal* ceased publication after the edition of June 19 — the day a strike began at its sister publication, the Nottingham *Evening Post*.

The *Post* had changed from 'hot metal' printing to photo-composition. The paper was redesigned and the first 40-page edition appeared on March 28.

With progress came problems. The replacement of stereo plates and magnesium etching with Letterflex plates prompted an inter-union dispute.

A strike began on June 19 and continued until July 31. But not a single edition of the *Post* was lost, and a reduced staff produced a 16-page broadsheet every day.

● Supermarket girls in the Victoria Centre staged a 'spend-a-penny' strike because they had to get permission to go the loo.

Capture of 'Panther' ends nationwide hunt ➡ Page 112

1974

SARTORIAL PRAISE: Nottingham band Paper Lace appeared at the Royal Command Performance in London. The Queen Mother congratulated them on their suits

Fan invasion cheats Reds

NEWCASTLE United fans saved their club from FA Cup defeat when they invaded the pitch as Second Division Forest went into a 3-1 lead at St James's Park.

Forest looked set for a semi-final place as they cruised into a 3-1 lead with goals from Ian Bowyer, Liam O'Kane and George Lyall.

With Newcastle down to ten men, Pat Howard having been sent off, and only 30 minutes to go, United fans spilled on to the pitch.

Reds players Dave Serella and Martin O'Neill were struck before referee Gordon Kew took the players off.

After eight minutes, order was restored and the teams returned but Forest's rhythm was gone. United staged a remarkable comeback to win the game 4-3.

But that was far from the end of the story as Forest lodged a protest with the FA over the game's outcome.

As letters of support poured in from fans in Nottingham and Newcastle, the two sides were ordered to replay the tie on neutral territory — Goodison Park being chosen.

But when the two sides drew 0-0, instead of Forest being awarded a home replay, the game was again staged at Everton and a Malcolm McDonald goal took United through to the semi-final and an eventual place at Wembley where they lost 3-0 to Liverpool.

● Notts County also wrote their own headlines — or at least their striker Ian Scanlon did. He recorded the third fastest hat-trick on record, taking just 165 seconds to put three past Sheffield Wednesday keeper Peter Springett.

Unfortunately, Wednesday battled back for a 3-3 draw.

Harris turns back years

FORMER world sprint champion Reg Harris, *pictured*, turned back the years and made a comeback in the UK sprint championships.

His 25-year-old Raleigh was recovered from the Nottingham factory — and the man who dominated his sport in the 1940s and 1950s prepared to take on men of less than half his age.

Harris fought his way through to the final against Trevor Bull, won both heats — and took the British title at 54 years of age.

Pit stance prompts three-day week

SEVEN million pounds in production was lost in the Notts coalfield during a four week strike by miners.

The dispute over pay and conditions led to a three-day week being introduced for thousands of workers.

Later in the year, there was another strike vote over a new productivity deal. The NUM won a narrow majority against the coal board's offer, even though Notts men voted to accept the proposals.

'Lion' sightings spark Notts big game hunt ➡ Page 113

HEROES: Gold watches from the Post Office for the men who captured Lesley Whittle's kidnapper ... PC Tony White, Roy Morris, Keith Wood and PC Stuart Mackenzie. Left: Donald Neilson

Cloughie signs for Forest

OUTSPOKEN Brian Clough became manager of second division Nottingham Forest.

The former Middlesbrough and Sunderland forward had started his management career at Hartlepool, but it was with Derby County that he made his name.

Under his leadership the Rams were promoted to the First Division and became champions in 1972.

"I don't see I have to prove anything," said Clough, "but I want to show the Nottingham public that we can do well."

The *Evening Post* wrote: "Clough will open up a new era for the sagging Reds ... the man has a charisma all of his own."

Clough took charge for the FA Cup replay at Spurs, which Forest won 1-0.

PCs capture the 'Panther'

TWO Notts bobbies were hailed as national heroes when the man they captured after a shooting incident turned out to be the 'Black Panther' — Britain's most wanted man Donald Neilson.

PCs Tony White and Stuart Mackenzie questioned a man walking in Mansfield Woodhouse.

He said: "Don't move," and the officers saw a shotgun stuck through their panda car window. Neilson forced them to drive him to Blidworth.

As the car drove into Rainworth, PC White grabbed the barrel. The weapon went off, perforating PC Mackenzie's eardrum, but the gunman was overpowered with the help of colliery mechanic Roy Morris and engineer Keith Wood.

The man was taken to Mansfield police station. When his fingerprints were taken, he was suspected of being the Black Panther.

Neilson was later jailed for life for the murder of teenage heiress Lesley Whittle and of three men at sub-post offices.

Both officers were awarded the Queen's Gallantry Medal.

IN CHARGE: Clough arrives at City Ground

Lilac Leopards take the strain

THE county council's controversial 'Zone and Collar' traffic experiment was introduced with the aim of controlling rush-hour traffic.

Eighteen luxury Leyland Leopard coaches were introduced to provide park-and-ride services on major routes into the city.

Because of their colour, the vehicles were known as the Lilac Leopards.

☐ ☐ ☐

NOTTS said Yes to the referendum question: Should the UK stay in Europe? In a 63.7% county turnout, 445,773 voters were 2-1 in favour of continued membership.

NOTTS County Council launched an inquiry into claims that the X-rated film *Confessions of a Window Cleaner* was shown to a youth club audience including children of 11.

☐ ☐ ☐

TRENT Bridge had a share in the first cricket World Cup, sponsored by Prudential. England beat New Zealand at Nottingham by 80 runs.

☐ ☐ ☐

RALEIGH survived a 50% slump in its £15 million US market without making immediate redundancies. But the 8,800 workforce was cut by 500 over two years.

☐ ☐ ☐

TWENTY thousand fans packed into Meadow Lane for County's 3,000th league match — the derby clash with Forest. The result: 2-2.

☐ ☐ ☐

DJ Jimmy Savile was presented with a huge cigar when he visited the British Red Cross at Beeston.

Doug Scott conquers Everest

NOTTINGHAM'S Doug Scott, 33, and colleague Dougal Haston became the first men to climb Everest via the south-west face.

When they reached the 29,028ft summit just before sunset on September 24, 1975, they became the first Britons to conquer the mountain by any route.

The expedition, led by Chris Bonington, provided Scott with a chance to conclude unfinished business.

He had been on an expedition in 1972 to scale the south-west face, and got to within 2,000ft of the summit but was beaten back by high winds and extreme cold.

Scott had caught the climbing bug as a Scout exploring rocks at Matlock.

TOLLERTON SAFARI: The hunt for the lion gets underway

City sweats in scorcher

NOTTINGHAM sweated through the worst drought for 250 years.

From May to the end of August the weather made the headlines as people were warned not to sit out in the sun, not to play with matches, not to waste water and even take extra care with their cycles — the heatwave had led to a sudden rise in bike thefts.

Hosepipes were banned from May, and at a trial at Shire Hall, the judge allowed barristers to remove their wigs.

Newstead Abbey grounds, municipal golf course, bowling greens, tennis courts, pitch and putt courses, putting greens and croquet lawns were all closed and Green Goddesses — fire engines from the emergency war reserves — were drafted in to help tackle grass fires.

Tollerton lion is a mystery

VILLAGES south of Nottingham went on lion alert in the summer after two milkmen reported seeing a big cat near Tollerton Airport.

"We both saw what to us was a lion," said one of the men.

"It was 50 yards away, had its head down and its long tail had a bushy end. It was walking away from us, very slowly."

His colleague added: "We would both stake our lives on what we saw."

Police were called to the scene, and although officers initially were disbelieving, a major operation was mounted. Householders in West Bridgford, Ruddington and neighbouring villages were warned to keep windows closed ... and eyes open.

Police deployed a helicopter and marksmen with high-powered rifles. Army units with infra-red nightsight equipment were called in and vets laid down doped meat in a bid to trap

the beast. As word spread, more sightings were reported.

A Norfolk couple who had passed through Lowdham a week earlier rang to say they had seen a lion in a lay-by — but had not reported it for fear of not being believed.

An Edwalton farmworker claimed to have seen a lion in a field. Passengers on the top deck of a bus travelling on the A52 said they had seen a big cat in a roadside garden — officers investigated and found it was an ornamental stone lion.

Just as police prepared to wind down the operation, the county's deputy coroner reported seeing a creature resembling a lion near his home in Stanton-on-the-Wolds.

Two golfers at the nearby Stanton club also said they had seen the creature. Armed officers searched the grounds, disrupting a tournament.

After eight days, the hunt was stopped. No lion was ever found.

BARE LEGS: Strollers at the River Trent

Mouth-to-mouth saves Charlie the fish

A TEN-year-old goldfish literally had new life breathed into it after it sank to the bottom of its bowl. Grannie Doris Jones spotted the ailing fish at her daughter's home in Carlton and decided to give it the kiss of life.

"I got hold of the fish in one hand and began to breathe into his mouth. I cupped my other hand across my mouth to make sure it didn't jump in!" Soon afterwards, Charlie was back in the swim.

AFTER just nine months of skating together, Jayne Torvill and police cadet Christopher Dean, 17 and 18 respectively, became regional ice dance champions. They beat five other pairs at the competition in Bristol.

Also in 1976, the Nottingham pair were fourth in the British championships. They were third the following year.

☐ ☐ ☐

MUNDELLA Grammar School became a comprehensive in spite of a fierce protest from parents.

☐ ☐ ☐

THE *Evening Post* made newspaper history by becoming the first newspaper in Britain to publish stories 'set' by journalists.

Th electronic editing system was developed in partnership with International Computers Ltd.

☐ ☐ ☐

NOTTINGHAM'S Victoria Hotel, £2m in the red and trading on a day-to-day basis, went into voluntary liquidation.

The situation was being made worse because no buyers could be found in the depressed hotel industry.

☐ ☐ ☐

NOTTS crime rate reached its blackest day — with more offences per person than London.

One in every 15 people in the county was a criminal, stretching the Notts' forces thin blue line to breaking point.

☐ ☐ ☐

NOTTS police inspector John Tordoff was awarded the Queen's Commendation for brave conduct after his rooftop rescue of an agitated woman in Tennyson Street, Nottingham, in 1975.

☐ ☐ ☐

DEREK Randall scored his first double-century (204 not out) but Notts lost to Somerset by six wickets at Trent Bridge, with Ian Botham hitting 80 and 167 not out.

New teaching hospital opens for business  Page 115

1977

Flags and fireworks for jubilee guests

Clough works his magic

AFTER three seasons of steady improvement under the Brian Clough and Peter Taylor management team, Forest were third in the Second Division in 1976-7 and promoted to the First.

Clough's men then began their surprising assault on the Division One title and by the end of the year were top of the table.

But controversy was never far away and Clough threatened to close the Trent End if the obscene chants were not stopped.

It led to an amusing exchange between manager and fans as Clough displayed a sign pleading: "Gentlemen, no swearing please, Brian."

Trent Enders replied with a sign of their own: "Brian, no leaving please, the Gentlemen."

There were dramatic developments over at Meadow Lane as well, as Ronnie Fenton and his assistant Mick Jones were sacked by chairman Jack Dunnett.

Mr Dunnett then turned to the Magpies' most successful manager Jimmy Sirrel for his second spell in charge.

Sirrel had left Notts during the previous season when they were sitting at the top of the Second Division table having just toppled Leeds United in the League Cup.

But his stay at Sheffield United was short-lived and within days of his Bramall Lane dismissal he was back with the Magpies.

Ex-con begins his ministry

COCKNEY church minister Roy Catchpole arrived at St Paul's, Hyson Green, with the confession that he knew more about *Police Five* than the Ten Commandments when he was young.

As he teenager, he was constantly in and out of trouble. First came probation orders and then the courts got tougher, sending him to borstal, only for him to abscond.

Then he gave himself up to police, dressed in top hat and spats he had stolen from a car.

But his life changed when he read his first Agatha Christie novel, followed by Shakespeare and then the Bible.

After serving 21 months in prison he was released, determined to become a chaplain, studied hard to pass examinations and was accepted for the clergy at St John's College in Bramcote.

□ □ □

THE Victoria Hotel was bought by the Glasgow-based Stakis Group for £645,000. The group said they would be spending £200,000 on upgrading the former station hotel.

□ □ □

PERCY CUTE — real name Simon Lester, son of Beeston's Conservative MP Jim Lester — a member of the punk rock band The Secret, had his first single released.

Drummer Simon, 21, and the rest of the band were signed to the Arista record label who described the single as "a rip-roaring, high energy form of the old Cliff Richard hit *The Young Ones*."

WALKABOUT: Nottingham greets the Queen in jubilee year

THERE cannot have been a more eagerly awaited day than July 28 when the Queen arrived in the city on her silver jubilee tour of the nation.

Flags were unfurled, the bunting came out and street parties were organised.

The Queen, with Prince Philip, spent an exhausting 13-hour day in the East Midlands, performing numerous official functions.

Every possible vantage point along her route was occupied and 15,000 crammed into Old Market Square to see the royal party arrive for lunch.

As the cheers rang out, the Queen made an appearance on the Council House balcony, before and after her meal.

During her day in Nottingham, she was presented with Nottingham Lace, a silver coffee set, a commemorative plate, leather-bound books, armfuls of bouquets, a red, white and blue teddy bear, jewellery carved from coal and even a prize cucumber — a Land Rover was laid on to transport them all back to Buckingham Palace.

The Queen visited Trent Bridge where England were playing the Australians, then she was then whisked off to the Queen's Medical Centre to perform the official opening and tour some of the hospital's wards and departments.

Her final engagement was on Trent Embankment where a fireworks spectacular was held.

Organisers expected 25,000 but by 9pm that figure had to be revised to 45,000 and the final count as the royal couple arrived at County Hall at around 10pm was around 63,000.

The Queen, Prince Philip and the crowd were then treated to one of the best fireworks displays ever seen in the county, plus a red, white and blue water display in the Trent.

Centenary Test: Randall is man of the match

IT was the year Notts batsman Derek Randall proved himself in world cricket — his greatest achievement being a spectacular 174 for England in the Centenary Test at Melbourne.

In an astonishing match to celebrate the first England v Australia fixture in 1877, both teams flopped in their first innings. Australia declared their second innings at 419. Needing an improbable 463 to win, England and man-of-the-match Randall almost got there, but eventually lost by 45 runs — the same margin as in the original 1877 Melbourne Test.

Randall was also at the centre of a memorable drama in that year's 3rd Test at Trent Bridge, where Geoff Boycott was both hero and villain. The Yorkshire opener hit a first-innings 107 — during which he went for an impossible single and caused Randall's run-out.

The crowd were unhappy, but all was forgotten in the second innings as Boycott and Randall scored the winning runs.

DEREK RANDALL: 174 earned Melbourne award

Clough leads Forest to one European Cup... Page 116

Teaching hospital opens for business

THE £80m Queen's Medical Centre finally opened for business, more than 40 years after the idea was first thought up.

The powers-that-be had been talking about such a project since before the Second World War and when University College was given university status in 1948, the proposal began to look a more practical proposition.

The catalyst was the 1962 Hospital Plan for England and Wales which pinpointed the need for a third district general hospital for Notts.

The university had a 43-acre site and, with the Sheffield Regional Hospital Board, came up with their vision of a medical teaching centre.

Two years later, after the City of Nottingham announced it would give £100,000 to the project, the Government gave the go-ahead.

However, it would be another six years before work on phase one could begin and it took a decade to complete the project.

By 1981, Nottingham had the first integrated hospital and medical teaching centre linked to a university to be built in Britain this century.

QMC: 40 years in the planning

With room for more than 1,200 patients and a purpose-built school, the Queen's Medical Centre contained the very latest facilities when it opened in 1978.

The first few years were marred by controversy as large sections of the hospital stood empty due to a shortage of NHS funds.

Rushcliffe MP Kenneth Clarke, who was then minister for health, described it as a 'monument to folly' after finding that some wards were still not open in 1982.

Since then the hospital has gone from strength to strength and is recognised as one of Britain's leading NHS facilities. It earned international recognition for the way it coped with the Kegworth air disaster in 1989.

It became an independent NHS trust, responsible for its own finance, in April 1993.

The hospital treats 170,000 people a year.

Reds are the champions

FIRST Division new boys Nottingham Forest enjoyed the club's finest ever season — winning both the League championship and the League Cup.

Peter Withe, Tony Woodcock and John Robertson were regular scorers as the Reds recorded some impressive League wins — 4-0 at home to both Ipswich and Middlesbrough, and 4-0 away at Manchester United.

The title was secured with the 0-0 draw at Coventry City on April 22.

The League Cup campaign included wins over West Ham (5-0), Notts County (4-0), Aston Villa (4-2), Bury (3-0) and Leeds United (two-match semi-final, aggregate 7-3).

At Wembley on March 18, the

PLAYER OF YEAR: Kenny Burns

final against Liverpool ended in a 0-0 draw after extra time. The teams replayed at Old Trafford four days later, and a Robertson penalty won the trophy.

Clough was named Manager of the Year and the Reds' hard-tackling defender Kenny Burns was the PFA Player of the Year.

Ice peril for firefighters

NOTTINGHAM was in the grip of some typically seasonal February weather with ice and snow blanketing the city.

It was so cold that firemen fighting a blaze in Nuthall were slipping and falling on ice caused by the water from their hoses, and one fireman got stuck up his ladder when water froze on the rungs.

Little Rebecca Glenn of Bulwell broke her left arm when she slipped in the playground — and a week later she did it again, breaking her right arm.

In Wales, Chilwell bridegroom Clive Jelley and his 19-year-old bride Diane were forced to carry on dancing at their reception until 5am because they and 60 guests were cut off by snow.

TWO enterprising rogues from Hucknall were before magistrates for fiddling fruit machines — using a coin attached to a fishing line.

The two men drilled a small hole in a 10p coin, attached the line and used it get free goes ... until they were spotted by an off duty policeman.

They were both fined.

□ □ □

THE *Evening Post* celebrated its centenary with a May Day party at the National Water Sports Centre at Holme Pierrepont. The sky was lit up with a £5,000 firework display.

□ □ □

JAYNE Torvill and Christopher Dean won their first British ice dance championship — which they were to retain for the next five years.

In 1978 the Nottingham pair also made their mark in their debut international season — finishing ninth in the European and 11th in the world championships.

The same year, Betty Callaway became their trainer.

□ □ □

CITY prostitutes were quizzed by detectives hunting the Yorkshire Ripper, who had killed six women, some of them street girls, in cities and towns in the north.

□ □ □

DEBENHAMS launched a £200,000 facelift to silence rumours that the city store was closing.

□ □ □

CITY comedian Larry Larkin turned the tables on the hatchet team of TV pundits when he appeared on the talent show *New Faces*.

While the judges were ripping in to Larry's act, he held up posters on camera declaring the critics to be "rubbish".

ATV loved it and Larry said: "I'm glad I got one in on them for a change."

□ □ □

GEOFF Boycott scored his 16th Test century as England beat New Zealand at Trent Bridge by 119 runs. Ian Botham's match figures were nine for 93.

...and another as Forest triumph in Madrid ▶ Page 117

THE George Green Memorial Society gave the Sneinton windmill to Nottingham City Council.

The mill had been built in the early 19th Century by a Nottingham baker whose son George Green inherited the business.

Green was the preeminent mathematics scholar of his generation. Largely self-taught, he was 40 when he became an undergraduate at Cambridge. He died in Sneinton in 1841.

The fund was founded by Prof Lawrie Challis amid concern over the future of the derelict windmill.

With support from Sneinton Environmental Society and Nottingham Civic Society, the mill was acquired and presented to the Lord Mayor in November, 1979.

❏ ❏ ❏

FIREMEN revealed a neat trick for removing stuck rings, using a piece of string.

When a caller asked for help at West Bridgford station, a fireman simply threaded a piece of string between the ring and finger and then one end was bound round the knuckle. The opposite end of the string was then unwound and the ring was forced over the bound part of the finger.

❏ ❏ ❏

A FINE arts auction in Nottingham set world record prices for a painting by 19th Century Dutch artist Klombeek (£14,500) and £4,600 for a seascape by Sir John Arnesby-Brown.

❏ ❏ ❏

DISABLED hero Gerald Whitehead, earned a police award after tackling an armed robber.

Raleigh worker Mr Whitehead saw two men running from police, after committing a robbery.

Despite a deformed left arm, he tackled the knifeman, parried his lunge and punched the man with his other arm.

❏ ❏ ❏

CITY MP William Whitlock called for a boycott of the 1980 Olympics in Moscow by British athletes because of the Soviet Union's record on human rights.

WINNERS: Skipper John McGovern with the trophy

Reds conquer the Continent

FOREST registered the highest achievement by any Nottingham sports team by winning the European Cup. The club also won the League Cup for the second year running.

Trevor Francis, who had arrived at the City Ground earlier in the season as British football's first £1 million player, scored the only goal of the European Cup Final on May 30.

After knocking out Liverpool, Forest had turned on the style against AEK Athens, winning 2-1 in Greece and 5-1 at home.

Grasshoppers Zurich were beaten 5-2 on aggregate. In the semi-final against Cologne, the City Ground leg ended in a 3-3 draw, and an Ian Bowyer goal settled the issue in the away leg.

Forest's opponents in the final were Swedish champions Malmo. Thousands of fans travelled from Nottingham to join the 57,000 who watched the Final in Berlin.

The opponents were Swedish champions Malmo, and they were undone by John Robertson and Francis.

Robertson outflanked the right side of the Malmo defence and crossed from the edge of the penalty area. Francis ran into space beyond the far post,

WELCOME: Forest's return

and headed the only goal of the game.

Forest would finished second in the First Division, but the League Cup was won with a 3-2 win against Southampton.

Showbiz mourns Beckinsale

TALENT:
Richard Beckinsale

THE world of show business was in mourning following the death from a heart attack of city-born actor Richard Beckinsale.

Richard, 31, had become one of the most popular figures on TV through his roles in *Porridge* and *Rising Damp*.

Richard decided to become an actor at the age of nine and his first part was in a school play.

He left school at 15 and was one of the first full-time drama students at Clarendon College, living with his family when they moved to Chilwell.

He left, having won a cup at the Nottingham Festival of Shakespeare, to study at RADA.

One of his earliest roles was at Nottingham Playhouse, carrying arms in the *Mayor of Zalamea* for which he was paid seven shillings and sixpence.

His first TV appearance was as a policeman in *Coronation Street*, arresting Ena Sharples.

He made several TV appearances in dramas and also made two films, *Rentadick* and *Give And Take*.

Stage strike: The show must go on

THE show went on at the Theatre Royal — but without a set. Technicians at the National Theatre in London were in the middle of a pay dispute and refused to load Nottingham-bound props for a performance of Somerset Maugham's *For Services Rendered*.

But in the best theatrical traditions, the director and cast carried on regardless. The theatre was staging a short season of mysteries with stars including Leslie Phillips, Nyree Dawn Porter, Kate O'Mara, Bill Pertwee, Molly Sugden and Christopher Beeny.

Car polisher finds his real name: Robin Hood ➡ Page 118

PANTO STARS: Chart-busting comedy duo Windsor Davies and Don Estelle, who had a surprise hit with *Whispering Grass*, topped the bill in the Theatre Royal pantomime *Cinderella*

Forest keep the Cup

ANOTHER glorious achievement by Forest, who qualified for the European Cup competition as holders — and repeated their 1979 success.

Oesters Vaxjo, Arges Pitesti and Dynamo Berlin were seen off in the early rounds. In the semi-final, a 2-0 home win against Ajax of Amsterdam proofed Forest against the 1-0 defeat in the away leg.

The final against Hamburg was at the Bernabeu Stadium in Madrid. As in 1979, one goal was enough to win European football's top trophy. John Robertson received a return pass from Garry Birtles and shot just inside the far post.

Back home, it had been a frustrating season. Despite extending a home unbeaten run to more than 50 matches, the Reds finished fifth in the First Division. They again went to Wembley as League Cup finalists, but lost 1-0 to Wolves.

RIGHT: John McGovern with the European Cup

City snub for Minsk appeal

NOTTINGHAM was at centre of an international nuclear arms row with the Soviet Union.

The twin city of Minsk had called on Nottingham to support Soviet opposition to the siting of NATO nuclear weapons in Europe.

The request came from Minsk's chief executive in a letter to the city council, just days before a Nottingham party was due to head out on a friendship visit.

The letter said that the NATO build-up represented a threat to both Nottingham and Minsk who had a common interest in condemning it.

The council's response was to dismiss the request out of hand and cancel the twinning visit — only a few days after agreeing it could go ahead, despite anger over Russia's invasion of Afghanistan.

● There were problems for local authorities nearer home when 300 people tried to block plans for an underpass at the junction of Derby Road and Middleton Boulevard.

Led by the Lenton and Wollaton Park Residents Association, they lodged objections when the proposal went to a public inquiry.

But the government inspector was told that the plan was the smallest and least obtrusive that could be devised to solve a rising tide of accidents and worsening traffic congestion at the junction.

The inquiry heard that 86 homes would need insulation grants to combat the high noise that would be caused.

Hands off our Robin Hood!

ROBIN Hood expert Jim Lees jumped to the defence of Nottinghamshire's greatest hero after another Yorkshire attempt to claim him for their own.

The people from the White Rose county claimed references to Barnsdale in Robin Hood ballads pinpointed his origins in Yorkshire.

But Jim, who spent a lifetime studying the legend, said the Barnsdale was actually Barnsdale in the parish of Basford: "The references to Notts are so many we can't doubt it."

THE Army decided not to take an action against a man who deserted — 37 years earlier.

The Meadows man failed to answer his call-up in 1943 and was posted as a deserter.

The allegation remained on file and was spotted when police checked his name on their computer during routine inquiries.

An Army spokesman said: "On humanitarian grounds, we will be taking no action."

❑❑❑

THE COAL Board launched a recruitment programme for Gedling, Cotgrave and Calverton collieries. A spokesman talked about up to 2,000 more mineworkers being needed in the East Midlands.

❑❑❑

T. GORDON Hepburn, one of Britain's finest railway photographers, died in 1980, leaving a huge collection of images of the steam age. Hepburn was born in Nottingham in 1905.

❑❑❑

ICE hockey returned to Nottingham after a 20-year gap as the Panthers defeated Solihull Barons 7-4. Within four games, the team was playing to capacity crowds at the Ice Stadium.

❑❑❑

DISASTER on the railway was narrowly averted when vandals laid sleepers across lines at Trowell. Three trains, two carrying passengers, hit the sleepers but, miraculously, escaped damage.

❑❑❑

MORE than 25,000 people greeted the Air France Concorde when it flew into East Midlands Airport. Among the passengers was Noele Gordon, star of TV soap *Crossroads*.

❑❑❑

CITY councillors were considering a two-way radio system to keep in touch with parties touring the complex cave system beneath Nottingham Castle.

Concert Hall: Elton John opens the big party ➡ Page 119

NOTTINGHAM gave a rousing sunshine welcome to the Queen when she visited the University for its centenary celebrations.

Thousands lined the Queen's route from East Midlands Airport, many of them waving Union Jack posters given away by the Evening Post, as she passed by in a glass-topped Rolls Royce,

When she arrived at the University, as well as the traditional bouquets, the Queen was presented with a silver boot by the President of the Students Union, the highest award they could bestow.

Queen Elizabeth toured the buildings, unveiling a commemorative plaque in the Great Hall and also pausing to look at the Royal Charter, granted by her father King George VI in 1948.

CITY relatives of businessman Stewart Christie were rejoicing with the news that he was to be allowed to leave Saudi Arabia after a 16 month wait.

The 46-year-old boss of a construction company had been refused an exit visa since the murder of the company's catering manager.

Although Mr Christie had twice been cleared of any involvement, his movements had been restricted.

NOTTS won the county cricket championship for the first time since 1929.

NOTTS County, managed by Jimmy Sirrel and coached by Howard Wilkinson, were promoted to the First Division — rejoining the top flight of English football for the first time since the 1920s.

Forest's dream of a hat-trick of European Cups ended in the first round, with 1-0 defeats home and away against CSKA Sofia.

THE Fellows, Morton and Clayton pub and micro-brewery opened in December, on the site once occupied by the canal haulage company whose name it takes. The late 19th Century building had previously been a warehouse and shop.

BEAUTY QUEEN: Michele Hobson of Notts won the Miss Great Britain title at the third attempt. Her prize included £3,500, a two week holiday for two and use of a car for a year

Your name is Robin Hood!

IT came as something of a surprise to Robert Leighton, at the age of 30, to discover his real name was ... Robin Hood.

The car polisher, who lived in Victoria Centre flats, was adopted as a baby by his aunt and uncle. He grew up believing his name was Robert Parkinson.

He became involved in a rock group and fancied a name change, so he registered himself as Robert Leighton.

But the truth finally dawned when he quizzed his adoptive parents about his background. It was then he learned that his mother's name was Bertha Hood, and she had given him the christian name Robin.

He had become known as Bobbie during a brief stay in a children's home after his mother's death, and from then on had been known as Robert.

Armed with his new persona, he dug out a copy of his birth certificate, proving he really was Robin Hood — but then he said: "I think I will continue to be called Robert Leighton."

Happy birthday, Alison

THE *Post* recorded a very special 18th birthday — of surviving Siamese twin Alison Fenwick.

Alison was born joined to her sister Beverley, who died after a 16-hour operation at St Bart's Hospital in London.

She celebrated her 18th birthday with her mother and Joan Clark, who looked after her virtually from birth.

For months after the operation, Sister Clark never left the hospital and, in the intervening years, often visited Alison at her home in Chilwell.

Later, Alison moved to London to receive special help with reading and learning, taking a job in a hospital supply department.

□□□

THE alarming rise in crime and disorder prompted a 77-year-old widow to seek a meeting with Premier Margaret Thatcher.

After collecting more than 80,000 signatures on a law and order petition, Sadie Tibbs of Nottingham appealed to any victims of crime to come forward and tell their stories.

● The continuing scourge of soccer hooliganism was illustrated by the plight of innocent victim William Adams of Aspley who was slashed across the face by a razor wielding thug.

The incident happened following a Forest v West Ham game when Mr Adams was surrounded by a group of visiting fans.

The one inch deep cut, stretching from his ear to his chin, needed 21 stitches.

Torvill and Dean skate to titles and MBEs

NOTTINGHAM ice dancers Jayne Torvill and Christopher Dean embarked on four golden years in which they were unchallenged as the world's best amateur ice dancing pair.

In 1981 they won the European championships at Innsbruck, then the world title in Hartford, Connecticut — and received MBEs. The following year they retained both titles.

Although injury forced them to withdraw from the European championships in 1983, they again won the world title in Helsinki, and received the team prize at the BBC Sports Personality of the Year awards.

In 1984 they won the European, world and Olympic titles.

CHAMPIONS: Chris and Jayne

Pop record bid to boost Nottingham's image  Page 120

RACE ACE: Barry Sheene, *right*, was back on the motorbike racing scene at Donington Park after almost losing his legs in a crash at Silverstone.

Sheene, his legs held together with metal screws, put in an appearance at a World Cup meeting.

Clarke besieged

HEALTH minister Kenneth Clarke was besieged by up to 50 angry protesters at his constituency office in West Bridgford.

The Rushcliffe MP was forced to use a back entrance to get into the office but eventually faced the crowd after a police appeal for calm.

The protest was over the Government's attitude to the health service pay dispute and there were many nurses among the crowd.

Elton leads party at new concert hall

ELTON John officially opened the £12m Royal Concert Hall, with two concerts on November 27 and 28, 1982.

Before the first show the superstar went walkabout among hundreds of fans and officially opened the venue by switching on the controversial £40,000 neon sculpture.

He then thrilled two capacity audiences — some of whom had queued more than 24 hours to get their hands on the cherished tickets — with some of his best known hits, including *Pinball Wizard, Blue Eyes, Song For Guy, Daniel, Saturday Night's All Right For Fighting* and The Beatles' *Twist and Shout*.

However, Elton John wasn't the first to perform on the Concert Hall stage — he was beaten to it two days before by the 13-piece Hunto Steel Band, made up of pupils and ex-pupils of Huntingdon Junior School in St Anns.

The Royal Concert Hall took nearly three years to build and opened as the city's largest venue with a seating capacity of 2,500.

Elton John's two shows

ABOVE: Elton John at the opening concert

were the first in a series of opening celebration concerts at the end of 1982. Others to appear included: Dire Straits, The Kinks, Haircut 100, Elvis Costello, Leo Sayer, The Stranglers and Ultravox.

Three years later Elton returned for yet another sell-out show at the venue.

Archie safe as Task Force sails

PREMIER Margaret Thatcher sent a massive military task force to the South Atlantic to kick invading Argentinian troops out of the Falkland Islands.

As the British forces won a decisive victory, Falklands resident Archie Short, pictured, watched the drama unfold from the safety of his daughter's home in Gedling.

The 84-year-old ex-shepherd had been flown out of Port Stanley following the invasion.

He had tales of tired, cold and dispirited Argentine soldiers preparing for battle.

Mr Short returned to the Falklands after the war, but died in Port Stanley in 1986.

Clough-Taylor partnership ends

IF one man could be guaranteed to knock a war off page one, it was Brian Clough. He reacted to the shock retirement of his friend and partner Peter Taylor by declaring he would never appoint another assistant.

Clough described it as a "tragic day" for Forest and said he could never have anyone work as closely with him as Taylor had done.

But their bond of friendship was broken when Taylor returned to football as manager of Derby County, and recruited Reds favourite John Robertson.

Clough and Taylor reputedly never spoke to each other again.

FIREMEN and police used water jets and CS gas to flush a man out of a loft in St Ann's after an eight-hour drama.

The man, wearing a hood and carrying an axe, kept officers at bay by hurling slates and chimney pots, smashing windows causing other damage running into thousands of pounds.

When he eventually came down, he was admitted to Mapperley Hospital.

❏ ❏ ❏

LUCKY 13 Notts women working at Cavendish Woodhouse furnishings in Talbot Street scooped £534,364 on Littlewoods pools ... a good £40,000 each.

After collecting their cheque from comedian Jim Davidson, the syndicate vowed to carry on working.

❏ ❏ ❏

DESTRUCTIVE Colorado beetles were found in a consignment of Italian spinach, causing a major scare among Notts farmers.

The public was put on beetle alert for the striped intruders as precautions were taken to stop the insect attacking potato crops.

Leafy imports from Italy were temporarily banned.

❏ ❏ ❏

A STORM of protest blew up over education authority plans to close Peveril Comprehensive School in Aspley.

The school was one of seven earmarked for amalgamation in the city.

Hundreds of pupils and parents staged a protest march from the Old Market Square to County Hall.

❏ ❏ ❏

NOTTS travelled to Lord's for the Benson & Hedges Cup final, but lost to Somerset by nine wickets.

❏ ❏ ❏

THE latest pet craze to sweep Nottingham was ... the skunk! A pet shop owner in Beeston reassured owners that a simple operation could get rid of the skunk's anti-social smell.

Perfect sixes from all-gold Torvill and Dean ⟶ Page 121

PRIMARY school pupil Natasha Shelton became the youngest winner of the Evening Post/Notts Police Citizen of the Month award for saving the life of an elderly pensioner.

The youngster from Hyson Green noticed copies of the Post, and mail, building up on the doorstep of 84-year-old Mrs Irene Lewendon.

And when Natasha's knock at the door failed to raise an answer, she went and found a policeman.

When the police got into Mrs Lewendon's home, they found her in a desperate state. She had been lying on the floor for five days after breaking her hip in a fall.

Recovering in hospital, she later said: "Natasha is my darling — wonderful. She saved my life and she is marvellous."

TEENAGE dancer Chantelle Hutchinson of Chilwell landed a plum job with the famous Bluebell Girls in Paris.

Standing 5ft 10ins tall, the 16-year-old was one of the first pupils of the Patricia Straw School of Dancing, winning 98 awards.

IT was all change at Meadow Lane as Notts County said farewell to an old stalwart and welcomed a new manager.

Pulling down the curtain on more than a quarter of a century at the club was Jack Wheeler, physiotherapist, former manager and jack of all trades.

He arrived at Meadow Lane in 1957 and until he retired he never missed a match in the dug-out — a record of 1,100 consecutive appearances.

And it was fitting Jack's career ended after a promotion season that saw Notts back in the First Division.

Forest's European Cup hero Larry Lloyd crossed the Trent to take over the hot seat at Meadow Lane.

Having walked out of Third Division Wigan, Lloyd brought every honour in the game as his credentials for managing a First Division club.

GONE FOR A BURTON: Burtons of Smithy Row, *left*, the fine foods shop, closed on February 5, with the loss of 75 staff.

Owners blamed the rise of supermarkets and the lack of nearby parking for customers

Disc idea for city's image

THE city council went into the record business with the release of a single called *Nottingham*, played by a group called Sheriff, whose lead singer was Mick Vaughan, once of Paper Lace.

Costing £16,000, the song was seen as a boost for the tourism industry. Lyricist Phil Wright, another ex-Paper Lace chart-topper, said the song was not designed to be a hit, but to provide a cost-effective way of promoting the city.

Copies were sent to travel writers and radio stations, while others went on general sale for £1.

However, not everyone was impressed. Tories dismissed the idea as "nonsense".

● Also in 1983 the council honoured two people who had done more to promote Nottingham abroad than anyone since the European Cup-winning Forest team.

Ice dancers Jayne Torvill and Christopher Dean were awarded the freedom of the city. Jayne became the first woman ever to receive the

NOTTINGHAM: It's a record!

honour when she and Chris collected their scrolls from the Lord Mayor.

A spectator was musical star Michael Crawford, who helped the couple prepare their *Barnum* routine.

Labour leader Coun Bill Maynard proposed the award saying: "They have always radiated overwhelming 'six' appeal", referring to their nine perfect sixes at the world championships in Helsinki.

Jayne said: "Perhaps they will have to change the title to Freeperson now."

Bridegroom was pen pal

THE Falklands War and the Evening Post combined to make a fairytale come true for a young sailor and his Notts sweetheart.

Kathy Burton of Clifton wrote to a chef on HMS Antrim in the Falklands after a reading a pen pal appeal in the Post and he passed it on to Petty Officer Paul Marriott of Castle Donington.

From there, romance blossomed and within a few months the happy couple had decided to tie the knot.

Graduate Paul and receptionist Kathy decided to make their home in Clifton after a honeymoon in Yugoslavia and Kathy's delighted mum said: "Kathy started writing to Paul to make him happy while he was away and now she's making him even happier by marrying him."

NOTTS was the "European hub" for a new pub craze from America. 'The Monster' was a kind of bar-mounted arm wrestling machine which had caught on in the USA and Australasia.

But after a fun launch at the Old Spot in Daybrook it quickly ran out of strength.

Showbiz guests for Barrie

ROYAL Centre director Barrie Stead brought showbusiness to Sneinton when he married Dutch dancer bride Brenda.

After a ceremony at the city's register office, the wedding was blessed at the parish church, guests arriving in a vintage Barton's bus with Bob Grant from TV's *On The Buses* acting as conductor.

Guests included comedians Keith Harris and Stu Francis, actress Barbara Windsor and drag artist Danny La Rue.

STAR TURN: Brenda's big day

Miners clash at pits and Notts men form UDM ⟹ Page 122

'Missiles' protest at Chilwell

THE controversy over the future of Chilwell Station spilled into the debating chamber at County Hall.

The Labour group confirmed its support for CND and the Reclaim Chilwell Group, who were planning a mass protest over the way part of the depot was being leased to the USAF.

They claimed spares for Cruise missiles would be stored there.

The County Hall row began as a 10ft banner carrying the message 'Notts County Council says Reclaim Chilwell' was unfurled above the main door by councillors Mick Warner and John Heppell.

That led to amazing scenes as first the Tory councillors walked out when chairman Bill Morris ruled it could stay ... and then Labour members walked out when a Tory took it down.

It led the *Evening Post* to publish a page one Comment which told councillors of both sides: "For heaven's sake grow up."

Hot-shot Chris wins 'just silver'

CHRIS Channon, the most disabled man ever to take up shooting in Britain, brought home to Nottingham a silver medal from the special Olympics in New York.

Ten years earlier doctors had described Chris, 28, from Arnold, as a hopeless case.

But thanks to his coach at Portland Training College, Don Price, and Chris's own determination, the dream became reality.

His proud mum Kathleen said: "Doctors told him he would spend the rest of his life in an institution, but Chris would have none of that."

When Chris telephoned his parents from New York his comment was: "I just managed to get silver."

But it was later revealed that the gold medal winner was much less disabled than Chris.

Chris excelled at several other sports and became a poet and regular contributor to the *Post*'s letters page.

ROYAL VISIT: The Queen and the Duke of Edinburgh on the Council House balcony during a visit to Nottingham in April

Chris, Jayne: Perfection

NOTTINGHAM skaters Jayne Torvill and Christopher became the greatest ever ice-dancing double-act when they won the European, Olympic and world titles.

Later during an unforgettable 1984, Jayne and Chris turned professional, won at the world professional figure skating championships, and were voted BBC Sports Personalities of the Year.

Their haul of gold medals began in Budapest in January, when there was criticism about the

THE GREATEST: Torvill and Dean

legality of some of their moves. It came from the trainer of their main rivals for the title, Natalya Bestemianova and Andrei Bukin, from the Soviet Union.

In the set pattern dance, Jayne and Chris received eight marks of 5.8 or 5.9 for content — but only 5.6 from the Soviet judge.

However he cheered up for their stunning Bolero routine, giving marks of 5.9 and a perfect 6.0 as the Nottingham pair skated to the title.

Torvill and Dean then moved to Sarajevo for the Winter Olympics ... where their Bolero won an unparalleled haul of perfect 6.0 marks (three for technical merit, and all nine for artistry).

The Lord Mayor of

Nottingham immediately sent a telegram of congratulations from the city which had sponsored the pair — as did Chris's former employers, Notts Police: "We all gave you a 6.1," the message read.

In March, the pair ended their amateur career by retaining the world title.

Twenty thousand people turned out in April to welcome Jayne and Chris back to Nottingham. Some 7,000 packed Old Market Square as they arrived for a civic reception.

They demanded balcony appearances from the skaters and trainer Betty Callaway.

The same week, Jayne and Chris were presented to the Queen, in Nottingham after distributing the Maundy Money at Southwell Minster.

FOREST were back in Europe, in the UEFA Cup. After wins against Vorwaerts, PSV Eindhoven, Celtic and Raika Sturm Graz, the Reds faced Belgian side Anderlecht in the semi-final, the winner going on to meet Spurs in the final.

Forest started with a 2-0 home win with goals by Steve Hodge.

Although they knew the away leg in Brussels would be a testing affair, Forest were confident.

But Forest lost 3-0 in the most dubious circumstances. The cruellest blow was a late goal by Paul Hart which was disallowed — no one knew why.

Suspicions about the referee's impartiality would eventually surface nearly 15 years later.

❑ ❑ ❑

WHILE Forest were bowing out of Europe, sadly Notts County were saying their farewells to the top division after an all-too-brief stay.

It was the start of a long fall from glory for the Magpies.

❑ ❑ ❑

A FOUR-month-old beer drinking pet calf was the guest of honour at a wedding in Lambley.

The happy couple were Gill Davis and farmworker David Colley whose boss Robert Martin thought Katie the calf would make an ideal guest.

Katie, Robert's drinking partner at the Robin Hood in Lambley, knocked back a couple of pints, three nights a week.

❑ ❑ ❑

THE world's greatest male ballet dancer Rudolph Nureyev made a one-night appearance at the Theatre Royal.

He danced in *The Sleeping Beauty* with the Northern Ballet Theatre, watched by an enraptured audience who gave him a standing ovation.

Explaining his appearance, at the age of 46, in Nottingham, Nureyev told the *Evening Post*: "It is the most important ballet in the repertoire of modern dance. If you tackle that ballet, you have a passport into life."

PICKET CLASH: Police try to keep rival factions apart at Babbington Colliery

A MEMORIAL honouring D.H. Lawrence was unveiled in Poets' Corner at Westminster to mark the centenary of the Notts-born writer.

The ceremony was attended by his nieces, Margaret Needham and Joan Frieda King.

At Eastwood, the writer's birthplace, a centenary festival was held in September, and Home Brewery launched a DHL Centenary Ale.

However, the celebrations attracted controversy. A professor from Manchester had complained about the trivial nature of the proposed Eastwood festival — and another critic branded some of the plans as "carnivalesque".

At Nottingham Playhouse, the centenary was marked by a performance of Nottingham writer Campbell Kay's *Phoenix Rising*. At the Theatre Royal, London Contemporary Dance Theatre performed Christopher Bannerman's ballet *Shadows in the Sun*, based on Lawrence's writings.

JAYNE Torvill and Christopher Dean presented their touring professional show in September, seen by 7,000 fans a night in a big top at The Forest.

PUPILS transferred from Mundella School to nearby Wilford Meadows School. Mundella was demolished later in 1985.

NOTTS County's slide continued. A year after being relegated from the First to the Second Division, the Magpies were demoted again, to the Third.

UDM split as pitmen clash

THE Union of Democratic Mineworkers was born on July 6 when representatives of 34 branches of the NUM voted to break away.

However, the UDM was conceived a year earlier when the national strike in protest at pit closures began, driven from the Yorkshire coalfield by NUM chief Arthur Scargill.

Notts miners, who were operating an overtime ban at the time, wanted a ballot on the strike. Mr Scargill restricted the vote to the national executive, who gave him their support.

They knew that decision would not rest easy in Notts and picketing of the county's pits began, with teams shipped in from Kent, Scotland and Yorkshire.

As Notts men continued to defy their union by working on, picketing became more aggressive and degenerated into violence against the police.

At Ollerton Colliery a Yorkshireman named David Jones became the first fatal casualty of the conflict.

With the lines now firmly drawn, both sides dug in with even greater determination. Scargill and Notts NUM secretary Henry Richardson called for peace while his miners held their own ballot.

It resulted in 75% of the men voting to work on.

At a massed meeting in the grounds of the union HQ at Berry Hill, area president Ray Chadburn pleaded with the men to "get up off your knees" and back the strike.

At that point financial secretary Roy Lynk interrupted, telling the men: "They can't fetch you out without a national ballot and whatever decision you take, I will support."

From that moment on, the NUM was facing a split that would never be healed. Relations among the NUM leadership became strained and Lynk was dismissed as an NUM official.

Within days the county branches had voted and the new union was launched. At first it did not receive favour within the Labour movement as it was snubbed by politicians and the TUC.

Lester 'retires' at Colwick

TURF LEGEND: Piggott cornered by fans at Nottingham Racecourse

LESTER Piggott chose humble Nottingham Racecourse for his final day's riding on October 29 — and a crowd of 5,000 turned up to watch the legendary jockey ride five favourites.

Before racing he said the one thing he looked forward to in retirement was eating. "It will be a whole new game," he said. "I may have to buy new trousers."

Piggott's 4,348 victories had included 29 Classic wins, nine in the Derby.

No. 4,349 came aboard Full Choke in the 18-furlong Willington Handicap.

His last mount, Gold Derivative, finished 23rd out of 24. The race? The Bitter End Selling Stakes.

Only it wasn't the bitter end. Five autumns later, Piggott was back in the saddle at Leicester, and in 1992 he won his 30th Classic aboard Rodrigo de Triano in the 2,000 Guineas.

Diana cheers rainy city

THOUSANDS turned out in Old Market Square in March for a glimpse of the Princess of Wales — making her first appearance in Nottingham since her marriage.

It was miserable weather, and the princess carried an umbrella as she and the Prince of Wales were welcomed at the Council House by the Lord Mayor. After a round of engagements, the couple flew out of East Midlands Airport.

Rice, Hadlee spearhead great Notts double ➡ Page 124

Rice angered by politics in charity

NOTTS cricket captain Clive Rice was at the centre of a race row as West Indian officials withdrew their support for a Sport Aid match against the Rest of the World.

It was the participation of the South African all-rounder which caused West Indies to take their stance, demanding the withdrawal of Rice.

They forced the names of the teams to be changed to a David Gower XI against an unofficial West Indies XI — and the game went ahead with the same players taking part.

Rice, understandably, was furious, launching a scathing attack on the West Indian administrators

"Surely, when there are thousands dying, we can pull together to help these people.

"It is not as if I support apartheid — and yet they are telling me I can't take part."

Denver starts famine race

THE *Evening Post* joined in the national response to pop star Bob Geldof's effort to relieve famine in Africa

CELEBRITY GUEST:
John Denver

by organising the Race Against Time.

Top American entertainer John Denver opened the event at Holme Pierrepont, timed to coincide with races in five continents raising huge sums for the starving in the Sudan and Ethiopia.

RISING STARS: Nottingham-born entertainer Su Pollard landed a starring role in the West End musical *Me and My Girl* and hit number two in the pop charts ... while BBC Radio Nottingham DJ Simon Mayo was promoted to a Saturday night slot on Radio1 before taking over the Breakfast Show

Health alert in big freeze

NOTTINGHAM shivered through the second coldest February of the century with temperatures plunging to -17F.

The big freeze broke at the beginning of March, bringing a huge sigh of relief to hospital emergency services, council workmen and sports officials.

Hospital admissions soared during the month-long freeze, more than 30,000 tons of salt were dumped on Notts roads in a £1m-plus operation to keep traffic moving, and Notts police dealt with 200 accidents in less than a month.

Three weekends of sport were virtually blanked out and the players of Forest and Notts County resorted to a practice match on plastic at Loughborough University.

Wildlife also suffered from the cold and appeal was made to bird lovers to come out and feed the ducks, geese and seagulls starving at Holme Pierrepont Country Park.

A more serious warning was aimed at children playing on frozen ponds — after two youngsters died in a frozen West Midlands canal.

NEW sails were fitted to Green's Mill at Sneinton following its rescue by the George Green Memorial Fund — dedicated to the Nottingham mathematician whose family had built it in the early 19th Century. Soon it was grinding flour for the first time in more than a century.

In one dramatic rescue, a fireman had to crawl along a ladder to reach a boy who had fallen through ice in Arnot Hill Park. The temperatures even plunged low enough for the DHSS to issue cold weather payments to pensioners.

FOLLOWING an *Evening Post* investigation, Notts police decided to look at ways of nailing car drivers who jumped red lights.

The *Post*'s bad driving survey prompted police to look at camera equipment used on the continent .

And in a scathing attack on driving standards, Chief Constable Charles McLachlan branded the 50-year-old driving test as "totally inadequate preparation" for the roads.

❑ ❑ ❑

BILL Anderson, who discovered stars like Duncan McKenzie, Tony Woodcock and Viv Anderson, died at his home in Radcliffe-on- Trent.

During a 50-year career he set a record in 1938 of playing for four different clubs in the same year — Barnsley, Bradford, Hartlepool and Barrow.

He joined Forest as assistant manager in 1966, had a brief spell as caretaker manager, and then became chief scout.

❑ ❑ ❑

TWO of the largest rides ever seen at Goose Fair were set up: Matty and Douglas Taylor's Magic Carpet, and Pat Collins' 85-tonne Pirate Ship.

❑ ❑ ❑

THE National Westminster Bank branch in High Street closed after 81 years. Staff transferred to the refurbished branch in Thurland Street.

47 perish as Flight BD92 crashes at Kegworth ⮞ Page 125

THE death of Nazi leader Rudolf Hess in Berlin's Spandau Prison brought to light the story of Nottingham man John Hartman, who met Hitler's former deputy once a week over a 19-year period.

Mr Hartman, from Sherwood, was chief censor at the prison from 1953 to 1972 and it was his job to read every letter written and received by Hess.

"He was always one hundred per cent Nazi," said Mr Hartman. "His thoughts were, 'Hitler was right. I did nothing wrong'."

Fluent in French and German, he was chief German interpreter with the Foreign Office in Berlin. He retired in 1972.

AN arsenal of more than 470 weapons were handed in during a two week knives amnesty in Notts.

The campaign, which was initiated by the *Evening Post*, yielded a frightening array of weapons including a wooden cosh encrusted with nails, a kung-fu style throwing star and 20 cut throat razors.

"If this amnesty results in five or ten incidents not occurring in the next few months, we will be delighted,"said Deputy Chief Constable Dan Crompton.

A DIRECTOR of Mansfield Brewery was among those who escaped the horrific Kings Cross tube station fire which killed more than 30 people. Stephen Holt escaped with his jacket over his head.

PLANS for two Robin Hood centres in Nottingham were unveiled. One, costing £2.5m, was to be built on the corner of Friar Lane and Standard Hill; the other, at £1.75m, was earmarked for Maid Marian Way.

CHART-topper Rick Astley and Rolling Stone Bill Wyman's ex Mandy Smith were in Nottingham to celebrate Ritzys first birthday.

Hyson Green's 1960s deck flats are levelled

EYESORE: Nottingham said a none-too-fond farewell to the Hyson Green flats which had been condemned to demolition. Built in the 1960s, their upkeep was costing the city a fortune

Famous double for Trent Bridge heroes

NOTTS completed one of the most successful seasons in their long history by taking the county championship and the NatWest Trophy.

And they were pipped to the Sunday League title on the last day of the season.

It proved to be a fitting finale to the Trent Bridge careers of all-rounder Richard Hadlee and captain Clive Rice.

The first leg of the attempted treble came at Lords where Notts defeated Northants in the NatWest final, thanks to a six and a four in the last over by Hadlee.

The New Zealander and Rice then spearheaded Notts to a county championship win over Glamorgan at Trent Bridge which ensured the title.

During his ten seasons at Trent Bridge, Richard Hadlee scored 5,854 runs and took 612 wickets at a cost of around 14 runs apiece.

"I shall miss playing for Notts," he said. "My career has really taken off while I have been here."

On the last day of the Refuge Assurance Sunday competition, Notts had to beat Surrey and hope that Northants would beat leaders Worcestershire.

Notts won ... but so did Worcestershire.

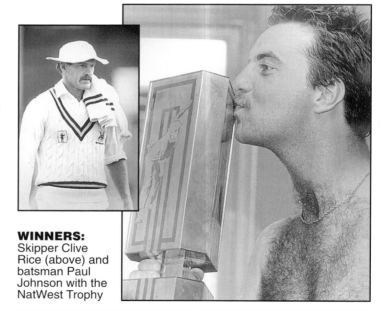

WINNERS: Skipper Clive Rice (above) and batsman Paul Johnson with the NatWest Trophy

'Arm the police' says LAPD guest

LOS Angeles police officer J.J. Leonard visited Nottingham and declared that British policemen should be armed.

"You are more than willing to have armed guards on jewels," he said, "yet are ready to send your policemen out on the streets with a little stick.

"Maybe the tragic incident at Hungerford could have been curtailed if that policeman had had a gun."

Reds fans see tragedy unfold at Hillsborough ➡ Page 126

Champion salutes Pickard

STEFAN Edberg praised the Brian Clough-style approach of his Notts coach Tony Pickard after winning the Wimbledon men's singles crown.

Swede Edberg defeated Boris Becker and said: "Tony has been a big part of my success. He has done a lot for me."

Pickard, who was born in Ripley, was a former Notts champion and Davis Cup player.

❑ ❑ ❑

HOME Secretary Douglas Hurd designated Nottingham a 'safer city' as part of a national crime crackdown.

Speaking at the conference in Nottingham, he said the city was the third of 20 to be included.

❑ ❑ ❑

A CAR bought for £6,500 by Peter Sellers at the 1962 Earls Court Motor Show, was snapped up by Nottingham man Tony Collins.

He paid a dealer around £20,000 for the Mercedes and found out by writing to Sir Harry Secombe that it had been a particular favourite of Sellers.

❑ ❑ ❑

A LETTER from screen goddess Greta Garbo fetched £1,100 at a Nottingham auction. The two-line note to well-wishers was bought by a postal bid from America.

❑ ❑ ❑

THOUSANDS of screaming fans welcomed pop idols Bros to the Royal Concert Hall. Matt and Luke Goss with Craig Logan seemed set to become a major force in the pop world.

❑ ❑ ❑

LIVERPOOL beat Forest 2-1 in the FA Cup semi-final at Hillsborough. The Reds had earlier knocked out Halifax, Orient, Birmingham and Arsenal.

❑ ❑ ❑

GOOSE Fair had a record number of new rides — including Pat Collins' Thunderbird, Manning's Break Dance and Willie Webb's Voyager.

KEGWORTH CRASH: The scene of devastation pictured next day from an aircraft over the M1

47 perish as BD92 crashes on M-way

FORTY-seven people died when a British Midland Boeing 737 crashed on the M1 motorway near Kegworth.

Flight BD92 was en route from Heathrow to Belfast when the Captain Kevin Hunt diverted to East Midlands Airport after detecting what he believed was engine vibration.

He flew low over Kegworth and was desperately trying to reach the EMA runway when the aircraft crashed on a steep embankment, splitting in two.

Wreckage was strewn across a wide area of the motorway and dozens of motorists and villagers raced to help. But 47 people lay dead or dying within the remains of the aircraft.

Incredibly, 79 people would be rescued alive.

Getting to the injured up a steep and slippery slope was a difficult and dangerous job.

Steps had to be cut into the bank to enable stretchers to move to and fro.

Doctors squeezed into confined spaces to administer help to the injured as fire crews shored up the structure.

Eleven members of Beeston Marina Boat Club, returning from London, joined the operation, staying for two hours amidst scenes which would haunt them forever.

They were among the 69 people who would receive Royal Humane Society awards for their efforts that night, the highest number ever given for a single incident.

Capt Hunt and his first officer David McClelland were dismissed by British Midland

Cartoonist and village resident Bill Tidy said: "At the end of the day we're still here talking and that's down to the pilot. I don't think you will find anyone in the village who's pleased they have been bounced."

A permanent memorial was later unveiled in Kegworth Cemetery.

RESCUE: Workers on the embankment

Pearsons closes after 99 years

THE Department store Pearsons of Nottingham, above, closed in February after almost a century. The site of Wrigglesworth Ironmongery was acquired by Frederick Pearson in 1889, and neighbouring properties were bought as the business expanded.

The Flying Horse Arcade, once the site of one of Nottingham's oldest and most historic inns, was sold for £9m to Friends Provident, one of Britain's largest mutual life offices.

Polo arm injury puts Prince of Wales in QMC ➡ Page 127

1989

Princess lifts city charity

PRINCESS Diana made another of her many visits to the city to mark the official reopening of the Albert Hall.

The Princess of Wales unveiled a commemorative plaque and signed the visitors book before moving on to the Turning Point charity's Alfred Minto project in Basford which provides rehabilitation for psychiatric patients who have been discharged from hospital.

□ □ □

NOTTINGHAM millionaire Mr Nat Puri and his wife Dagmar were bound and gagged by armed robbers during a raid on their city home.

The four gunmen escaped with £20,000 worth of property and during a dramatic chase along the M1 motorway, shot at Nottingham police officer Carl Handford.

Detectives warned the public not to approach anyone they thought might be involved because of the danger of them using the firearms again.

□ □ □

NOTTS won the Benson and Hedges Cup at Lord's, beating Essex by three wickets.

□ □ □

THE Showman's Guild celebrated its centenary year at Goose Fair.

□ □ □

FOREST won the Littlewoods Cup, beating Luton Town 3-1 at Wembley.

Earlier victims were Chester City, Coventry City, Leicester City, Queen's Park Rangers and Bristol City.

The Reds also won the Simod Cup.

REMEMBERING: Nottingham pays its respects to the Liverpool fans who died

Fans united as 96 die in Cup tragedy

NOTTINGHAM Forest fans watched in horror as 96 Liverpool supporters were fatally injured in the Hillsborough football disaster.

The FA Cup semi final, on April 15, was one of the most eagerly anticipated matches of the decade — and there were not enough tickets to accommodate all the Liverpool fans wanting to get into Sheffield Wednesday's ground.

And that led to tragedy as thousands of supporters, many of them without tickets, arrived minutes before kick-off, overwhelming police on duty at the Leppings Lane end.

To avert the potential for disaster outside the ground, the order was given to open a gate and let the fans in.

It was to prove a fatal move, coming with the game only a few minutes old and just as Liverpool's Peter Beardsley struck the Forest bar, sending up a mighty roar inside the stadium.

Excited Liverpool fans flooded through the gate and into the packed centre section of the terracing.

Fans at the front had no escape as they were squeezed against the metal barriers.

At the Kop end, where the Forest fans were gathered, the mood changed from anger, at what appeared to be a pitch invasion, to horror as young men and women were given the kiss-of-life down on the ground where minutes before a thrilling football match was being played.

The fans applauded Liverpool supporters who ripped down advertising boards for makeshift stretchers.

In the following week, Liverpool was a city in mourning as a carpet of flowers was laid in tribute over the grass of Anfield.

In Nottingham, flowers and scarves were piled up at the City Ground and collections were held to help the grieving relatives.

Forest manager Brian Clough and his players attended a service of remembrance at St Mary's.

The match was replayed six weeks later, at Old Trafford, in an unreal atmosphere. The game ended 3-1 to Liverpool who went on to take the FA Cup, defeating Everton 3-2 at Wembley.

The repercussions would rumble on for years to come — and would lead to the biggest upheaval in the history of football.

Lord Justice Taylor was appointed to head the official inquiry.

As a result of his findings, safety fences at all grounds around the country were ordered to be removed and a time frame was established for grounds to become all-seater stadia.

Students get cleaning bill after Rag Week

A THOUSAND Trent Polytechnic students allowed their Rag Week celebrations to get out of hand — and landed a hefty bill to clean up the mess.

Students bombarded each other outside the Poly library, leaving pavements covered with eggs, flour, water, ketchup and raw meat.

Police inspector Dave Williams commented: "It was totally over the top." A 27-year-old student replied: "It was hysterical."

Alert Notts sailor saves battleship Missouri ➡ Page 128

Notts pair flee Saddam invaders

HUNDREDS of British citizens were caught in Kuwait when the Iraqi forces invaded — among them health technician Peter Bunting from Bramcote and Kathy McGregor from West Bridgford.

Mr Bunting drove his own car in a convoy of eight vehicles who made a 600-mile dash across the desert to reach the safety of the Saudi Arabian border.

And as Iraqi troops began to round up foreign nationals to use as hostages, Kathy dressed up as a Bedouin and joined a 13-car convoy making its escape.

"The gentleman who got us out was a real hero. He took great risks to get us out. He was part of the resistance and we got to know him through some Kuwaiti friends," said Kathy when she returned safely to West Bridgford.

As the civilians arrived back home, 30 Notts soldiers were among a contingent from the 1st Regiment of the Royal Horse Artillery embarking for the Gulf.

2,000 witness Robin pageant

THE first Robin Hood Pageant took place in Nottingham with more than 2,000 people packing Old Market Square.

Hundreds of children were among the crowd, booing as Robin Hood was brought before the Council House by the Sheriff's men and sentenced to be hanged.

And then they cheered as he broke free after a riot by the outlaws — actually, more than 200 cubs and scouts.

That was the prelude to a week of feasting, jousting, archery and merriment on the Castle Green.

Kegworth: Call for rear-facing seats

A REPORT into the Kegworth air disaster revealed that rear facing seats would have reduced the casualties.

And investigators said a more effective bracing position could possibly have cut the death toll, which claimed 47 lives.

PATIENT PRINCE: Health authority chairman David White welcomes the Prince of Wales to the QMC

QMC arm op for Charles

PRINCE Charles arrived at the Queen's Medical Centre to undergo an operation on his right arm, fractured during a polo match.

During his week long stay in hospital, he was visited by the Princess of Wales and received hundreds of gifts and get well wishes.

They included a giant card from the Ritzy nightclub in Nottingham — and a bottle of Shipstones bitter.

He left hospital with the aid of a walking stick, which he cheekily waved at the nurses before being driven away.

Princess Diana, who visited her husband in the QMC, was in Nottingham on another occasion to open the new luxury indoor tennis centre.

The tennis-loving princess toured the eight indoor courts at the £1.5m centre, but turned down the chance of a quick game with British ladies

GET WELL SOON: The card from Ritzy

number one Sarah Loosemore.

The Princess also visited the Nottingham and Notts Society for the Deaf on Forest Road West which was celebrating its centenary.

GOAL POST: England soccer captain Gary Lineker catches up with the news in *Football Post*. He was in Nottingham to launch a new menswear range at a Victoria Centre store

FORMER Notts all-rounder Richard Hadlee made his final appearance at Trent Bridge in the drawn 1st Cornhill Test between England and New Zealand.

Days later he was knighted in the Queen's Birthday Honours. For the 2nd Test, he was listed on the Lord's scorecard as Sir R. Hadlee.

The Kiwi celebrated with four wickets and a quickfire 86. He retired as the world's leading test wicket-taker — 431 at 22.29 apiece.

□□□

BRIAN Clough prepared to take the first steps towards an acting career by filming a role in Boon — playing himself.

The Forest boss was told to go to the Star pub in Beeston to film his part, without knowing the name had been changed to the Drum for the purposes of the plot.

After a struggle to find the venue, he eventually strode in to say: "Right lads, let's get cracking!"

□□□

NOTTINGHAM University student Dominic Cullen celebrated clearing his £1,000 overdraft — after a £2 bet won him £3,200.

He had £1,700 riding on the last leg of a seven-horse accumulator, and Moscow Dynamo obliged.

□□□

WEMBLEY goals from Tommy Johnson and Craig Short saw Notts heading back to Division Two. The Magpies beat Tranmere Rovers in the play-offs final.

□□□

FOREST again won the Littlewoods Cup, a Nigel Jemson goal beating Oldham at Wembley.

□□□

AFTER a five-year absence from competition, Jayne Torvill and Christopher Dean won the world professional championship and were named American Skating World Professional Skaters of the Year.

□□□

HONORARY degree recipients at Nottingham Polytechnic included Radford-born writer Alan Sillitoe.

Poly becomes university ... with name problem ➡ Page 129

SIR Andrew Buchanan became the new Lord Lieutenant of Notts, succeeding Sir Gordon Hobday.

A working farmer and occupant of the family seat at Hodsock Priory near Blyth, Sir Andrew was anticipating a major change to his lifestyle.

"People say I'll have a busy year," he told the *Evening Post.* "They don't realise it lasts until you retire."

□ □ □

NOTTS won their first seven games in the Refuge Assurance League and went on to take their first ever Sunday title. The season ended with Notts (13 wins in 16 matches) two points clear of Lancashire.

The West Indies beat England by nine wickets in the 3rd Cornhill Test at Trent Bridge. The series was drawn 2-2.

□ □ □

GEORGE Miller became the first blind chairman of Notts County Council with a pledge to fly the flag for the disabled.

The Stapleford councillor, an ex-*Evening Post* reporter, took up his post with his German Shepherd guide dog Sarina at his side.

□ □ □

THE day after the ballerina Dame Margot Fonteyn died, at 71, *Post* theatre critic Emrys Bryson recalled the great dancer's visits to Nottingham.

As well as remembering great performances, Emrys revealed that the wafer thin star enjoyed tucking into steak ... and was partial to a plate of jellied eels.

□ □ □

ANOTHER promotion season for Notts County — again, after a Wembley play-off. Tommy Johnson scored twice as Brighton were beaten 3-1 for a place in the First Division.

□ □ □

FOREST were back at Wembley, this time for the FA Cup Final. Skipper Stuart Pearce scored for the Reds with a thunderous free kick, and Mark Crossley was to save a Gary Lineker penalty — but Spurs won 2-1 after extra time.

GULF HERO: Steven Bunbury is welcomed home by his family

Sailor saves the Missouri

THE war to force Saddam Hussein's Iraqi troops out of Kuwait began on January 16.

While the world's media concentrated on hi-tech bombing of Iraqi targets and a brilliant land campaign, a Nottingham sailor made his own contribution to the effort.

In HMS *Gloucester*, 17-year-old Steven Bunbury was manning radar when he spotted the track of Iraqi Silkworm missiles with enough explosive power to destroy their target, the American battleship USS *Missouri*.

With less than a minute to impact, Steven identified the incoming rockets as hostile, informed the gun deck and Sea Dart missiles destroyed the Silkworms. They were within 17 seconds of destroying the American ship.

Stephen, nicknamed Hawkeye, was praised by MPs.

The ground war began on January 30 and by February 2, Iraqi resistance was all but over but the operation to liberate Kuwait would take until February 26. Two days later, exactly 100 hours after Operation Desert Storm began, Iraq was defeated.

A total of 26 British servicemen died in the Gulf War, the survivors returned home to a heroes' welcome.

But for many, a new battle was just beginning — to win recognition for the affects of the war on the rest of their lives. Gulf War Syndrome was about to become part of the dictionary of war.

Tennis stars come to town

THE Federation Cup, the women's team championship, was held at the Tennis Centre.

And among the enthusiastic fans who turned up for matches involving the likes of Steffi Graf and Jennifer Capriati, was Princess Diana.

She watched from the Royal Box, seated between Cliff Richard and Virginia Wade.

The British team consisted of Jo Durie, Clare Wood, Sam Smith and Monique Javer. Needless to say, they made an early exit.

Gary Glitter at the Theatre Royal

LEADER of the gang, Gary Glitter was in town ... as an actor.

The king of Glam Rock, starred in *A Slice Of Saturday Night*, set in the Sixties, at the Theatre Royal.

Stella Rimington heads MI5

FORMER Nottingham schoolgirl Stella Rimington, 56, was appointed director-general of MI5. She was the first woman to hold the post — and the first director-general to be officially named.

Mrs Rimington, who was educated at Nottingham High School for Girls, took up her appointment in 1992. In 1994 she became the first head of MI5 to speak publicly about the secret services when she went on BBC television to give the Richard Dimbleby Lecture.

SPYMISTRESS: Mrs Rimington with pupils at her old school

Five Notts cult members die in Texas tragedy Page 130

Reds race to complete new stand

BUILDERS were working feverishly to complete Nottingham Forest's new Bridgford End stand in time for the opening match of the new Premiership season against Liverpool.

But the project to cover and reshape that part of the ground was not going down well in the neighbourhood.

Residents formed a committee to voice their complaints about noise and disruption.

Committee chairwoman Margaret Grabowiecki said: "It's like hell living here."

And resident Janette Mulvaney said she had been told the disruption would be no worse than if a neighbour was building a garage extension.

"It's more like living next door to a shipyard."

Completion of the stand was still some weeks away and its occupation on match days was gradually phased in during the early part of the season.

There were complaints about too many seats going to away fans, lack of atmosphere and even the affect the stand was having on ground conditions.

But the finished article did help Forest secure three European Championships group games four years later.

World tour for missing luggage

WILFORD holidaymaker John Haslam waved farewell to his family before jetting off for a holiday in Turkey — a luggage-free holiday.

He expected it to be there when he arrived in Turkey, but instead it went its own way to Sicily, Frankfurt, Addis Ababa in Ethiopia and also Izmir (right country, wrong airport).

Handlers at Gatwick dubbed his baggage "one of the best travelled suitcases in the world".

It was little comfort to John when he returned to be told: "We are not sure exactly where it is now ... we think it might be in a bomb proof container in Germany."

OLYMPIC FIRST: Gareth Marriott from Notts won Britain's first ever Olympic canoeing medal in the Canadian singles slalom at Barcelona. He lost the gold by the slimmest of margins

University challenged

IDENTITY was the name of the game as Nottingham's two highest seats of learning exchanged verbal volleys.

At issue was the new name for Nottingham Poly after it had been granted university status.

The college had plumped for City University, Nottingham — but elders of the University of Nottingham were not impressed.

They said the new title would be confused with their own, and the registrar confirmed: "We've already had mail addressed to the polytechnic's departments.

"We don't want any mix-ups. Yes, it's causing a little friction."

Back at the newer university, they were taking a slightly different view.

"We are in the city and we want to be associated with it," said a spokesman. "If we lose, we won't take it lying down."

The title of Nottingham Trent University was finally chosen — and it is now firmly established among the most popular in the country.

WEST Bridgford-born entertainer Leslie Crowther, 59, *above*, was severely injured when his Rolls-Royce crashed on the M5 in October. Later in the month his wife Jean sent a message of thanks to wellwishers as the patient emerged from a coma.

Rumpus over youth camp condoms

YOUNG people at an international camp at Holme Pierrepont were given free condoms by the county council.

They were handed out at the breakfast and dinner table to visitors, aged 16 to 25, from Holland, Germany, France and Latvia.

A Tory councillor said: "This is just carte blanche for experimental sex."

But the director said it was inevitable that some of the visitors would sleep together.

EX-goalie Ken Oxford pulled off the save of his life ... stopping armed robbers stealing cash he was taking to a post office.

The former Derby County keeper was delivering for Securicor in Ilkeston when a gang attacked him with a hammer.

Helped by an off-duty police officer, he fought them off. The three thugs turned and fled, straight into the path of a car.

One of the villains was seriously injured and ended up in hospital, but the other two escaped.

❏ ❏ ❏

MORE than eight million gallons of water were being lost in Nottingham every day, according to Severn Trent.

Nearly a fifth of the city's daily supply of 42 million gallons was escaping through leaks or unaccounted use.

❏ ❏ ❏

BT revealed plans to change telephone numbers in Nottingham.

Out would go the old 0602 dialling code, to be replaced with 0115 plus a 9 in front of the original six-digit number.

Nottingham was one of five cities singled out for a telephone shake-up, joining Leeds, Bristol, Leicester and Sheffield.

❏ ❏ ❏

OLD Market Square hosted the 1992 Pitcher of the Year competition and a Notts man scooped the Best Newcomer prize, worth £500.

Super salesmen from across the country turned up for the event, but it was six times winner Bobby Halket from Stoke who shouted the rest of the down.

❏ ❏ ❏

BOXING legend Muhammad Ali was in Nottingham in June, visiting Dillons to sign copies of the new biography by Thomas Hauser.

❏ ❏ ❏

IN another dramatic season at Meadow Lane, Notts finished 21st in the First Division and were relegated. High-scoring former Sheffield United star Tony Agana scored just once in 13 games.

Hospital abduction: The hunt for baby Abbie Page 131

FORMER Radio Trent disc jockey Dale Winton got his big break — hosting Central Television's made-in-Nottingham version of the hit American game show *Supermarket Sweep*.

Winton was contracted to record 75 shows in 1993. His TV career blossomed later in the Nineties when he hosted shows including *Pets Win Prizes* and the National Lottery Draw.

THE Princess of Wales made her first visit to Nottingham since the break-up of her marriage.

She was at Nottingham Playhouse to see members of the CandoCo Dance Company for able and disabled people, perform before visiting Turning Point's Corporation Oaks mental health project and Challenge House, the British Red Cross care home in Beeston.

RUSHCLIFFE MP Kenneth Clarke, *pictured*, was Prime Minister John Major's choice to take over as Chancellor from Norman Lamont.

NOTTS' season began with the county's first tied match in first-class cricket — the honours at Trent Bridge being shared with Worcestershire.

NOTTS-born entertainer Leslie Crowther, recovering from serious injuries after a car crash, received the CBE.

WORLD champion power lifter Wayne Buck from Bestwood Colliery Village wed his sweetheart Jeanette Saunders in All Saints', Nottingham.

'Pleasant surprise' for DHL niece

KEN Russell's BBC-1 version of D.H. Lawrence's novel *Lady Chatterley's Lover* was serialised in June, starring Joely Richardson, with James Wilby, and Sean Bean as the gamekeeper Mellors.

Lawrence's niece Peggy Needham, 84, from Heanor, said she had been apprehensive about the adaptation of the work which had been the subject of an obscenity trial in 1960 ... but was "pleasantly surprised" by the result.

LADY C AND MELLORS: Joely Richardson and Sean Bean

Waco: Notts five die in Koresh cult siege

FIVE Nottingham people were among 23 Britons who died when a siege at a Texas ranch ended in tragedy.

On February 28, US authorities tried to raid the headquarters of the Branch Davidian religious cult in Waco.

The raid prompted a 51-day stand off at the compound before the FBI again attacked. Fire swept through the buildings, killing 75 people including cult leader David Koresh.

Survivors later told of a suicide plan using fire, tanks, or for people to be shot.

Three separate blazes started within minutes of each other following the FBI operation to spread tear gas through the buildings.

The situation was made worse because windows were boarded up or barricaded.

A two year investigation into the massacre on behalf of the UK victims strongly criticised the role of the American authorities in the tragedy.

A US Justice Department report said Koresh was responsible for the deaths of 50 adults — including four FBI officers — and 25 children. Of the dead at least 17 died of gunshot wounds and only nine cult members, including a Nottingham woman, survived.

Livingston Fagan, from Nottingham, was later jailed for 40 years for his part in the siege.

TOP SHOT: Broadway Cinema's 'Shots in the Dark' crime festival was building an international reputation. Visiting stars in 1993 included Herbert Lom, best known for his portrayal of the hapless Inspector Dreyfus in the *Pink Panther* films

Cloughie: Unhappy ending as Reds are relegated

NOTTINGHAM Forest chairman Fred Reacher made the announcement which shook the football world: "Brian Clough will retire at the end of the season."

The great man was about to bring down the curtain on a glorious career in the game, and an 18-year stay at the City Ground which had brought promotion, the Championship, two European Cups and four League Cups.

Sadly, his parting was filled with sorrow as Forest were heading back where Clough had found them.

After 41 years in the game, as both striker and manager, Old Big Head said: "I suppose I'm entitled to sit back and enjoy my pension."

Trucker the hero of Belgian motorway inferno Page 132

Sorry, we demolished your home

HOLIDAYMAKER Dora Molik was given the shock of her life during a stay with her brother in Nottingham — the home she left behind in Australia was accidentally knocked down!

The mistake was made by the Queensland railway company which chose the wrong house to remove to make way for track.

She heard about it while staying in Aspley.

Headlines in Australian newspapers read "Oops! Wrong house", and even Dora was able to see the funny side.

"It was a mistake, but what a mistake. The house was in the process of being sold but I didn't think I would lose it that quick."

Jailed 40 years for Waco involvement

CITY man Livingstone Fagan was jailed for 40 years by a court in America for his part in the Waco siege which ended in the deaths of more than 80 people.

Fagan and seven other members of the Branch Davidian religious cult who were involved in a shoot-out with police and FBI agents were jailed.

They had faced charges ranging from carrying a firearm during a violent crime to aiding and abetting the voluntary manslaughter of federal officers.

Bronze comeback for Chris, Jayne

A CHANGE of regulations allowed Nottingham-born ice dancers Jayne Torvill and Christopher Dean — professional skaters since 1984 — to reclaim their amateur status.

In January they gained their seventh British title, and followed up with gold at the European championships in Copenhagen.

But there was to be no repeat of their 1984 Olympic triumph — although they did win the bronze medal in Norway.

Abbie drama grips nation

FOR the first 15 days of July, the nation followed news of the hunt for new-born baby Abbie Humphries who had been snatched from the maternity unit at the Queen's Medical Centre.

A woman dressed in a nurse's uniform took the child from her father Roger's arms, claiming the baby needed a hearing test, and then walked out of the hospital.

A massive police hunt was started as parents Karen, 32, and Roger 33, pleaded for their baby's safe return.

As an immediate debate over hospital security began, people with information began contacting the police inquiry room.

Less than two weeks after the incident, new, improved security measures were introduced at the QMC.

The hunt for Abbie and her abductor was now nearing its conclusion.

REUNITED: Abbie and overjoyed parents Roger and Karen Humphries

On Day 16, at around 1am, following a tip-off, police returned to the Wollaton address they had visited earlier.

They find baby Abbie asleep and unharmed.

● A young woman was put on three years' probation, with a psychotherapy condition, for the abduction.

TWO DEGREES: The University of Nottingham awarded honorary Doctor of Letters degrees to Ilkeston-born stage and TV star Robert Lindsay, and Radford-born novelist Alan Sillitoe

EXTRA security had to be brought in when the bad boys of Nineties rock came to Nottingham.

Oasis were due to play to a sell-out concert at Rock City on August 15, 1994.

A few days earlier a show in Newcastle had to be cancelled after fighting broke out between the band and the audience.

The Rock City gig went ahead as planned, without incident.

Two years later, as the biggest band in Britain, they played to 250,000 people over one weekend at Knebworth.

❐❐❐

JIM Lees was nominated for the Guinness Book of Records as the world's longest serving Scout.

Mr Lees, perhaps even better known as Notts' greatest expert on the legend of Robin Hood, had totted up 73 years in the movement.

❐❐❐

JEAN-Pierre Varet of Broxtowe Estate appeared on Channel Four's *Big Breakfast* after winning the title Most Fantastically Good Looking Man in Britain.

The martial arts expert from the South of France was nominated by his wife Donna.

❐❐❐

TODDLER James Wright gave his parents a scare when he fell 12 feet out of his Hucknall bedroom window — got up and knocked on the door to be let back into the house.

❐❐❐

FRANK Wise retired after 35 years washing cars. The super soaper, boss of Nottingham's Five Minute Car Wash, had cleaned around five million cars during his career.

❐❐❐

NOTTINGHAM Forest clinched promotion back to the Premier League at the first time of asking under manager Frank Clarke. Forest, thanks in main to the goals of leading scorer Stan Collymore, clinched promotion at Peterborough.

Miners win fight for wider lung illness benefit ➡ Page 133

NOTTS student Paul Wells was one of four holidaymakers kidnapped by Kashmiri terrorists.

Paul, 23, a photography student at South Nottingham College, was captured with another Briton, two Americans and a Norwegian.

Three fellow trekkers, including Paul's girlfriend Kath Mosley, were released.

The Kashmiri separatist group Al Faran claimed responsibility and demanded the release of 30 jailed militants.

Fears for their safety were heightened in August when the decapitated body of Norwegian hostage Hans Christian Ostro was found.

As the months went by with no word of the hostages whereabouts, Paul's father Bob, from Blackburn, and girlfriend Kath would make trips to Kashmir to try to find out more for themselves.

The campaign was given a higher profile when Beirut hostage Terry Waite visited Paul's brother in Nottingham and agreed to become patron of the Hostages in Kashmir Campaign.

Nothing more was heard of Paul and the other hostages.

STAPLEFORD mum Kathleen Needham was dancing with joy after scooping a one-fifth share of a £2.6m lottery win — followed by a £300 bingo jackpot.

THE Andrew Lloyd Webber musical *Cats* became the Theatre Royal's first £1m blockbuster when Strelley mum Barbara Pellicciari bought two tickets which took sales through the six-figure barrier.

NOTTINGHAM'S most celebrated living author Alan Sillitoe brought out his autobiography *Life Without Armour* in which he told of his early life in Radford, followed by RAF service in the Malayan jungle.

NOTTS County were relegated after finishing the 1994-5 season 24th in Division One.

STAN THE MAN: Stan Collymore, whose goals helped get Forest promoted, was transferred to Liverpool for £8.5m. The Reds used some of the cash to buy Kevin Campbell and Chris Bart-Williams

Trucker Alan saves three in gas tragedy

A NOTTINGHAM lorry driver was hailed a hero when he dragged three people to safety after a gas explosion in a motorway service station in Belgium.

Alan Sharpe of Arnold was sitting in his truck when the blast ripped through the Wally-stop cafeteria.

With the help of another British driver, Mr Sharpe risked his life to save two waitresses and a German trucker from the flames.

More than a dozen people died.

Mr Sharpe said: "I was the first man on the scene and I could see a young girl lying in the wreckage. She seemed to be terribly injured ... I pulled her out and called for help and my mate and I went in to lift out a really big German driver.

"We pulled the rubble off him and got him clear and went back for the other woman."

Moments later, the whole building went up in a ball of flame, making further rescue impossible.

King Albert of Belgium travelled to the scene to meet the two drivers and thank them for their heroism. Nearly a year later, he travelled back to Belgium to receive the country's highest civilian honour, the Medaille Civique from the King.

RESCUER: Arnold trucker Alan Sharpe

Rolf rules OK with Nottingham fans

HUNDREDS of fans queued up for autographs when Rolf Harris, *pictured*, visited the Virgin megastore to promote his new album *Rolf Rules OK*, hot on the heels of his controversial hit version of Led Zeppelin's *Stairway to Heaven*.

And to prove he bridged the age gap, 20-year-old student Dawn Collins announced: "I have always loved Rolf."

City, county shake hands on split

A TWO year war between the county and city councils ended when Nottingham was allowed to run its own affairs.

The city achieved its aim of unitary status, despite County Hall's argument that it was too inexperienced to look after education and social services.

But once the decision was made, the two council leaders leaders shook hands.

After 30 years, rock legend Bowie hits town ➡ Page 134

1996

Reds prepare ground for take-over

THE first shots in the Nottingham Forest take-over saga were fired by chairman Fred Reacher who announced to stand aside and let the club be sold to the highest bidder.

One of the first people to throw his cap in the ring was businessman Grant Bovey who talked about a £25m investment, but he just as quickly withdrew.

Other names came and went, including that of an Indonesian multi-millionaire.

Forest's board whittled the bidders down to two serious applications, from an East Midlands consortium headed by Sandy Anderson, and a group including former Tottenham chief Irving Scholar and author Phil Soar, a lifelong Reds fan.

But the agony for Forest fans would drag on into 1997 before a final decision would be taken.

☐ ☐ ☐

A CONVICTED murderer saved a Nottingham prison officer from death inside the Perry Road jail.

Officer Michael Bugg choked when a segment of orange became stuck in his throat.

Lifer Terence Hughes, who was trained in first aid when he was a miner in Wales, performed the Heimlich manoeuvre — squeezing the victim's chest — to force the segment into the stomach.

Grateful Mr Bugg, of Toton, said: "I wouldn't be here if it hadn't been for him."

☐ ☐ ☐

A VILLAGE garden was at the centre of a major planning row when a council told its owners to dig it up.

Retired GP Martin Leadley and his wife Pauline had lovingly created a beautiful garden in their Cropwell Butler home, using an adjacent field they had bought.

But because the field was Green Belt land, they needed planning permission.

Eventually, the Leadleys were allowed to keep the plot, but as a woodland and not a garden, which meant they had to replace hundreds of plants with shrubs and saplings.

Farewell to Dennis, Leslie and Tommy

TWENTY thousand fans lined the streets for the funeral of broadcaster Dennis McCarthy — 'the voice of Nottingham'.

Traffic came to a standstill as the cortege, led by a horse-drawn hearse, progressed from BBC headquarters in Mansfield Road to St Barnabas' Roman Catholic Cathedral in Derby Road.

In Old Market Square, the Lord Mayor paid her personal tribute, doffing her hat. The flag at the Council House was at half-mast.

Mr McCarthy, 62, had collapsed and died at his Bingham home just hours after presenting an edition of his BBC Radio Nottingham show *Afternoon Special*.

● West Bridgford-born entertainer Leslie Crowther, 63, died in September.

The host of TV shows like

VOICE OF THE CITY: Broadcaster Dennis McCarthy

Crackerjack, The Price is Right and *Stars in Their Eyes* had been a major charity fund-raiser and a supporter of Notts Cricket Club.

● Soccer legend Tommy Lawton, who in his later years was an *Evening Post* football columnist, died at the age of 77.

Tommy played for Burnley, Everton, Chelsea and Notts County, as well as winning 23 England caps.

It was a mark of his stature that at his funeral, mourners included Sir Stanley Matthews and other greats football. Wreaths included one from Everton in the shape of the club badge.

Hundreds of people turned out, on a crisp November afternoon, to pay their last respects to one of the greatest centre forwards of all time.

In the 1980s Tommy, who had settled in Nottingham after a spell as manager at Meadow Lane, began a long running column in the *Post* which he provided for readers until shortly before his death.

Pitmen win benefit battle

THE *Evening Post*'s Pay It Today campaign to extend benefit to more miners suffering lung disease finally ended in triumph, nearly two years after it began.

It was in 1994 that the *Post* first revealed that only nine per cent of more than 40,000 claimants nationally had been successful in gaining benefit.

Over the next two years, the Post pressurised ministers, supported sufferers, backed union leaders and enlisted the help of people like Ken Clarke and Jim Lester against their own party.

When the benefit breakthrough finally came, campaigner Ron Blair of

Cotgrave said: "I cannot describe in words the admiration I have for the way the *Post* has helped us."

Union of Democratic Mineworkers president Neil Greatrex said: "All mineworkers owe a debt of gratitude to the Post."

City Hospital respiratory expert Dr John Britton said: "All credit to the Evening Post for taking this on and carrying on the argument when other people were silent on the issue."

The *Post*'s campaign was even backed by the cast of the hit film Brassed Off which dealt with the issue of serious lung disease.

BIONIC: Three-year-old Jason Fowler became the youngest child in Britain to be fitted with an above-the-elbow bionic arm. The £2,000 device fitted City Hospital would enable the youngster, born without a lower left arm, to ride a bike and use a knife and fork. The hospital's disablement services centre helped 1,800 patients a year.

A TERRIFIED family claimed they were driven out of their Forest Fields home by ghosts.

And despite the efforts of two local vicars to exorcise the spirits, the family said they were too frightened to return after a series of inexplicable incidents that included:

● Rooms turning cold.
● Banging on the ceiling.
● Lightbulbs jumping out of sockets.
● Cupboard doors opening and closing.

The last straw came when a ghostly figure, dressed in black, was seen.

☐ ☐ ☐

BREWING giant Scottish Courage announced plans to turn Home Brewery into a supermarket.

Arnold traders objected to the move at the Daybrook site.

The issue even brought political rivals together with Tory MP Andrew Mitchell joining Labour leaders on Gedling Borough Council in opposition.

☐ ☐ ☐

A COUPLE of Moody Blues fans who met through the internet were married in the US. David Evans of Clifton met Marion Carlson of New Jersey through the '60s hit band's fanzine and love blossomed through a series of telephone calls.

PIERRE van Hooijdonk, *pictured*, joined Nottingham Forest from Celtic for a fee of £4.5m.

He was signed by player-boss Stuart Pearce to help Forest's bid to avoid relegation.

In an exclusive interview from Scotland, Charlie Nicholas told Forest they had got a bargain, while the Dutchman said: "I heard that Forest were being taken over by three

men who were ready to put a lot of money into the club.

"They want to make Forest great again. Forest were a big name in Europe. I want to help get that name back again."

After an unhappy stay, Van Hooijdonk was transferred in 1999 to Vitesse Arnhem.

◻ ◻ ◻

A NOTTINGHAM psychiatrist warned teenagers to beware surfing the internet.

Dr Mark Griffiths of Nottingham Trent University said users could develop the same obsessive behaviour as drug and alcohol addicts.

◻ ◻ ◻

HOMES in Notts were swamped when torrential rain produced flash floods. Hucknall was one of the worst hit places with 16 homes suffering serious damage.

Litter shames city

ACCORDING to a national survey, only Aberdeen and Newcastle stood below Nottingham in a litter league of shame.

And in a bid to beat the litter louts, the *Evening Post* joined forces with the city council in a Trash Buster campaign.

The Grot Spot enabled residents to pinpoint the city's worst sites and city officials vowed to do their bit by cleaning up the streets.

The result was a blow to Nottingham as it anticipated the visit of Tidy Britain competition judges later in the year.

To combat the problem, more staff were taken on and the number of street sweeping cars was doubled.

At last ... it's David Bowie

THE legendary rock star David Bowie took thirty years to come to Nottingham to perform ... and when he finally did, on August 4, 1997, the fans were waiting for him.

The 50-year-old Bowie arrived at Rock City in the afternoon with his wife Iman, stopping in the car park to sign autographs for fans who had been waiting for the star since early morning.

Despite still managing to fill arena sized venues around the world, innovator Bowie had announced a tour of "small" venues to promote his latest album, *Earthling*.

Considering the drum and bass nature of the album, Bowie was intent on playing to the right "clubbing" audience.

Staff at Rock City described it as the biggest coup in the club's history, and a further boost for Nottingham's reputation as an after-dark entertainment centre. They were well prepared for his arrival — his dressing room was transformed with

LEGEND: David Bowie in action

leather sofas, rugs, plants, candlesticks and a plentiful supply of his favourite Marlboro Light cigarettes.

City mourns Diana

NATIONAL mourning for the Princess of Wales was reflected in unique scenes in Nottingham, where citizens queued up for days on end to place floral tributes in front of the Council House and to sign the books of condolences.

On the Saturday afternoon following the princess's funeral service at Westminster Abbey, a memorial service was held in Old Market Square.

Thousands turned out for a multi-faith act of remembrance, during which speakers included representatives of charities the princess had helped.

Ice stadium: Protest at loss of pub

AS plans were revealed for a £30m ice arena in the centre of Nottingham, drinkers were defiantly proclaiming — "We would sooner keep our pub!"

Furious ice hockey fans called for a rethink after learning that the development plans meant the Old Cricket Players in Barker Gate would have to be demolished.

A petition was organised by Panthers fan Ray Marvin of Thorneywood who said: "If they want to knock it down they will have to do it with me inside."

But city council officials insisted the pub had to go to make way for emergency access for the new stadium.

Princess sets seal on recovery

PRINCESS Anne put the royal seal of approval on a city firm's fightback from a £13m blaze.

Aspley-based British Printing Company lost two of its four presses in the blaze.

Fifty workers had to be evacuated following an explosion and subsequent fire, threatening the future of the company.

But an investment of £25m in new equipment help BPC rise from the ashes and, according to managing director Andy Robinson, the Princess Royal's visit was "the icing on the cake."

'Worst ever' city centre blaze: Two youths detained

TWO teenagers were ordered to be detained for four and five years after admitting they started the blaze which wrecked the former Pearsons building.

The youths had lit a fire on the roof of the old building to keep warm and it got out of hand.

They were the first to dial 999 and as more calls came in, fire engines were already on their way to the scene.

At the height of the blaze, more than 100 firefighters were on duty and 18 fire engines were present. Water pressure has to be increased because so much was being used to fight the flames.

It was described as one of the worst city centre fires Nottingham had ever seen, causing millions of pounds worth of damage and costing at least 26 people their jobs.

Jambuster for 2002: The return of the tram ⏩ Page 136

NEW OFFICES: Castle Wharf House, Nottingham

Post moves HQ after 120 years

THE *Evening Post* left its Forman Street home after 120 years, moving into purpose-built £10m offices at Castle Wharf House in the city's booming canalside district.

The move followed the acquisition of the business in 1995 by Northcliffe Newspapers. Following the take-over, Nottingham Post Group turned its flagship paper into a full-colour tabloid, printing on new presses.

Former owners Forman Hardy Holdings retained the Forman Street site, which was levelled in 1999 prior to redevelopment.

A 'BRING him home' campaign was launched when reports reached Nottingham of the delapidated state of D.H. Lawrence's resting place in Taos, New Mexico.

The memorial in which the Eastwood-born writer's ashes are interred was said to be in need of renovation by the owners of the site, the University of New Mexico.

But British literary scholars argued that Lawrence would not have appreciated any moves to return his remains to England. The memorial was later repaired.

□ □ □

INMATES at Nottingham Prison, Perry Road, became published writers in the book *Beyond the Wall*, edited by writer-in-residence David Swann and illustrated by photographer Mike Usiskin.

The 28 contributors wrote both poems and short stories for the volume, and attended a prison exhibition of Mr Usiskin's black and white photographs.

□ □ □

TA volunteers Sue Pennant and Karen Hughes were hailed as heroines after scrambling down a cliff to rescue a scooter accident victim on the island of Madeira.

The two nurses administered first aid to the man, while perched on a ledge 200ft high, until an ambulance arrived.

□ □ □

NOTTINGHAM film director Shane Meadows, received critical acclaim for his movie *TwentyFourSeven*, starring Bob Hoskins.

But nothing came of plans to cast *Easy Rider* star Dennis Hopper in Shane's next movie ... as a Sneinton milkman!

□ □ □

A CIRCUS worker whose arm was bitten off by a tiger had his new limb made at the City Hospital.

Nigel Wesson was attacked while feeding the 25-stone Bengal tiger featured in the Esso advertisements. Specialists fitted his new limb — so that he could go back to working with tigers.

Aggressive patients anger '999' crews

AMBULANCE chiefs called for tough action against violent patients after a series of attacks on staff.

More than 40 attacks were recorded in the first three months of the year, with 12 people being injured.

In one incident, leading paramedic Wayne Foster from the Stapleford station, answered a call to Chilwell where a woman was reported by a man to be unconscious.

"I examined her and found nothing wrong. I told him I thought she was pretending.

"Then when I tried to move her, she lashed out and punched me in the groin and kicked me in the abdomen."

Notts ambulance chiefs said such attacks were part of a growing trend and the only way to combat it was to start prosecuting offenders.

"We are there to treat sick and injured people, but that seems to have gone out of the public consciousness."

Exasperated fire chiefs also complained of mindless attacks on their crews.

Youngsters in the Meadows were even starting fires deliberately and lying in wait for the fire service to respond. The youths then pelted the firefighters with stones.

PANIC OVER: Randall and Teresa Weber and their son Brandon after the emergency

BABY Brandon Weber was saved by the kiss of life — but the incident was kept secret from his father Randall until the Nottingham Panthers ice hockey star had returned from a playing trip to Scotland.

The tiny tot collapsed at his Bulwell home with a viral infection.

His frantic mum Teresa called for the child's aunt Ellen, who lived across the road, and she acted immediately despite having

Baby drama kept from ice star

no first aid training. "I held his nose and began puffing into him," she said.

"It took six puffs and my massaging his chest before he started breathing."

Teresa kept the news from her husband until after his vital match against Ayr.

A grateful Randall said: "Ellen saved Brandon's life."

NOTTINGHAM Forest were relegated from the Premiership for the third time in six seasons. During the season they sacked manager Dave Bassett and replaced him with Ron Atkinson.

However, he could not pull off a miracle escape and the hunt for a new manager began as soon as the season was over.

The number one target for prospective investor Nigel Doughty — and the fans, according to an *Evening Post* poll — was former City Ground favourite Martin O'Neill. But he chose to stay at Leicester City.

Former England coach Glenn Hoddle was also linked with the job, but the City Ground still secured a high-profile manager in former England midfielder David Platt.

He arrived in early July, and hinted that he would be available to play for the club as well as manage it.

THERE was outrage in Nottingham when the Home Office announced plans to move newly-released paedophiles to bedsits within the prison at Perry Road.

Furious residents demanded to know why up to three potentially dangerous ex-offenders were being brought to a residential area with several schools nearby.

The Home Office said the ex-offenders would be monitored both inside the prison and, if they chose to venture on to the streets, outside, too.

But residents pledged to continue their protest.

A CONSORTIUM put together a package of improvements in the hope of winning Government backing for a massive regeneration scheme at Radford.

The £50m 'urban village' scheme aimed to improve housing, health and the environment in the inner-city district, to cut crime and to promote a mutually-supportive local economy.

At first the Government had reservations — but later in the year the consortium was given £200,000 to take their plans a stage further.

● A £5 million homes scheme was announced for bringing new life to the Alfreton Road area.

NON-DEBUT: Sam Fox

No-star show folds early, but Neville returns

INVESTORS pulled the plug on a Nottingham show that would have given an acting debut to singer and former Page Three model Sam Fox.

It happened in late February, ten days before the curtain went up on *Virus: The Rock Musical* at the Theatre Royal

After extra backers were found, the show went on — without Sam Fox — but closed before the end of its two-week run.

● One long-awaited theatrical event that DID go ahead was the return to the Playhouse of the theatre's former director John Neville, who since emigrating had been one of the most influential figures in North American theatre.

The 73-year-old actor flew in from Canada for his first Nottingham part since the 1960s — the solo role in *Krapp's Last Tape*, part of a Samuel Beckett double bill with Endgame.

Both shows were staged by Martin Duncan, his last at the Playhouse in a five-year spell as artistic director.

Duncan was succeeded by Giles Croft, who arrived at the Playhouse in August.

Go-ahead for £167m supertram system

NOTTINGHAM got the go-ahead for its £167m supertram system — a fast passenger service to link the heart of the city with its north-western suburbs.

The plan was a reaction to a disturbing traffic report a decade earlier which predicted that Nottingham streets would be gridlocked by the year 2000.

The scheme will be operated by Arrow, a consortium including Nottingham City Transport and private sector partners including Adtranz and Tarmac. The first trams should be running by 2002.

The main line will run from Hucknall to Nottingham Station, via the Robin Hood railway line, Bulwell, Hyson Green and The Forest, Nottingham Trent University, Old Market Square and the Lase Market.

There will be a spur to Cinderhill. If the scheme is a commercial success, there further lines could be considered, possibly to West Bridgford, Clifton and Eastwood

Supertram is expected to carry ten million passengers a year, with the hope of relieving traffic congestion on major routes like Mansfield Road, Hucknall Road and Alfreton Road.

Trams will travel at speeds of up to 55mph, with services every five minutes between the station and Wilkinson Street, then every ten minutes to both Cinderhill and Hucknall.

TOGETHER: Dennis with Iris and Marjorie

THE *Evening Post* launched its campaign for the millennium: 'Together for 2000' — aimed at reuniting long-lost relatives and friends.

By the summer of 1999, we had already fixed it for scores of readers, and shared some heart-warming stories.

None more so than that of Dennis Riley, 81, who, during the Second World War, found a photograph floating down a jungle river in Borneo.

He looked at the picture and recognised two girls from his home town, Beeston. He kept the picture as a memento of his years as a prisoner-of-war — but never tracked down the pair.

Yet within days of the *Post* telling the story, he was chatting with the girls he knew as Iris Baker and Marjorie Redfern.

It was a reunion for them, too. They had worked together at Boots in their teens, but drifted apart.

They had no idea how their picture came to be floating down a river on the other side of the world.

"It's a fairytale ending," said Dennis, "thanks to the *Post.*"

Index